The
SILVER
CORD

*Finding
Truth Along
the Roadside*

JOHN JOHNSON

Copyright © 2022 William Johnson

This is a work of fiction.
Names, characters, businesses, places, events, locales, and incidents are either the products of the author's imagination or used in a fictitious manner. Any resemblance to actual persons, living or dead, or actual events is purely coincidental.

All rights reserved. No portion of this book may be reproduced, scanned, or distributed in any printed or electronic form without permission. Please do not participate in or encourage piracy of copyrighted materials in violation of the author's rights.

Purchase only authorized editions.

Paperback ISBN 978-1-945169-87-8
eBook ISBN 978-1-945169-88-5

Orison Publishers, Inc.
PO Box 188
Grantham, PA 17027
717-731-1405
www.OrisonPublishers.com
Publish your book now, marsha@orisonpublishers.com

Printed in the United States of America

Other books by John Johnson
The Byzantine Chronicles series
    The Blade – ISBN 978-1945169-29-8
    The Brothers of the Blade – ISBN 978-1945169-40-3
    Sons of Light – ISBN 978-1945169-45-8
The World Chronicles series
    In the Shadow of Babylon – ISBN 978-1-945169-55-7
    Babylon Revealed – ISBN 978-1-945169-72-4

This is a book about a young man's travel through the United States in the latter half of the 1970s. This is a coming- of- age story, a story about questioning, and not fitting into life. In it, you may find solace that you were or are not alone in being the odd man out. You may find answers to life within the covers of this book. Make of these travels what you will but know there is at least one person hoping that you find peace and success.

Remember also your Creator in the days of your youth, before the evil days come, and the years draw nigh, when you will say, "I have no pleasure in them." Before the sun and the light and the moon and the stars are darkened and the clouds return after the rain; in the day when the keepers of the house tremble, and the strong men are bent, and the grinders cease because they are few, and those that look through the windows are dimmed, and the doors on the street are shut; when the sound of the grinding is low, and one rises up at the voice of a bird, and all the daughters of song are brought low; they are afraid also of what is high, and the terrors are in the way; the almond tree blossoms, the grasshopper drags itself along and desire fails; because man goes to his eternal home, and the mourners go about the streets; before the silver cord is snapped, or the golden bowl is broken, or the pitcher is broken at the fountain, or the wheel broken at the cistern, and the dust returns to the earth as it was, and the spirit returns to God who gave it. Vanity of vanities says the Preacher; all is vanity.

Ecclesiastes 12: 1-8

CHAPTER 1

I hear the sound of traffic, cars, trucks, motorcycles, at the intersection below my opened windows. A breeze comes through the windows, of car exhaust, oil and gas, faint odors that don't offend. These are mixed with the aroma of newly cut grass, flowers, earth, cement, macadam. The heat pulls scent from painted wood, brick. The air is a summer's air, a summer's breeze, gently billowing my curtains. The curtains are sheer and white; they move away from the window, enlarging my view.

I see the church across the street. Methodist—but it could be any denomination; gray stone, stained-glass windows, looming, the steeple above the shade trees of the street. The church has a manicured lawn, yew bushes, a sidewalk, a signboard: "He who comes to me shall not hunger, and he who believes in me shall never thirst." The massive church is like a medieval fortress, a bastion, out of step with the architecture of this age. The red, heavy wooden doors are locked. The building is only used on Sundays. There are treasures inside that thieves would like to steal, or vandals to destroy.

On the street, a tractor trailer caught by the signal light has been set free, is beginning the spasmodic, fitful shifts through the gears. The diesels roar; the wild power is caught in the teeth of the gears, held fast, trapped, tamed, and the truck rolls. The ground trembles, and the windows of my apartment shake. When the light is red, I hear the sound of air brakes hissing, farting, struggling to hold back the rolling weight. Sometimes the sound is the tires locking, shuddering to a halt.

Sometimes the trucks aren't trapped by the signal light. The trucks roll under the green light, the great weight coasting, drivers with their feet off the pedals, glancing down the intersecting streets. The engine seems silent; there is no sound except for the rolling wheels over a manhole cover. Then the pedal is stepped upon, when the driver thinks himself safe from an accident, or the eyes of the police; the diesels roar, growl.

The green light says, Go! Go and find the open road; clear this town of narrow, confining streets, of bicyclists, dogs and cats, aged men and women in their senility, slow, heavy-hipped housewives, darting children. The man in the cab hears, obeys; the truck is gone, the green light says Go! to an empty street. The intersection is barely a memory in the driver's mind.

I hear the deep throbs of chopped Harleys, mounted by men in black leathers or jeans jackets of Confederate flags, oil and gas company patches, insignias, emblems. Black grease lies under their fingernails. I hear the oily burpings of frantic dirt bikes. The kids on the dirt bikes want excitement, want to defy the laws of physics, the obstacles of nature and man. There is the short, rapid explosion of foreign-car pistons; tires squeal.

There are the bored and lost youth of the town and outlying suburbs and farms; high school kids or just graduated, slipping into their twenties. They are in the heavy-muscled American cars made to cut the houses, the people, the town to a blur. You hear the engine gulp the gas; the sound system is blaring; the riders chug their beer. The boys in the machine rock in the metal cradle; the chassis vibrates, the engine hums their lullaby—until the beer rages for the power trapped in the engine. Then the town, civilization is discarded, cut up, flutters behind like confetti of the mind; as the boys are pushed into their seats, laughing in amazement, cursing in admiration.

I hear and see these things, think these thoughts within my room. My room within an apartment, an apartment within a building, a building within a block, the block within a town. The town called Mechanicsburg, named for the founding fathers, mechanics of an earlier age, near the beginning of machines and mechanics. This town is twelve miles from where I was born, in Harrisburg, Pennsylvania. A person has to be born somewhere, and that was my place; and twenty-five years later, this is my place. Who knows if it matters that I have lived twenty-five years? God knows; I was taught as a child.

I went to a church much like the one across the street. I liked to sit in the church when it was empty; lofty vaulted ceiling, stained-glass windows, colored light, shadows, sunbeams, quiet. Then God's presence would appear, appear as the invisible can. I wanted Jesus so desperately then. Church means nothing to me now, perhaps because I never met a man or woman in that building who had any more answers to life than I did. Perhaps I am bitter because He never helped me with my little boy problems, hurts, anxieties to my satisfaction. Perhaps I like my sin. I don't know; I do know there is a God and there must be a purpose.

I do know it is the time of year when the grass has had its third cutting and the lilacs are in bloom, hanging sweetly. The trees are fully leafed, and still the leaves are curled slightly on their edges as if they have not stretched, yawned from their spring awakening. There is a maple tree outside my window; I like the jagged, five-tongued shape of the leaves. I like the smell of the greenness; my eyes are soothed by the color. On the church grounds, the dark yews are tipped with the lighter green of the new summer's growth.

If I were to leave this town, go into the country, the fields would be a foot high with green wheat. The wheat would appear soft, cushiony, in orderly rectangles, like thick towels laid on the body of the earth. Beside the green fields would be furrowed fields, expectant. Farmers would be spreading fertilizer or weed suppressors over the brown furrows; a cultivator may be bumping through the lumps; a haze of dust would arise around the tractors. In the pastures the cows would have calves; the horses, knobby-legged colts.

I am not in the country. I am in my room in the town called Mechanicsburg. This is where my body is. The breeze blows through the screens, the air is hot. Hot for this time of year—early summer almost

The Silver Cord

and eighty-seven degrees. The sunlight is bright. Not a light that pounds into your head, but a diffused white light that has a softness from the humidity within. Even the humidity is gentle, a haze like a sheer curtain.

I sit in the center of the high-ceilinged, empty room at my card table. A breeze walks over the dusty wood floor from the window and touches me. Sunlight slowly creeps out the window as silently as it came. The traffic on the streets is increasing; everyone's going home, the day's work is done. I always sit here at this time.

Sometimes this time stretches into night, into a yawn, into a sleep that brings no rest to my mind. My mind twists and turns during the night, and in the morning, I say to myself, "Wake up!" And I wish to God that I was, that I was alive, within life. Reality and dreams play within my head. Is there some separate place between what we think is—what we think day and night, reality and dreams, conscious and subconscious are? Have I glimpsed a vision of another place? If I were to give this visionary land some name, it would be Hell.

The sunlight receding from the floor darkens the wood. I see the sky—it is dark. I hear the sound of thunder. The sound is in the distance, it travels through the great vault of the sky. The electric sound within the intestines of cloud bodies is an internal sound, eternal within men. The sound rolls across fields, woods, farmhouses, suburbs, over the thousand-foot ridges of the Appalachians to the north, miles away. The thunder rolls: over the broad sheen of the river named Susquehanna, which cuts the mountains; over the capital city of Harrisburg to the east, which found purpose in the crossing of the river.

The thunder rolls over the scattered city/towns of the broad valley, Carlisle, Chambersburg. The thunder comes to this town, this apartment; it comes from somewhere and passes over me. The cool, almost cold wind of the storm bursts through the windows; the grumbling thunder does not want to end. The sound runs up my arms, chest, back. The white curtains are blowing back—running women in nightgowns. The papers on the table flutter.

The sounds of the traffic are urgent. The wind carries the heavy scent of rain. The wind is working into a rage. The sky is black/gray now. The trees are rustling, shushing in the wind. The people want to get home, before the roads are sudsy with oil, gas, water; before the traffic slows; before they will be soaked between car and house. The people don't consciously think of these things, it isn't necessary. They hurry because a storm is coming and something deep, instinctual says *shelter*.

These people will go home, or to a health club, a bar, another job. They will eat, bathe, perhaps watch TV, read the paper, drink, smoke, go to church, watch their children play, putter around the house, do whatever people do. They will go to bed—single, double, queen size, bunk beds. They sleep alone or with someone. They dream or look into the past. Some will talk to themselves or their bed partners, some pray, some worry, some cry or laugh into their pillows.

They are all filling the time that is called life. The event that is between birth and death, the beginning and the end. Birth and death are real; they are the solid ground, the canyon's edges. We are all in the leap, between the truths—the two realities that we did not ask for nor can control. The leap is frightening if you are foolish enough to think upon it.

Most people don't think—they grasp whatever whirls around them, like debris in a tornado, whatever happens by, by chance or circumstance. By grabbing something, they forget the leap. Some grab people, sexual lust, money, a job, a new car, a three-piece suit, the title of doctor or lawyer. The possibilities are endless, and it doesn't matter what the object is; they grab and hold it close to them, or they grab and grab, filling their arms until it's spilling out. People will do anything, grab anything, believe anything to forget the leap. Ask them what living means. Ask them why they are alive. I can't tell you why I am alive, and I don't pretend to know. But I do know I am in the leap.

The narrow, brick home across the street has a second-story porch along its side; the floor is battleship gray, the railings white. Braided oval rugs are draped over the railing. A young woman is gathering up the aired rugs. She hurries; the rain will come any moment. Her hair is long and dark, thin hair that is raked, pulled from her head by the wind that pulls at the maple tree beside her porch. The dark hair and leaves blow together in the wind. If my hands were the wind, they would press against her temples, feel the shape of her head, run back, twine in the cool tangle of soft hair. The sound of the rushing leaves is the woman's hair. The woman's trunk is long and thin. Her eyes are dark. Her skin is cool white. She is as beautiful as the wind in her hair is beautiful.

Above the porch, in the eaves of the roof, the pigeons gather. The wind throws open their feathered jackets, touches the bare flesh. The pigeons shake their wings, snap them in an audible crack, then huddle deeply in the recesses. The air is cold, an autumn air. The pigeons will listen to the hard rain fall on the roof, on concrete, on brick; through the maple trees they will hear the rain fall. They will be warm and dry. The recesses will collect their heat, their scent, their excrement. The eaves are their shelter, their home.

One pigeon remains outside, on the rooftop, like a sentinel. He is like me. He likes the storm, won't leave till he sees it in, till he feels the cold droplets on his body. The storm is his delight.

The woman is gone. Her lights blink on. The darkness of the storm has overtaken the natural light. It is afternoon, but deep dusk has come, night seems so close. I see the gray-black thunderheads, ominous, powerful. Lightning is cracking, ripping, tearing the sky. Lightning that finds lonely trees, tall roofs. Brilliant, sharp lightning that squints your eyes; thunder that pounds in your guts, shakes the heart. A storm that drowns out the wail of the fire sirens.

The rain comes in the blackness, throws itself against the apartment building, the windows. The rain reaches across the floor to my table. The rain seems to carry a message to me. What does it want? My papers explode from the table into the air. I close the window. The rain's sound is muffled. The room has taken on a stillness, a silence.

I love this storm. It aches in my soul, is a hurt within my mind. I've seen storms on the Dakota Plains or coming out of the Pacific waters. I've seen storms swirling over the jagged peaks of the Rockies, the Sierra Nevada. I've seen storms born in the tropics coming out of the Gulf of Mexico. All the storms of the past swirl in the winds of this storm. The past is all I have. This is what I grasp in the leap called life.

The storm reminds me of what I had and what I have now. I've got nothing—a dishwasher's job, a fading memory of when life was good. I once had life, confidence, hope; life conformed to my commands. Life is just a haze—chemicals within the mind, say the scientists. Thought, perception, love, hate, everything that we are comes from a vial of chemicals within the skull. We taste, touch, see, feel, smell, and that is life, they say.

I once had a country to roam. I was free, seeking life. I rambled like the first man over highways, roads, trails, paths. Mountains, deserts, seacoasts, plains were mine. The minds of a nation were mine to explore—farmer, housewife, surgeon, factory worker, student. I had a vibrancy. Now there is a deadness. The images within the mind, the chemical stains like iridescent gas upon a wet street, are turning to vapor, are washing away. A man's mind is finite; memories are the decaying past.

I have allowed the past to surround the present, and so there is no present and no future. When this happens, a man becomes a shadow; he falls into himself. I am the shadow of the clouds of words upon the paper. Each letter is an atom, each word a cloud, each paragraph a cloud bank; cloud banks are a front—a high or a low. I exist when clouds appear upon the paper. There will be a time in my life when all that I lived will seem as if it never happened, as if someone else had lived my life and was telling me about it. Life borders on illusion.

Sometimes I awake from sleep at an hour in the early morning when the light is gray; the birds haven't awakened, aren't singing in the stillness. People haven't stepped out their doors in bedclothes into the humid cool to leave out a pet or collect a newspaper. The milkman is still about, striding between truck and house. The traffic light beside my window clicks its colors, and I hear the electric box whine like film coming from a camera. The streets are empty.

My windows are open, and the morning chill is in the room, so the room and I, who breathe the air, are connected to the outside. My insides, my lungs are a continuation of the air. If the air is in my blood, then even my body is the air. There is a rawness, a density to the air, each particle vibrates. The sound that is carried on the molecules of air substance is the sound of the highway miles away.

The Silver Cord

The highway's sound is the concrete and the tires, the tires and the engine, the engine and the grade, the wind upon the steel. The tires whine, pressed between the earth and the weight upon them. The sounds remain on the highway so that the sounds seem to be within the concrete, poured into it as it was first laid. It is as if the concrete is taut, stretched to the verge of breaking, so delicate that the wind blowing upon it gives it a sound.

The truckers give the sound its volume—the eighteen wheels, the shifting gears, the diesels complaining against the load. The sound is like a high-tension wire in that it is unremitting, surging, always flowing. Sometimes the sound seems to end, but it doesn't; it just sinks below the consciousness of the mind. Wherever the road is, there is the sound. Even if you do not hear the sound, the sound is there. If your ears were more sensitive, your mind more attuned, the sound could be heard, for it is within the concrete.

One highway I hear is the turnpike, stretching from Philadelphia to Pittsburgh. Philly was once the city of brotherly love before it became leprous with slums of unloved and unloving people. The pike lies across the Amish country found between Philadelphia and Harrisburg. The Amish are frozen in time, live in the past on their fertile land of solid houses and big barns. What do they hold onto in the leap called life? Is it God? Is it their culture? The pike brushes Harrisburg before burrowing through the ridges of the Appalachians. Near the end of Pennsylvania is Pittsburgh, a steel town. Here the Ohio River begins.

I hear another road. It doesn't receive the toll money. It is pitted concrete, slabs with black tar oozing from the cracks. It is a road that thumps under your tires, is worn to a sheen, shines in the sun; the right lane shadowed by the spilled oil, fluids of cars long since rusted and quiet. This road stretches from South Carolina to New York, comes up along the Great Valley from Virginia to Maryland and brushes by a small town named Gettysburg, not far away. There, in 1863, many men of unmovable convictions made it to the solid ground of death.

On these roads, in the morning, the diesels are roaring. The sleepy-eyed man is watching the line, bouncing in the big seat before the big wheel. Truckstop food turns in his stomach, he listens to tapes or his

CB, he smokes. The air is stale inside the cab, or a cold air from a partially opened window is stiff on his neck. He watches the line that keeps him safe, keeps him on the back of the curving, twisting, sliding, looping cord. The cord that binds and secures a nation. A cord soaked through with the blood of patriots.

I can't describe the sound of the road in the early morning hours. I can talk of the sound, but I can't say what it is. Sometimes the sound builds within my mind, and I'm ready to name the sound, understand the sound; and then the words sink back into my mind. The sound is elusive, carries a vague sadness; the sound makes me remember.

On the road I would awake an hour or more before sunrise. I always awoke with an excitement. The world was new, the newness an expectation. At times the newness was staggering to the mind—looking upon the vastness of the Great Plains or seeing the snowcapped Rockies. Sometimes the newness was as subtle as an unfamiliar caterpillar, plant, flower. The people were different, unique. A Californian is not like a Texan, who is not like a Pennsylvanian. All the differences swarmed in the senses, tickling, delighting. You are where you are only once in a lifetime, in thought, perception, place; then that unique moment is gone. Knowing this, you grasp, hold all that your senses collected. Life was good and new.

I was a college boy, so the differences, the permutations had structure. This is the Midwest, this is the Pacific Coast, this is the South. They call it *geography*. Geography is the dividing of what *is*, division by rainfall, soil, climate, topography. A man can learn the list of criteria so that he can say with confidence, "This is the Northwest. This is the Midwest." Doing this pointing and knowing makes a man feel good. He has fragmented life into a piece he can grasp.

I would wake up, stretch, laugh at the daring of my adventure, yearn for the newness the day would bring. Sometimes I would build a fire if the morning had a chill, or if I wanted tea or oatmeal. I would sit my sticky, brown-stained aluminum pot over the fire, cedar in the Northwest, sage in the West, locust in the Midwest, pine in the South, oak almost anywhere. Ashes, black and gray, and bugs would blow into my boiling water. The smoke would billow into my face, cure my skin, and lie in my clothes. I would huddle by the small fire, wrapped by a sleeping bag. My hands would be stiff from the cold, brown hands, white skin under the nails and upon the palms seeming to shine. I'm a person who tans easily and deeply. My hands would wrap around the cup of oatmeal or tea.

My body sucked food of nourishment. I ate from cans and an occasional fast-food restaurant. My stomach was never filled, but it was good. There is something good in having less than you want but enough for your needs. You become dependent on providence. Food tastes better when you don't get your fill. You feel disciplined; the hunger keeps you alive. My body did not live on food but on the wonder of the trip.

I would break camp in minutes. It was an art. My only task in a day was to set and break camp. Breaking camp was setting the tent, if it had been used, and my sleeping bag, in the sun. Knocking dirt and grass from the bottoms of both, folding each tightly so that they could be crammed into their carrying bags. I washed my cup, spoon, pot. If there was running water I washed my face, hands; brushed my teeth. The water was always cold, as if I were scrubbing with ice particles.

All my possessions were placed tightly in my pack, never a loose jangle; articles of frequent use near the top. My equipment was always battered. I went army/navy, didn't have the money to go any other way. My worn pack and equipment were good. You don't become upset when inexpensive items are lost, forgotten, torn, battered. No one ever wanted to steal my gear. I felt like I was beating the system that says spend, spend, spend, then be anxious for what your hard-earned money bought.

My pack made me feel like the complete vagabond, a man as old as the first trail. I was the first man, a man before villages, towns. I was a man in the Garden of Eden, wandering the earth, trusting the day for his needs. When I broke camp there was nothing to show that I had been there. I was a shadow of a different sort then.

In the summer I wore cutoff jeans, T-shirts, ankle-high work boots. I was never cold in the mountains, upon the plains as long as my body moved. My legs were lean and hard. I liked to walk, liked to think I could get to wherever I was going without a ride. In the beginning there was fatigue, hunger, soreness, stiffness. The body adjusts as you step out of the twentieth century. My stomach was flat, my arms swollen from restrictive pack straps; I was tanned, smelled of woodsmoke and sweat. My hair was greasy and unkempt. My eyes gleamed at life.

The body will walk by itself if you give it a chance. While the body walks, the mind walks. The mind is on the land, its history. You don't want to leave the land and yet you want to go on, see more, keep traveling. You think of the people who have given you rides, food, beer. The empty stomach grabs the food or beer, there is a warm glow. The mind is happy, content. The arms swing.

At night you can barely sleep; you await the day expectantly. Now I don't care if the day comes or not. It is all the same. Life runs past me. I allow it to run; there is nothing I want from it. Time stands still, but life runs past me. Why were men made? What is life? Why has it turned upon me?

The rain still beats upon the homes, the streets. The sewers are clogged with leaves, sticks, the stuff of tree blossoms and seed pods. The edges of the streets are flooded. A stream runs along the curbing of the street by the church. The water hits an obstruction by the sewer, the water leaps and froths. The earth, the streets, will smell clean when the rain has ceased.

I would like to go back to the road, relive the past times, if it were possible. It isn't. Even remembering doesn't bring back the past; only what you think the times were like. You forget the bad moments or glorify them; you accentuate the good or unique; you might give a twist to a common incident to make it seem special. Because the mind is the mind, the feelings and emotions attached to the people and the land fade. The spirit of the times is gone, it will evoke little within the mind—no passion, no welling in the soul.

CHAPTER 2

I can't go back. I have tried—twice—since coming to this town. One weekend I stood beside the turnpike. Horace Greeley was there in my mind, saying, "Go west, young man. Go west. " So I went. I went past barns, farmhouses, fields, rectangles of trees within the fields, suburban houses in cornfields. Everyone grabbing his or her little acre of serenity. Middle American squires leaving the city's problems behind—they think.

Mountains almost at the vertical, trees struggling to hold to the sides, long strings of mountains. Tunnels through the mountains. The road stops for nothing. The mountain ridges break apart, the land opens; hills are between the distant mountains. More farmhouses and smaller barns. The weather is humid, the sky gray. My shirt is soaked with perspiration.

Most of the ride was from a trucker, gas engine, hauling something up to Oil City. Up in the corner of the state where the first oil was drilled. He didn't say much. I didn't talk. There had been a time when I would have talked. I paid for my rides in talk. After a time, you find no one knows any more than you do.

This trucker had a seallike quality. I say this with no unkindness. He had shiny black hair, crew cut, and long stubbly sideburns, perfectly shaped. He was overweight, perched on his seat like a circus seal on a barrel. He shifted the gears. He was part of the machine. The machine told him what to do, the land told him what gear to be in, the boss told him where to go. There wasn't much left over for the man physically, unless his mind was free to wander and wonder. The man was the machine, the machine was the machine. The machine was what it was. This guy had his fragment of life. He could have told me things I didn't know—probably in the same depth and volume as any college professor. He could have told me about the engine, toll roads, cargo specifications, truck laws, truck terminals, state police, the Teamsters Union, independents, anything associated with the truck he could have told me. It is good that he might know these things; it is why the trucks roll, why there is food in the stores, clothes on the racks. It is why America is prosperous. Yet something was missing. He wasn't all a man should be. He had grabbed a truck in the leap called life. Or was the *something* missing in me? Where were his thoughts? Who am I to presume?

A violent thunderstorm brought torrents of rain that reduced visibility. He pulled over at a rest stop and said he was going to catch some sleep. He was trying to shake me. For some reason he was uneasy. I guess I wasn't what he had in mind for a traveling companion. I hadn't talked much, hadn't kept him amused. I understood, I had no bitterness; no one was forced to give me a ride.

I was on the outskirts of Pittsburgh, waiting for a ride by a toll station. A truck broke down fifty yards from me. The driver came up and asked if I was a mechanic. I had a work shirt on—I suppose that was the stimulus of his hope. The man was an optimist or grasping at straws. His truck breaks down at a random place at a random time. He sees a man standing by the road and hopes he has found a truck mechanic. We all want a break, for luck to be in our favor.

I know the feeling when the machine breaks down. The waiting for help or the searching for it. The thought of the cost, wondering if you will get a fair deal from the towman, the mechanic. The inconvenience of a broken schedule, lost time that will have to be made up. You think that because it is a machine, made of what you can see, touch—made of steel—that human weakness would have been built out of it. Men had time to think before they built; time being the filter of mistakes, miscalculations. The machine should be pure, filtered of human weakness so that only strength remains.

It isn't so. Men's weaknesses are built into the machine. The broken machine needs special men or special machines and tools to be repaired. A long time ago, the machine became more complicated than one man. Machines are built by hundreds of men, hundreds of machines. There isn't one man who can say, "I know how to build a truck." A man with grease under his fingernails and machine thoughts in his head can say, "I can fix parts of the truck." I wasn't the man.

A thin man in a luxury sports car pulled up. He was wearing a suit and tie; the hair, jet-black, greased back; skin a deep tanned brown. I didn't like the eyes; they wanted something from me. My inner sense said danger, said homosexual. I don't like to judge people—I could have been wrong. Life forces you to judge sometimes. I said, "No thanks," and he was gone. It was the end of the line for me. The rain was coming again, my heart was empty. I crossed to the other side of the road and was homeward bound.

A man in his thirties picked me up, six-packs of beer on the floor, a beer cradled between his legs. He looked like a man whose diet consisted of cupcakes and beer—flabby, loose skin. He seemed overly eager to have me drink, offering his beer more than once. It seemed to frustrate him when I said no. His speech was slightly slurred from the alcohol. I had that inner voice again, and I asked him if he was queer. He said yes. I needed the ride, it was raining hard, it was dark. He was no physical threat. I asked him how it happened.

He was in a restroom, drunk; some guy began talking to him, contact was made, and so now he is a homosexual. I saw a sad man, who probably never had any human warmth as a child, a man who was in the leap and had nothing to grasp, whose mind was sick from loneliness. The only human warmth he would receive in his life was from a stranger manipulating his penis. In the leap called life, he had grasped homosexuality. His story took me a third of the way home. I couldn't hate or despise him. I said thanks for the ride.

The rain had stopped, a lull in the storm. I didn't have a tent, only a poncho. I walked through a collection of gas stations and motels clustered

The Silver Cord

near an exit from the turnpike. I thought about sleeping in back of a building, under a recess. I would have felt like a derelict, so I kept walking. I slept by the turnpike under some high trees. Most of my sleep was in a sitting position with my feet tucked under the poncho. The leaves of the trees shielded me from the heaviest downpours. Early in the morning the rain stopped, fog hugged the earth.

I waited for a ride near a line of tollbooths. Two hitchhikers passed by, then stopped between me and the booths. One was a young girl—fifteen, maybe; thin build. Her hips were still narrow; they would always have a narrowness. She had long blond hair with the glint of red within. Her hair was dry, brittle from exposure to the sun. She had skin that freckled and burned easily. The cheekbones and nose were sunburned. She had blue eyes. The freckles were faint. She had a woman's face; there was no softness as in a child's skin. Her face was pleasant, appealing. She traveled with an Indian; a Sioux, I guessed. He was about five ten or six feet, stocky, with a heavy bone structure and little fat. Plains Indians are like that many times—sturdy, heavy boned. He wore a vest; his hair was loose and long.

The girl was looking at me as a red pickup truck, with a construction company symbol on the side, pulled up between us. The driver said he would take the three of us. I volunteered to ride in the back. The girl said thank you. A person's use of *please* and *thank you* will tell you more of their upbringing and character than most would understand. The Indian threw their bundles into the bed, I hopped in, we were moving.

The fog lifted. The sun shone in a clear blue crystal sky. The mountains were puffy in their forested greenness. The trees along the creek bottoms, in ravines, within the rectangular stands within the fields, had the puffiness, the exploding softness of green cotton balls. The trees had retained the clean rains; the roots had sucked the wet soil of water and minerals. The heat of the summer had boiled the stored waters, the juices; and the trees had exploded like popcorn.

The light coming through the cleansed skies gave the trees and forest depth, shape, accentuated their unique forms. The trees seemed to hover over the land. The day was made for a traveler in the back of a pickup, feeling the sun and the wind, smelling the forest and the fields. My mind felt the goodness of life again; but deeper, in my soul, the emptiness sat, waiting patiently.

The farms across the fields were painted white; metal roofs and domes of silos reflected the sunlight into a blinding glitter. The trees planted by the homes, buildings, billowed and gave shade, gave the rustle of their leaves, a branch for a swing, a cool place to park the car. The trees broke the heat that rose from the bare fields. The trees caught the wind. It seems strange that man is such a fragile creature that he needs the shade of a tree, that the sun is so hot he must hide from it, as if he would pop, boil like an overheated radiator if he remained long under its rays.

I noticed a large book had fallen out of the Indian's pack. I asked to look at the book and was given permission. A book of photographs, of Indian faces from the past, the turn of the century. A man had caught, in the leap called life, the faces, each wrinkle, each scant facial hair, each thought behind the eyes. Suspended in time. The book had a library card holder on its back jacket that said, "Cancelled." The worn book had been discarded. I knew the book from before, the college days, anthropology. The photographer was Curtis.

We passed a yellow bus and a string of cars with safety lights blinking. Behind the bus ran Indians. Native Americans were gathering from across the nation, from the red sandstone of Monument Valley, from the cedared coasts of Washington, from the plains of the Dakotas and Montana. They were marching to Washington, DC. What did they want? Their land? Their pride? I knew then but can't remember now. I know the land isn't theirs anymore, and they cannot possess it as they did, for that is the nature of land, of men, of time. The time of first man is gone. They are holding onto the past in the leap called life.

The girl and the Sioux left, joining the bus and the cars. I sat with the driver of the pickup. He told me about his passengers. The girl was fifteen. She had lived in Mozambique and Tanzania. Her father was a radar specialist. They called California home even though they were never there. Her mother, brothers, sisters were with the march. The Indian was a friend of the family and her escort. That was her story.

The Silver Cord

I was home. The first trip to find what was lost was over. It wasn't the rain that sent me back, it wasn't my job, it wasn't family. The ache was in my soul, the consuming emptiness. The question, "Why?"

I should have stayed put, but man is a stubborn creature, or perhaps it is that he knows desperation. I went out again to the road that didn't have the answer. The road was my only hope.

I went up Interstate 81. From Harrisburg, you run along the Blue Ridge for a while, then the highway cuts through the ridges and rides the Appalachian Plateau through Pennsylvania.

You know you're on the plateau when the trees are stunted because of poor soil and winter winds. The land has been mined for coal, and the waters are acid. Scars, gashes in the earth, old mining timbers, deserted roads, coal piles, rusting metal, acid ponds are what you see.

The summer day was warm, a man in a Chevy Blazer picked me up. Tennessee plates, going to Hartford, Connecticut. His daughter was in Hartford, at a prestigious college. He had a slight southern drawl, wore shorts; his thoughts were disjointed. The hum of the engine, the static on the radio, the monotony of the land, the length of the drive forced his mind toward sleep.

I knew he was a southerner of book knowledge and abstract thought, who had lost his southern accent in the northern world of academia. I was given other clues besides the loss of an accent. His truck was the standard model off the lot, well kept, clean inside, no little piles of earth in the corners, no grease stains, no additions to the vehicle like heavy-duty shocks or wide, knobby tires. He did not make his money from the earth—he was no horse owner or farmer, no construction site foreman, no garage owner. He did not have a glib tongue of honed cleverness, phrases that had been crafted, constructed with thought over the course of time. Such traits seem common in the southerner, where the spoken word, the story, have an honored place. He was quiet, introspective even beyond his weariness. He wore dress shorts, a knit shirt; and this told me something.

I made him talk so that we wouldn't slip off into a drainage ditch; though I would have been content to watch the land stream by. He was a psychologist. He had difficulty choosing words through his weariness. He began to talk of a case. He said most people don't know they're unwell. They hear voices and think the voices real—not just one person but whole families. A woman came to him saying she heard God speak; her family had heard the voice. He couldn't make them believe they hadn't heard the voice.

If a person hears voices, who is to say the voices aren't real? The question, I believe, is, is the voice dispensing soundness and goodness? What good could come from this woman and her family who believed they had heard God? Why shouldn't God speak? I wish He would speak to me. If the words they heard were enlightening, kind, good, and produced good in the hearer, then who should deny her reality? I would deny her reality if she were told to burn her home to ashes or do any act that was not authored by love. I would help her destroy the voice if it kept her from hearing the audible voices of loved ones.

I left the psychologist; he was continuing east on I-80, I was going north. I caught a ride with a construction laborer my age. He told me glaciers had scoured the land up above Scranton, plenty of lakes and ponds for fishing. Then a retired truck driver gave me a lift, left the highway so that I could pick up some food at a supermarket. He waited for me and took me back to the highway. He said I should think about becoming a truck driver. I'm on the highway traveling, so why shouldn't I get paid for it? Up in New York, I went through a gentle valley of green fields and dairy cattle. A truck, with empty cages in its bed, stopped. The driver said the cages usually contained beagles, used by the army for scientific experiments.

Turned east at Syracuse. One ride, a grocery-delivery driver, talked of his quarterback son and stopped at a harness-racing track. Stables, huge tents, horses being walked, groomed; horses pulling heavy men on light sulkies. I should have stopped but I didn't. I continued up through the Adirondacks from west to east.

Pines, sandy soil, swampy ponds, then the land rises, becomes mountains. The lakes now are clear blue, rimmed with summer cottages. I see canoes on the lakes, people swimming. The pines turn to hemlocks, birches. The mountains are peaked, not ridges like in Pennsylvania. Some of the mountaintops are treeless, bare rock, looking majestic and foreboding.

A construction foreman gives me a ride. He points to the bike path along the road and says his company built it. He talks of beaver, bear, solitary lakes filled with trout, the winters, trappers.

I'm over the Adirondacks. Lake George is long, blue; the eastern shore is flanked by a mountain ridge of green. The sky is clear blue. I see Fort Ticonderoga and think of the French and Indian War and the Revolution. The lakes, George and Champlain, were a strategic route between the colonies and Canada. The green trees have caught the yellow of the sun and sparkle in the light. I go north to Plattsburgh and cross Lake Champlain on a ferry. The land is flat; a strong wind presses the land, the lake is whipped to white waves. The wind is clean, the earth cold; Canada is very close.

I come down through Vermont. The forest was there, is still there. The forest amazes me—it astounds me with its resiliency, its vastness, its rolling, flowing sanctuary. Man has cut into it, cleared the flat land, crept up the slopes. The forest hugs the mountains. Men have their cycles of cutting and clearing; the forest endures, returns down the slopes into the flat land. From Maine to Florida, from the Atlantic to the Plains, I've seen the forest. I've seen the forest end, shrink to the banks of rivers and streams in the West.

A navy man gives me a ride. We buy beer and drink as the mountains and forest blur by the windows. The towns are small, there are few homes in the countryside. The day of sun and clear skies is coming to an end. Coolness is creeping out from under the trees, out from the soil. I smell pines, hemlocks, fermenting oak leaves, wildflowers, lush grasses along the roadside. The smell is cool, damp. I smell rotting wood, moss, lichens, rock, grainy rock. The pine smell is tangy. The forest is darkening; beneath the canopy there is skimpy undergrowth; the rocks, tree trunks stream by. A mysterious world is under the trees.

I am drunk. That I am drunk on the road tells me the days of the road are over. The alcohol is sadness and yearning. Alcohol takes my body away. I am vapor. I want to hold the scene, the smells. I want to be the very trees, the grainy rocks, the coolness that is pungent in the nostrils. I want this life—so much that it aches. I love life, and it fades even as I grasp it. It fades away, and I ache. The forest cannot give me what I seek.

Near Concord, in the night, my ride ends. I sleep behind a Baptist church. I feel safe there, as if no one has the right to tell me to move. The next day is Sunday. I see the first man come to church. He does not talk to me but he tolerates my presence with a smile. I wish he could give me the answer. I am gone. A black guy picks me up, then three teenagers, two of whom are girls. I circle around New York City with a drug addict from the Dominican Republic or Puerto Rico. He is small, thin-boned, scrawny. He's on drugs, shouting gibberish, making nervous motions, wild gestures with his hands. He runs through every tollbooth. His speed is above what the law allows. He is gone. I cross the Hudson, enter Pennsylvania and the Poconos.

A car on the highway spots me as I am walking the long grade of an entrance ramp. I had bought a soda at a gas station and was returning to the road. The day was humid, a slight breeze brought no relief. Father drives; oldest daughter, son sit in the front. I am in the back with youngest daughter and my pack. Their mother is at home. She is confined to a wheelchair due to multiple sclerosis.

Father is a geologist. The oldest girl is eighteen. She would start Syracuse University in the fall. She has prominent cheekbones; brown, fine hair; skin that deeply holds a tan. I wonder what it would be like to be her boyfriend, to meet her on the porch on a summer's evening. The son looks like his father. The son is quiet, reserved. He listens to everything and sometimes snorts a laugh to himself. A gentle humph from the nose with the mouth immobile. He's probably sixteen, his shoulders widening, his muscles just filling.

The youngest daughter is fourteen or fifty, that is the kind of person she is. She has a calmness as if she has already lived life. Her face is like that of a doll from my mother's childhood. Not a doll of plastic bumps of breasts and buttocks, but a soft doll of cloth, round of form, with a porcelain head. Youngest daughter's skin is white as snow with peach cheeks. The girl's face has a stiffness like the doll's face, and there is always an enigmatic smile. I can still see her face.

The Silver Cord

These people love to talk. They talk one after the other, father, older sister, younger sister, a humph from brother. They respect each other's right to speak but it sometimes strains their patience. I had never met people with so much to say. They talk, and talking is good. Perhaps I was annoyed at life because they didn't speak what I need to hear.

Father would talk and his voice went on and on. As he spoke I would notice his oldest daughter pick something from the flowing mass of words. Her mind would leave his words, his thoughts, his conversation, as she examined that idea that had been extracted. She did not hear him to the finish, because she was in her mind, thinking her thoughts. There was a gap. There always is a gap. When father stopped, there was no pause of silence, no reflection; from his last words, hers began. Even my precious doll, who spoke slower, with less emotion, no gestures, no facial expression, no raising or lowering of the voice, joined the unending words and was heard as they were heard, till something pricked their own memory banks and they were within themselves. Only the boy heard everything; for him there were no gaps.

They talked of their vacation in San Francisco. They told me how the city had been rebuilt after the earthquake and fire of 1906. They talked of New York City, the restaurants, the sights, the Village, operas, plays, concerts, the good times they had. They told of the friendliness of the people toward their mother. They told me of a black doorman named Henry, who was from Jamaica and who helped wheel their mother around. Henry was kind and pleasant. They liked Henry. I liked Henry. I liked this family, and yet there was something wrong. Or was it me? Was I wrong?

My ride ended in Scranton. It had begun to rain; a gray mist, coldness hung upon dreary mountains. A soldier on leave picked me up. He was proud of being in an airborne support unit. That was what he held in the leap. I am thankful he took pride in his work.

***

These were my abortive attempts to find what was lost or perhaps what was never found. The rain has stopped. Night has come. My windows are open. Drops are falling from leaf to leaf, from leaf to cement or puddle.

Leaves have been torn from the maple trees and shellacked to the black macadam by water and road film. The traffic has almost disappeared. My street is quiet for the moment. My mind expects the sound of a car; even when there is quiet, there is no peace.

The mechanical eye produces a dull glow of red on the street. The wind gusts, but there is a constant gentle median to the power. The trees rustle. The sound is like crinkling lens paper. No, it is softer, less harsh—perhaps like a sheet being pulled from a bed. No, the sound is mysterious, tormented. Or is it I who is mysterious and tormented? The sound tells me to live, live intensely. There is no intensity left.

I am alone in my room. Traffic breaks the silence. Tires hiss on the damp street. The air smells so clean—even the summer smells of greenness have been washed away. I look across the street to my neighbor's house. A light shone in her room; the woman with the long soft hair is in the light.

On the flat roof that extends from my back entrance I stand, feel the gritty cold roof shingles under my bare feet. I take my shirt off; the wind gusts against me, raises goose bumps. I've loved storms since a child. I would open my bedroom window to them, sit in the darkness, alone, and watch. As a child I would feel the warm air turn cold, sting upon the skin. The beating rain would thump upon the window sill. I would listen to the trees sigh then toss and rage. I would wait expectantly for the pink-white light, like the color of a new penny, to light the sky. The storm clouds would be revealed, jumbled, tossed, rolling through the sky. The rain would end, the heat lightning would appear, and my eyes would struggle to see all there was to see before the blackness.

As a child the storms came directly from God, and I would compliment Him on a good flash of lightning, a deep roll of thunder. Then I would ask Him why life was as it was. I sat like an Indian in ambush, never moving, feeling my limbs tingle to deadness. I wanted to train my body to be patient—like a rock, a mountain, a tree. Storms were solid ground.

I remain on the roof till I don't care that I am cold, till being cold means nothing. I am on empty. If you see me on the street, my eyes will not look into yours; they will wander away. If you talk to me, stand in front of me, I will hear only half of what you say. The sound of the road is humming in my ears like a gnat, like a woman's whisper. Tomorrow I will be at work. I will do my job, come home, sit at my card table. Clouds will pass across the paper. I will tell you about the beginning. But there is no beginning, just a place I say is the beginning. It is arbitrary, and it will be the beginning.

CHAPTER 3

I left home at the age of twenty to attend the University of Wisconsin in the city of Madison, the state capital. I had attended a community college for two years and was ready for the big time. No, that's a lie. I just didn't know what else to do with my life, so I followed the course of least resistance. College bound, seven hundred miles from home, or thereabouts. I remember the first drive with my father; since then, I've traveled that stretch of road from Harrisburg to Madison, Wisconsin—Route 11/15 North, to I-80 West, to I-90 West—five more times. It is possible I will travel it again. Of the hours of driving, which total days, I retain a few impressions.

Route 11/15 takes you north along the west bank of the Susquehanna River, through some small towns, shopping center/gas station/motel/restaurant sprawl, and traffic lights. It is a slow road built for a time past. Eighty West is highway, an interstate, built for the future so that it can catch the corner of the present before it is obsolete. Eighty West carries you through the dissected, wooded hills, pastures, meager farms of the Appalachian Plateau. In Ohio, the mountains vanish, replaced by gently rolling hills. Then the hills cease, and there is flatness, the Midwest, Youngstown, Canton, Cleveland, Akron, Toledo, South Bend, Gary, Chicago. These are the names on the signs.

The Silver Cord

Chicago as seen from the interstate is tollbooths, restaurants built over the highway, constant light all night from the high metal poles, O'Hare Airport, jets in the sky, engines screaming, flaps down or up. Glimpses of neat-rowed homes; modern, antiseptic office buildings. You pass Rockford, Illinois, and you are in Wisconsin. An hour or two beyond the setting of the sun, the speedometer falls as you drive the streets of Madison. Fourteen or fifteen hours of driving, if you take no breaks and drive the speed limit.

The long drive is my passion. I drive according to the rules. The drive means nothing if I break the law. It would be like cheating in a game of solitaire. My left arm is outside, resting on the window ledge. My right arm is at my side, holding the wheel as if it were a level, the speedometer needle an air bubble in water. My right leg is locked, holding the needle steady, as if the needle were painted on the speed limited. Now we use cruise control.

The drive begins on the earth, the grade, the contour, the height and depth of the land. The concrete on the land has holes, lumps, crevices; debris is scattered upon the concrete—blown truck tires, boards, rocks, the bodies of deer, what has flown from a car window or a badly tied load. The concrete has a line. The concrete meets the tires, and the tires are connected to the power.

The engine is of the earth; it is earth shaped by man. At rest, the engine is like the earth—unmoving, docile. The engine has an ignition and a pedal. Step on the pedal, and the animal that is the engine roars. The animal was born to run. It will run to its death, your death, if you wish. The machine wants perfection from the concrete so that it can run to its fullest, but the concrete is imperfect. The man must be the broker in the game between the stillness of the concrete and the movement of the car.

I glide on the concrete. Other people, the traffic, do not glide. The slow ones I pass and never see again. The fast ones, they are gone; but I always find them behind me again and passing. There are those who accelerate, decelerate, pass, and are passed. We play a game of leapfrog. They wear me out because they can't glide, can't remain steady. And so it goes on and on. It is monotony, and it is never exactly the same.

I have seen gypsies at an Indiana rest stop, in the parking lot before the chain restaurant and gas station. Black curly hair, skin of olive tones, earrings, an Eastern-European accent, different body scents. They have three big cars pulling little mobile homes. One car is without a roof—not a convertible, just a car without a roof. They are approaching people, attempting to give away a beagle pup that they say is sick and eats their baby's food. I do not want the pup. I notice they offer the pup to people going into the restaurant, not coming out. Take the puppy, put it in your car. You can't take it inside the restaurant. Leave the window open a crack. Go eat, save the pup a piece of hamburger, come out and find your car ransacked. Suspicious? Perhaps.

Once I picked up two hitchhikers outside of Chicago going to New Jersey. They were coming from Alaska, two seventeen-year-old kids who had built a raft and floated down the Yukon. They had seabags of gear, even rifles were within their bags. They had some hard luck tales, not of the Alaskan wilderness but of the road. They had been given a ride by a group of men driving a van. They had been treated as friends. They went into a restaurant to eat. That is when their friends stole two pairs of expensive hiking boots. They had a ride with a trucker who they thought was a decent guy, until he reached over and grabbed hold of the nearest thigh. They practically jumped out of the truck.

The road taught them lessons the wilderness couldn't. You've got to know who you are before you begin, or at least have others think you know who you are. You've got to have some grit and know how to judge a man. I became older brother to them. They relaxed. I took them all the way into Harrisburg.

I am on the road in a wide, low beast named for an antelope of the African plains. I'm hurtling toward a slow-moving car, even as a truck is fast approaching in the left lane. I step on the beast; the big engine likes to be stepped upon. I shoot out as the needle points toward the limits of the speedometer. The beast wants to run; I force the needle to fall. I am in the right lane, past the slow-moving car, when the truck passes, hugging the line, sucking me into its vortex. The driver is half-asleep at the wheel. I am not. I nudge the beast out of the vortex.

The road stretches out. My head is on the headrest. Radio stations surge and weaken. I drink coffee from the thermos. My stomach complains, but my mind is clear, euphoric. I sing as I glide on the back of the beast. A time comes when the caffeine buzz breaks. The concentration slips, the needle sinks and rises. My heart is thrashing in my chest. The fear is that the thousands of pounds of metal wishes to fly from the road. The beast wants me off its back. I struggle to remain the master.

Then the earth is moving, and my beast is sitting still. The engine hums. I glimpse objects from the blur. A home. Then the mind is empty, staring at the stuttering line. The mind saw much more than a home; the number of windows, the human touches, the style of roof are buried in the subconscious, never to be uncovered.

I step out of the car and feel the weight of my body upon my legs. The drive, the caffeine has drained my strength. My mind is no longer sharp, it is burned out from the concentration of the drive. I feel as if there is a wall in my head. My stomach is empty, but I am not hungry. I leave the car, slightly dizzy, staggering so no one would notice but me, and walk the streets.

Madison, Wisconsin, state capital. Population somewhere around two hundred thousand. On the whole, the land is flat, scoured by glaciers, yet there are swells, dips, rounded hills, ridges. The fields around the city have prairie oaks, corn, hay, alfalfa, and cows. Madison is situated on an isthmus between two lakes. There are five lakes altogether. The city is flat for the most part, except for a rise of land on which the capitol building sits.

Along Lake Mendota is the university; the first buildings were built on the high ground before the lake. It is a good college, a land grant college, with a spacious campus; Greek columns, ivy twining somewhere. Age, stability, reputation, vibrancy. Sailboats dot the wide blue waters as racing skulls hug the shoreline. The city and the university have plenty of parks, bicycle paths, an arboretum. It is a good place to live.

I notice the breeze immediately; there is always a gentle breeze in Madison. This and a certain lack of humidity make the city different than the summer city I left. The scent in the air is not Pennsylvania. The scent comes from the wind that flows over lakes, prairies, forests, over expansive farms. The wind pulls from the earth the chemicals and minerals within the soils, the warmth and coldness of the earth, the wetness or dryness, every piece of vegetation that grows on the earth, every animal that lives upon the earth. Men are on the earth, and the wind pulls the scent from men and their endeavors, what they grow, what they build, what they produce.

The wind holds such scents. You can know a land simply by the wind. The wind picks up the variation, the infinitesimal differences, and makes a perfume that is pressed against a man's senses, his thoughts, his life. The man and the scent bond. The wind brings you the joy of the new land.

You remain in the new land, the wind tantalizes slowly, the earth and the men on the earth reveal the uniqueness of their land. I found that leaves dropped earlier in the fall and yellow was the predominant color. The winters are colder than in Pennsylvania, but the dryness takes away the bone-aching dullness of damp Pennsylvania winters. I remember the first day my nostril hairs froze—such a simple, unimportant thing, yet it was new to me. Seconds from a warm house, they froze. The new snow, so clean and dry, squeaked under my boots, and the sky was crystal blue. There are Scandinavian names on the mailboxes; cross-country skiing, ice skating is popular. People call bags *sacks*. It goes on and on, little difference that make traveling a drug, make life new and exciting, an adventure.

I walk along State Street; State Street runs from the Capitol down to the corner of the campus, the Student Union Building, the shore of Lake Mendota. The street has restaurants, bars, stores—clothing, hardware, sports, book, and others. The street is always crowded with students. I have this perception while watching people that each is the last of their species. That each has nothing in common with the other. They were made in the mold of man. They speak, laugh, cry, but it is to themselves, to that difference that is them and not you. The body you see—the flesh—is merely a form sculpted from an elastic, fragile medium. Tucked within the sculpture is a spirit of love and hate. The spirit, either love or hate, within the sculpture cringes or expands in response to words or actions, or to some real or imagined obstacle.

State Street is usually crowded with the students who have come to learn. I remember entering a bookstore on State Street to buy my books for the first semester. An attractive girl—girl to me now, woman

The Silver Cord

then—searched the shelves for books she would need for the coming semester. Wonderment, amazement, happiness was shining in her eyes. She said, "I wish I could read them all." She spoke to no one in particular, only another guy and I were in the aisle. She had to express her joy. It was true, it was what I felt, what I had always felt when looking at books.

She knew the pull of knowledge. I knew the pull; that is partially why I left home, traveled seven hundred miles. The quest for knowledge was an adventure; diplomas seemed irrelevant. Any hardship I would endure would be seen as noble because I was on the quest. I lived in a room, in a house, in a residential area. I ate peanut butter and jelly sandwiches, sardines, cheese, snack bars. I used the window sill as a refrigerator in cold weather. I drank dehydrated milk and Kool Aid. Suppers came from a mom-and-pop restaurant across from the stadium. An extra order of mashed potatoes or bread kept me filled, cheaply. I walked or rode my ten-speed. I had no car. Snow, rain, sleet—I walked. My room had a bed and a desk and a chair. I enjoyed every minute of learning. I enjoyed staying under my meager budget.

I've forgotten most of what I have learned. Is the knowledge gone forever or is it simply waiting to rise to the surface of thought at the opportune time? Perhaps it will rise of its own accord—the mind is a churning place. I often wonder why we think upon what we think. How do thoughts come into our minds? Where do they come from? Knowledge is fact; it exists outside of you. Man's ability to remember limits him. Everything a man learns is real, and if it is forgotten, then he is a shadow floating across the hard rock wall of facts.

I went to college with my hammer; my hammer is called *why*. I used the hammer to become a bright boy, college material (they were fooled). The hammer is used on the rocks of knowledge that come your way. Hit the rock with your hammer, keep pounding until the rock crumbles, then sift through the rubble. Is there anything in the dust you've seen before? Are there pieces you've never seen? Get out the hammer and pulverize. The dust becomes like quicksand in a way; the dust dulls your mind like sand in a watch.

My rocks were anthropology, American literature, philosophy, Spanish, geography, history, statistics. I was looking for answers—anthropology was my major. I wanted answers that wouldn't turn to quicksand, answers that I could build a life upon. If that is what you want, then forget a college education, for the answer isn't in college. I worked in the rock quarry; the sweat came, my brain ached. Each moment when the quest seemed a sham, the books would reveal one more interesting piece of knowledge, the professor would give one more impassioned lecture. He would get out his snake oil and praise its virtue. I would buy the elixir, drink, feel refreshed till the percent of alcohol would dissipate, and I was at the beginning again.

We had the crystal ball, too, and gazed eagerly within—the science journals, the latest archeological finds in Africa, the latest sociology study or psychology experiment. I longed for the day when man's faults and the ills of the world would be uncovered. I wanted the knowledge that would make me the kind of person I wished to be. What do I wish to be? How can I know? I, at the least, wanted the power to not be what I didn't want to be. It is far easier to know what you don't want to be than to know what you wish to be.

But there really wasn't a me, just stains of chemicals soaked up in flesh. A little more of this or that, a little less of something else, and I would have been different. A different genetic code. A little more of this hormone, a little less of that. Psychology bound me to past actions, traumas, anxieties. I have so many it would take a lifetime to conquer them—if there were a way. Sociology tells me I'm a lump of clay molded by my surroundings, usually meaning other people as confused as I am, all of them in the leap. Anthropology tells me all that man does is just fine, it's all relative. There is no such thing as barbaric, cruel, bestial, right and wrong. What's right for one culture isn't right for another; just sit back and watch the show—don't make judgments.

Philosophy said I could make choices even though I was a bag of chemicals. What choice could I make when no man upon the earth, from his knowledge, knows what life means? Even if he knew, where would he find the power to live the truth? I made a choice when I went home for winter break; I told my parents I wasn't planning to continue with my education. A college degree had never meant anything to me, and now I knew that college had no answers for what I sought. Knowledge is still good, interesting, but it isn't life; it isn't the answer. I couldn't make myself sweat for knowledge anymore; the desire was gone. They had me in the groove, on the path to security, money, modest success, a safe, comfortable life; I felt as if I were walking into a trap.

The trap goes like this: college degree is proof of knowledge, college degree equals job, job is at least twenty years as a machine part, even while your soul is in the leap called life. When you are worn and worthless to yourself and the machine, you are thrown away—that is called retirement.

My parents wanted this for me because their lives were bound by fears that only routine, job security, health insurance could lessen. If I had seen something good in their lives worth having, I would have followed their example. I was rebellious; I wanted to live intensely, not rot away day by day in some dull job just to say I was secure. Happiness is living intensely, searching, taking risks. Out there somewhere was the answer.

I completed the semester and returned to Harrisburg for winter break. I was purposeless and lonely and without the will to overcome. I was lost in statistics and Spanish and didn't want to endure more of the same. I had been poorly grounded in those subjects or perhaps that part of the brain never existed or had been given too many blows in sandlot football. I was returning to Madison with every intention of leaving. The arguing, the fighting with my parents was behind. The spilled emotions, the bitterness, the emptiness still hurts to remember. Why couldn't they tell me what life was for? A friend named Kit, a fraternity brother from my community college days, returned to Madison with me. We were going to pick up my belongings and take off. California? Mexico? Anywhere. The future did not happen as we had planned.

Kit and I went downtown to State Street. We sat in a bar and drank Seven-and-Sevens—whiskey and 7 Up. The swizzle sticks piled up. That was living to us—now, I am ashamed. When I stepped out onto the dark, windswept pavement,

I felt elation. Behind the elation was an emptiness, a mind so wrapped in confusion, conflict that it was ready to break. Knowledge gave no pleasure. I was trapped by my parents and society into leading a life I could not accept. Or was it the fear that I could not succeed? There was the inevitability of a process begun. I had filled out the forms, paid the money, come seven hundred miles, attended classes. I hadn't been taught to be a quitter, but no one had ever shown me how to gracefully and confidently abandon a sinking ship. My parents said the chance at a college education would never come again. I understood.

I wanted to feel life before I became a part of the machine and life dulled, was abraded from my soul. I would willingly join the machine if someone could give me a solid reason. The alcohol was saying, "Feel, live, experience." The alcohol mocked me, but I was not aware of the treachery then. The alcohol said, "Do something, even if it is the wrong thing; but don't live *between* life."

These were the thoughts moving through the alcohol-soaked mind, pulling and tugging at each other. The pulling and tugging ended; my mind snapped. On that January night, I walked down State Street, kicking in storefront windows. Some windows didn't break because saner men had invented plexiglass—knowing people like me exist.

Glass broke, shattered. I kicked in a jewelry-store window. The glass fragments mixed with the diamonds on the sidewalk. The glass and diamonds appeared the same to me, and this seemed to legitimate my rage. The glass and diamonds were equal in beauty; people weren't interested in beauty, only wealth. I was wrong; the thinking so childish. Is glass made as a diamond is made? How many thousands of years does it take to make a piece of glass? Diamonds have beauty deeper than the naked eye. The evil of my own mind astounds me.

I knew I was wrong but couldn't admit this to myself. I knew I felt emotion. I was alive even if living wrong. I did not blame the store owners for where I was in my life. I had no desire to make their lives more difficult. The drunkenness drowned out my feelings for other people. I had broken my own sense of morality, rules—that is what the alcohol had wanted me to do, and I had followed.

Kit was laughing, but not to encourage. His mind saw something it hadn't thought probable or possible. A new reality had burst upon his consciousness unexpectedly. He was also laughing because I had told the world to leave me alone.

The Silver Cord

Someone yelled at me from across the street. A couple came over to me. I met them in the deserted street. He said, "What do you think you're doing?"

I said, "What does it look like?" Then I stared at him hard, filled my lungs with the frigid air, clenched my fists. He was a small guy, a student. He walked away. I respect him for that now. Hitting him would have only increased my shame the next day. If he had beaten me, he wouldn't have been any more of a man. Violence solves nothing, proves nothing. The police came, I walked past them as they picked jewelry from the glass.

Kit and I went back to my room, drinking and talking loudly at three in the morning. Kit was staggering. Each time he lost his balance, his foot went down on the floor like the floor was a ship's deck in a tropical storm. One leg was numb, like a wooden leg. He continuously banged the leg down, trying to feel the floor. Bang, bang, bang. The landlady, who had a voice like a frog from chain-smoking, who was in her seventies, hair in curlers, body in a robe, came up, angry. She raged and raged, was going to throw me out. I laughed at her.

The next day I had a hangover, a raw throat, an emptiness deeper than the day before. Remorse, guilt, shame. I could not justify my actions. That day, I decided to remain one more semester. I would leave in the spring. In the spring, the weather would be warm, I would be twenty-one. Kit understood. He drove back to Harrisburg alone through raging snowstorms.

CHAPTER 4

I left Madison near the end of May, the afternoon after my last final. The day was cool, windy, the sun was shining. I had left my personal belongings with a friend, Ed, an alumni and neighbor. I walked away from my room with everything on my back, feeling free and slightly apprehensive, through the arboretum toward the open road. I walked in the middle of the road, following the yellow line, my yellow-brick road. The dream of this trip had carried me through the last semester. I had planned, studied maps, become hypnotized by the names of states, rivers, cities, and towns. To give order and purpose to my trip I made the national parks my destination. Now imagination was becoming reality.

A third of the way through the arboretum, an attractive woman in a yellow Volkswagen picks me up, takes me to the highway. An older man in an RV stops. I climb on board. He has his granddaughter in the back. She appears to be five or six. It seems strange, as he does not seem alert, and she seems cranky. He doesn't go far before I exit. As I am standing there and the RV pulls out, a state trooper pulls up—probably to take me off the highway. I tell him my concerns, show my student ID, and he is gone in pursuit. Two rides later I am in Mauston, Wisconsin, at the home of John, who had roomed across the hall. His wife and boy live in

The Silver Cord

Mauston. For the summer break, they are moving to his father's farm on the Door Peninsula. I will help them load the U-Haul truck.

I meet John's wife and his seven-year-old son. John is strict, demanding of the boy—annoyed at his presence or just wanting quiet time with his wife? The boy is not John's by passion, by flesh and blood, sperm and egg. John is reminded that someone else loved his wife. Maybe the boy is a symbol to John, not a child who needs love and attention. The kid is full of life—he wants to show what he can do on his bike; he rides his dirt bike in figure eights. He shows off, is daring, beaming at the attention and praise. We get his kite airborne. The last day of moving, we take pictures of each other against the side of the truck. John gives me his address. I lose it before the summer is over; I've never seen them again.

I head down to the Wisconsin dells. This is where the Wisconsin River has cut into the soft sandstone rock of the surrounding country. I have read it is something to see, so I go. I continue my hitchhiking initiation. When to shoulder your pack, when to carry it by the straps. How to take it from your shoulders with ease and grace, how to place it upon your shoulders with the same virtues. Where is the best place to stand? What clothes are most convenient in seemingly fickle weather? How do you place a bulky pack into the back seat of a car or a trunk? How do you judge a man or woman in a few seconds of eye contact? I learn.

By the dells, a young kid picks me up, probably sixteen. He's drinking, driving a fast car, a road runner. He offers me a beer, and I accept. His concentration is between the gearshift and the road. He grinds gears and wanders off the road a few times. He's had no experience driving a stick, and he is slightly buzzed. We drive through the little town by the dells.

The main street is long, bordered by businesses capitalizing on the dells and tourists—restaurants, souvenir shops, places to buy tickets for tours. Hundreds of tourists walk the sidewalks, mostly families or retirees. The kid turns up his music, raucous, rowdy music that makes the mind turn to movement, energy, lustful passion. The beer and the music mix in the brain. The engine is growling. The young women with their parents turn for sly glances. The young girls want to leave their families, enter the machine, feel the power as their hearts beat to the speed and rhythm of the music.

The kid drops me off at a campsite a quarter of a mile outside of town, where the corn rows begin. He pulls the growling beast onto a dirt road flanked by picnic tables and the bare earth of campsites. I step out with an empty beer can as families watch. The kid revs the engine and spins out from the dirt road. A light powder is in the air, and exhaust; stones rip out from under the tires. The stones rip past the legs and faces of the watching children; I place the beer can in a trash container, and I am thankful none of the children are hurt.

Looking for water, I meet the owner of the campgrounds, a woman in her fifties. She says they are not open for the season yet—no running water, no bathroom facilities. Instead of telling me to leave, she says I may stay free of charge. She asks about the driver. I tell her what little I know. She says children could have been hurt. She is right. I wonder at this woman who gives a hitchhiker a place to sleep free of charge, who judges the hitchhiker to be good, who doesn't associate him with the irresponsibility of the kid in the growling car.

In the evening I go over to the old farmhouse to fill my canteens at the outdoor faucet. The woman invites me in. Her son is there; he is in his late thirties. She offers me food. She asks about the driver of the car again, then calls the sheriff. The sheriff wants to talk to me. I'm nervous, my mind racing through different possibilities. Is the car stolen? Has the woman already talked to the sheriff? Could this be the second call, since so much time has elapsed since the incident?

I tell my story. I believe the car is not his, but I don't say it is stolen and refuse to give an opinion on that subject. The sheriff doesn't ask questions about me. He says thank you, and that is the end. Later the sheriff calls back and talks to the woman. She tells me the kid took the car without his friend's permission. Both were known for general rowdiness at the motel where they were staying. The kids were told to leave town.

As I eat my apple pie, the son talks. He has been to Wyoming to hunt. He tells me of the beauty of the mountains, the dusting of snow covering his sleeping bag as he awakes in the morning. I am going to this country he finds so beautiful. He says he admires me for traveling with everything on my back, alone. I think maybe I am loose in the head.

The Silver Cord

The next day, Sunday, the woman promises to take me into town, but first she must stop at her church. The day is hazy, the morning cool. The church is built of wood, painted white. The bell is ringing in the tall steeple. The church sits in a grove of mature maples, whose tops just touch the base of the steeple. The parking lot is full; men congregate outside the steps, shooting the breeze. The sun breaks through the clouds, the maples; the beams light up the grove. People are coming to worship God. I think about that, it is an amazing thought. No one living has seen Him—but you know He is there. He must be alive—you don't worship the dead if you have sense. People who don't believe there is a God must think these people crazy. "Where is God?" they must say. For the first time in many years, church seems like the right place to be on a Sunday. Maybe it is because I am happy, truly happy for the first time in many years; perhaps it is the adventure of the trip. Or is it the kindness of this woman that makes God real? No, I know God exists; it is that she *lives* God.

I sense I am looking at America there in the maple grove. What we are comes from that place, it is where we learn what is good and what is evil. I sense this as an outsider looking in, as an alien traveler observing a strange custom. The woman invites me to the service. I say, "No, thank you." She smiles and drives me to the edge of town. I say good-bye. I have the feeling that she is happy to have met me. She wanted to do something good for someone, and I was there. What would I have discovered if I had walked into that church? Just memories of the past?

I take a boat tour of the dells, then head south, through the sandhill country, or perhaps just a sandy country. Long rows of pine trees are planted between the fields. The rows are deep. A ride tells me they were planted in the Depression years when the land was becoming a dust bowl.

It is not difficult to imagine a farmer, sand stinging his face, staring out across his fields. He has a large family depending upon him. His wife is lean and sunburned with dried, sagging breasts. Her rough, bony hands are large; she has high cheekbones. She has the same eyes as he does—lost, unbelieving eyes. Unbelieving that the land could pick up and leave them barren. The eyes hold resignation but also patience, an unfounded determination to survive.

This is my imagination. But my eyes see that the land is in its place and giving abundantly. The people who held it down are dead or dying. But the land is in its place for those who came after.

It is Memorial Day weekend. I stop at a bar for directions. I meet a young guy in the bar who says he will give me a ride to a nearby state park. I hop into his van with a group of guys not far out of high school. They are from Chicago, work in factories, come from ethnic neighborhoods; they act tough and are tough.

The state park is full, the campgrounds in the park are full, the commercial campgrounds are full. They wrangle a site from a campground owner. He told them no vacancy, but they persisted till he said they could have a spot if it was big enough for their van. They find a spot; they say I can pitch my tent. They are drinking. One has red capsules of speed wrapped in his handkerchief, shows them to me discreetly. He offers me one. The road is my drug.

The weekend is a circus. A holiday is when the machine shuts down; the machine parts rush to live, they all rush to the same places. They crowd and harry each other, are dizzy in their rush to enjoy. The state park has beauty—a lake, Devil's Lake, faced by a protruding granite boulder of a mountain. Huge boulders line the base of the mountain. I climb the trail to the summit. The next day I leave.

I make my way toward Prairie du Chien. A woman in her fifties, who lives in a houseboat on the Mississippi, gives me a lift. I thank her for picking me up, compliment her on her confidence. A glimmer comes to her eyes. I have made her feel good; I am an adept talker by this time. You need to put people at ease and to give them an idea of who you are.

My mind is always sharp in those first few seconds of a meeting; no matter how tired I am or where my mind has wandered to, I concentrate. My eyes have a sparkle, a humor. I laugh at the game and the alertness within my eyes; I look into their minds to see what they hope I will be. Some want me to be a philosopher, others a drifter, others a mellow flower child, others a college student, others a jock type.

I can give them any of these, for these are facets of my personality. If they search for immorality, perverseness, dishonesty, crudeness, they

The Silver Cord

will find nothing. From their words I pick up information on the heaviest-traveled roads, places to camp, location of stores, things to see. I learn about their lives. What I really listen for is the essence. The essence has to do with right and wrong, goodness and evil; not so much what a person says but what a person will do.

In the beginning I always asked people about their jobs. I thought that if I found the right job, a profession, life in the machine could be good. I know a man should find that work that is his passion because work is most of your life, forty hours a week, forty years of your life or more. What time is not the forty hours a week has no real meaning.

It consists of taking care of your body, haircuts, dentist and doctor appointments, sleeping, grocery shopping, preparing food, eating, washing clothes and yourself, housework, car repairs, driving from here to there, resting before the TV, a few hours a week for a hobby. All this means nothing but that you are alive.

What you do at work is all that you will have to show for your life. I have found that it isn't the work that gives happiness or fulfillment. I believe the work is only the expression of the happiness. What is happiness, what is fulfillment? You must know who you are, what life is, before you can know what to do. I don't know who I am.

I am in Prairie du Chien. I visit two historic sites; a priest buys me lunch. For some on the street—store clerks and shoppers, or farmers driving by in pickups, the sight of me raises an uneasiness, a vague feeling they do not like. They wonder if I can be trusted in their little town. Why isn't he working? Some might be secretively envious, others seem disgusted.

I cross the Mississippi, enter Iowa and a small river town. I see old buildings that were once warehouses, stores, hotels, and are now empty. The streets are narrow; the town nestles by the river. The town is lazy, the heat lies on the peeling paint, on the painted tin roofs. The river scent wafts up to the town but cannot break the smell of hot macadam, cement, stone, greenness.

I walk through the town and out a road crowded by bluffs. The road, the railroad bed, the river. I walk the railbed for a while. The tracks shine.

I hear the cracking, popping sounds of wood and metal expanding in the heat. I smell tar, oil, rotting fur. I see bones from raccoons, skunks, opossums who have met the night trains. My sweat streams, my feet are hot and aching. There is no traffic on the road.

The road is lined by wooden posts, painted white, joined by drooping wires meant to keep 1935 roadsters on the road. A delivery truck stops. A driver offers to share a joint; we smoke. The smoke was good then; now it paralyzes my mind, deadens me, and I shun it. Then it seemed good. I smell the river, the orange lilies growing by the road. The smell is sweet. I have a heavy weariness as I enter Effigy Mounds National Monument.

I drop my pack at the visitor center; I walk the quiet trail up the bluffs. The summit of the bluffs is crowded with mounds shaped like animals. The Native Americans are gone; I am the nearest man to an Indian—I am first man, the wanderer, who lives one day at a time. I am alone under the tall oaks and hickories; the heat presses the smell of the trees deep into my memory. A slight breeze finds my sweat-soaked skin and tingles. I see the winding Mississippi below me.

My eyes scan the shoreline on my side of the river. Wooded bluffs disappear up the band of water miles in the distance. Beneath me the water is brown; but up the river, the band is silver and winding. The silver cord loses itself in the haze of the distance, trails into the sky as if it became sky, as if it were an umbilical cord to heaven.

Below, the river is wide; the wooded islands are large, hovering green clouds over the water. Some islands have green pastures with silver ponds. The river is lush, exotic, more like a tropical river. Buoys mark the barge channel; I wait patiently for a barge that never comes. Pleasure boats streak the water; I hear the pounding of their hulls on the hard water.

The haze breaks, cumulus clouds pile high, pressing the limits of the atmosphere, stretching over the curve of the earth. The bridge in the distance, an arc with vertical lines, seems a silver spider web. The roofs of the small river towns sparkle, the exteriors of homes shine white or blue. I watch a vulture soar over the river. Then I am gone from the national monument, walking the river road to a state park where I will camp.

The Silver Cord

The view of the river from the bluffs of the state park seizes me and will not let me go. I don't want to stop looking at the river. The winding band of silver, brown—my umbilicus of life—tugs at me. The verdant green of trees and towering clouds pulls out all the knowledge I have stored. Six-foot catfish, migrating ducks, geese, the muskrat, beaver, the deer. Indians found fertile flood plains, plentiful game; the French found a water road. They have left their names on the towns, on the mailboxes. The steamboat came and Mark Twain, and every book he has written about the river flashes through my mind.

My mind swims in the thoughts of the makers of the mounds, their settlements, raids, wars; French men and crosses, keel boats, river pirates, slavery and cotton, bayous, steamboat races, the Civil War, on it goes. The knowledge floods me; I am lost in it.

The Mississippi is now real to me, and I am thankful to be upon the bluffs. Whom am I thankful to? To life? To God, I believe, though I would not speak it. I look across the river to where I have been. This piece of Wisconsin dairy land tilts into the river from miles back on the horizon. The crest of the tilt is wooded. The woods appear dark and cool. The corn fields are dark green, barn roofs sparkle. I see miniature cars, cows, homes.

Day turns to evening. I watch the change of light alter the river, and I must pull away. At night I wonder at all the life I have crammed into such a short amount of time.

Crossing the river is like a graduation ceremony. I am now nature's guest, a rambling dreamer, a wood-fire cook, a stream bather; I sleep upon the earth. I have walked through blisters, aching shoulders and feet, sweat, fevers, sun, rain, insects, hunger. I do not thirst or hunger like you; sustenance comes to me, and yet I do not need. There is nothing more the earth can do to me, it cannot hurt me; all that is left is pleasure.

The river is the beginning of a new world. Farmland, prairies, vast empty plains stretch before me; the height, wildness of the Rockies looms in my mind. These will demand more from me. I have no experience with craggy heights. I look through my atlas, see the distance between towns and wonder. In the morning, even before the sun has risen, I take out all the unnecessary equipment and clothing and leave it on a picnic table.

***

The sun is over Pennsylvania or Ohio, the earth is turning. The tops of the tall oaks and hickories wait for the sun. The food-stained picnic tables are damp, the sparse grass is wet, the mosquitoes have not taken wing. The rays of the sun are coming. I break camp, walk a limestone road from the bluff.

The sun comes with a burst of heat. I yearn for the day. I find the yellow line. The day is hot and cannot become hotter, that is the type of summer morning it is. The grasshoppers, insects are insane with life, buzzing, screaming. The noise in my ears tickles like electric barber shears against the skull. The red-wing blackbirds complain of my presence; they dive from wires not caring that I am a man.

My feet slap the road, my cutoff jeans are already wet with sweat. I pull my baseball cap visor closer to my eyes. I see the moisture rising from the fields of corn, hay, soybeans. The moisture rising seems like static on a radio. I hear a truck on a dirt road, stones kicking up underneath the chassis, upon the hubcaps. Though there is no wind, I smell the dust rising from the dirt road. I look across a field and see an old black pickup emerging from a wooded depression. As the pickup touches the paved road, it stops.

I am beside the battered, rust-spotted, repainted truck. In the bed are the ends of hay bales, gray chaff, mud, cow manure. I smell the dust falling back to the earth. Within the fine, hot dust smell, I smell hot metal, gas vapor, rubber tires. Through the window, I smell the old, cracked seat, the stuffing within. The smell begins dusty and ends as a tartness.

The man within the truck is lank, with bib overalls that are loose, torn, faded. His work shoes, once black leather, have been scuffed to a brown whiteness. Eyelets are missing the metal reinforcements. He wears a dirty straw hat with a piece missing as if a goat had taken a nibble. The man has a red neck and sallow skin. The hairs on his arms are gold with a tint of red. His hair is stubble short. His eyes are dark gray.

He has been a farmer all his life. His thoughts are upon the weather, the heat's danger to his chickens, the lack of rain on his crops, the frayed fan belt of the tractor, the cow that was sick, the meal his wife would cook for supper, the pipe he would smoke on the porch in the cool of the evening. His eyes are merry because he never sees anyone walking the road, and now, on this day, out of the monotony that is not unpleasant, there is someone walking with a pack upon his back. He will have news for his wife.

I step into the truck. Dead, cleaned chickens sit in pots of water. The silver taste/smell of the naked chickens is in my nose. He is going to town to sell his chickens for a little pocket money. He has regular customers. The moving truck creates a breeze, which brings a silent sigh.

We enter town. The town is not up yet, but it is the type of town that never gets up on a hot summer's day but sort of oozes its people into the fields, offices, stores, household chores. There is no reason to get up in a rush; there is nothing to rush to, life is not crowded. My farmer says, "I hope this is a good place to leave you off." Then he adds, "I wish I could take you further."

I say, "Thank you, this is fine. Have a good day." That is what I say, that is what I feel.

CHAPTER 5

I am in Illinois near Dubuque, waiting by a bridge, for a ride to carry me back across the Mississippi. To this day I don't know why I recrossed the river, or if I am just confused as to where I was. A guy on a motorcycle offers a ride. I accept, as I've watched traffic stream by for half an hour. He deposits me on the other side. Again, the traffic has no interest in me, I have waited an hour. A truck with a stake bed, bales of wool rising over the cab, stops. A man and a woman are in the truck; the man, driving, offers me a ride.

He is not going directly to where I wish to go, but I will get there, he assures me. I accept; movement is better than waiting in a haze of car exhaust and the noise of heavy traffic. He says he picked up a hitchhiker at the exact same spot four years ago. The hitchhiker had a sign that said, "Anywhere!" The hitchhiker had been waiting for a ride for four days. He took the hitchhiker to Cedar Rapids, helped him find a job. The hitchhiker realized Cedar Rapids was as good as anywhere, stayed, married, had children. I suppose he is still there.

I will call the driver Jim; the woman, I will call Sally. I have forgotten their names. Jim has the slim, athletic body, wiry, that belongs to a twenty-year-old—Jim must have been pushing fifty. His face is flushed

The Silver Cord

or sunburned. He is drunk—not sloppy drunk; his head is buzzing. He is in his memories, thinking in a pensive, wistful way.

He has regular features; his hair is cut close around his temples and neck, with barely enough on top to push to one side. The pores are open, the eyes have creases. Jim is lonely, but he knows the loneliness is his and that is the way it has to be. The loneliness is manly with no self-pity. He gives me a ride because I need a ride, not because he is lonely. He wants company even as he knows I have no answers.

Sally sits beside Jim like a newborn owl chick. She is dumpy, formless in appearance; grease oozes from her skin. She has straight black hair; she claims to be an Eskimo. Lots of Indians like to claim that—a private joke on the non-Indians. How she arrived in Iowa might be a mystery even to her. She is sloppy drunk, an alcoholic. Her drunkenness is of emptiness; no thoughts, no memories, nothing; just the hollow buzzing in her ears.

We cross the Mississippi south of Dubuque. The river doesn't appear majestic, no depth or width. I ask, "Is this the Mississippi?" with doubt and incredulity. Jim laughs slowly, delightedly, in a sad way because the river isn't what I expected, as life isn't what he expected. He repeats my sentence in a low voice to savor the last drops of delight. He says, "This is it."

I say, "You've seen a lot of country?"

He says, "Yes."

"What does the river look like farther down?"

"The same, only wider."

"What is it like out west?"

"It's flat, and it all looks the same after a while."

At the time I didn't understand because nothing looked the same to me. Now I understand.

We ride through rolling hills; farms are in every crease. The overloaded truck tilts around corners and bends. Jim has tipped overloaded trucks before but has never been seriously hurt. We stop at a town, enter a bar. Jim buys me a beer. I refuse a second beer; I'm tired, and more beer would put me to sleep. He looks me dead in the eye and says, "You wouldn't be owin' me nothin' if you take it." I see that he believes taking from another might carry some obligation or denote some relationship. He must speak clearly, so that I know what kind of man he is.

I say, "No thanks," and tell him why.

He drinks two more to keep the buzz going till the next stop. Sally drinks four. When Sally leaves, to go to the lavatory, Jim says Sally belonged to a friend. He feels bad about taking her away from his friend. He wants me to lessen his guilt. I say she has a mind of her own and can go where she wants. If Jim weren't so lonely, he would realize he didn't have a woman beside him, just a hollow piece of flesh, a mind rinsed of personality by the river of alcohol. Who am I to judge? A childhood of sexual abuse? Beatings? Or just no love from a parent? The relationship was working at the moment, and neither could see beyond the moment. Sometimes that is good enough.

Jim takes me to Cedar Rapids, invites me to stay with them, go fishing out on a nearby reservoir in his boat. His offer has no ties, no demands. Why is this man lonely? He has a job, a woman, friends, a home. He has all we're told we need, and he is empty. I decline his offer, express my gratitude for the ride. I was twenty-one, the road was filling the emptiness in me. I had to keep moving.

I wonder what Jim is thinking today. Is he alive or in his drunkenness did he tip a load once too often, or did the alcohol act slowly, rotting out his liver? Did he ever find something to fill the emptiness?

I am on Interstate 80 in Iowa; it is past five in the evening. The land is opening up, an anticipation wells within me, the plains are ahead—ranches, cattle, Indian reservations, antelope, buffalo. Beyond the plains, the Rockies, grizzly bears and beaver, snow-capped peaks. The vast fields of corn won't last forever, yet I am content with this farmland. The sun is yellow-orange through hazy clouds.

The Silver Cord

The air is cooling; the grass along the road is distilling cool moisture. Pigeons and starlings fly over. They fly as birds do when the sun is sinking and home is far away. An element of haste marks their flight. There is always one bird in the flock who wants to play, nip another's wing, crowd a friend. The others ignore him. They race; there is no time for games.

An anxiousness possesses me. I feel the need to find a place of rest when the earth is turning from the sun. The road beckons, says, "Live a little more this day." Far over the horizon, it is still day. I must keep pace with the sun, I must live intensely. I don't want darkness. I want more life. I wait by the highway. A sixties station wagon stops.

The driver is a farmer. His car is filled with tool boxes, greasy used rags, tools. He wears gray, grease-stained overalls. His skin is the color of coffee, his face rutted, the nose heavy for the face. He has an unkempt beard that is scraggly and remains in whatever position he slept the previous night. The beard looks like smoke from a forest fire, gray tendrils amid the brown.

The eyes are unfocused, glazed. The mouth is snarled in a quizzical expression, part apprehension, part the menacing snarl of a cornered man who is vulnerable and haunted. His words are blunt and aggressive; they are the screen for a hurting heart. He was a father who raised a "cruel and hateful son." The son had a son, a grandson, who was beaten and abused until he could take no more. He ran away to that place homeless, rootless people go, west till there is no more land, no more west—California.

The man asked if I knew a way to find the boy. How do you find a fourteen-year-old runaway? The man seemed to talk to himself. When I spoke, he was jolted from his world. His words always seemed to snap, snarl. I suggested a private detective. He and his wife had hired a detective. Did he think I could find his son?

I thought that if the son was hateful, the father might have had something to do with it, creating the hate, or at the least not alleviating the source of the hate. Sometimes a person can have perfect parents and yet develop a personality of hate. Placing blame wouldn't have helped the situation. The ride ends, and I wish him good luck in finding his grandson. That is all I can do. A part of my mind imagines an ugly life for his grandson—drugs, sexual exploitation, death.

I am running out of daylight but search for one more ride. Three high school girls, compressed in a small car between suitcases, pocketbooks, travel bags, books, furniture, and a huge hairy sheepdog, make room for me. They have graduated from high school; they will spend the summer in California. For two of the girls, I am part of the adventure. One girl is uncomfortable with my presence. They are three attractive women. To walk down the street with any one of them at your side would bolster your self-esteem. I am polite. They tell me about themselves, as much as a high school graduate can. California is a place to have fun, relax for the summer.

The land becomes flatter, the fields are growing crops, though there are no farmhouses in sight. The sun, now a lurid ball, is sinking into the flatness. I tell the girls to drop me off anywhere. The two in the front seat are concerned, searching the map for a park or campsite. They drive me to a campground, though it's out of their way. The kindness in them impresses me. I had become their responsibility. I remember the girl looking, studying the map for an exit. Where does kindness come from? How do we acquire it?

I am outside a little town called Adair. I see no town, just railroad tracks, a gas station/restaurant, a campground. I remember Jesse James committed the first train robbery at that spot. The campground has high, soft grass; sleep come easily. The next morning, I eat at the restaurant and promise that this will be the single expenditure of the day.

I walk to the highway feeling very much alive. I want to put miles behind, watch the land stream by; Nebraska beckons. I don't know what to expect from Nebraska, but I know I will like it. The morning begins cool, the air clean. A car stops, a guy in his middle twenties, thin beard, brown hair, wide face, playing classical music. He asks if I like classical music. I say, "Yes." He picks a cassette, plays it; we do not talk again until Omaha, Nebraska.

I fantasize the ride is the beginning of a movie, the music is the soundtrack. The sound of the tape deck are the cameras rolling. The flat

The Silver Cord

land, the highway strung taut, already shining silver in the light. The orange-red sun behind us, the car, are my props. Life is focused on me. My search is good, necessary, something will be learned. I am the leading actor—the star. I have no conceit, only thankfulness. I am not better than you or anyone, but I am here, searching.

It is good to believe that your life has a purpose. If I have an audience, it is God and all the angels. What are they thinking, what will they think when the film has run its course?

***

I am in the interstate sprawl that surrounds any metropolitan area; this time, it is Omaha. I dread these places. People are too busy switching lanes to see the hitchhiker. Much of the traffic is local. The traffic isn't heavy. A large, air-conditioned car stops. The day is hot, the sun bright. The driver is a year or two older than me. He says he saw me from the far lane and turned around to pick me up.

He has a couple of joints rolled. He tells me of a book he has just read called *On the Road* by Jack Kerouac. Never heard of the book. He is excited about the book and says that I am like one of the characters in the book. The book is about a guy who hitchhiked around the United States, partied, ended up in Mexico.

I ask if there is more to the book—a theme, a message. He says no, that is it, a guy who liked to travel, who liked to drink, do an occasional drug, and live intensely. I would hear of this book again, from a woman. She would give me the book to read, farther up the road, in Montana.

Somewhere near Omaha, a beat, red pickup truck, fifties model, solid, rounded, with a flimsy plywood cap, stops. Three college students are in the truck; two are bound for Lake Tahoe to spend the summer working as waiters and to enjoy the nightlife. The other is bound for Oregon to visit with a sister. He is thinking of living in Oregon permanently.

I ride in the bed of the truck with the guy going to Oregon. We cross the hundredth meridian; this is where corn can't grow without irrigation. The Midwest has ended, and the West has begun. The soil is sandier;

dust devils play on the vastness; you see no human activity for miles and miles. Bare rock ridges stick out of the ground. Off in the distance is a line of trees sunken into the land. The trees follow the Platte River, a river of sand with only a trickle of water.

My ride ends at the exit for Sidney, Nebraska. I am headed north; my friends in the pickup, west. The western horizon consists of a black, blue, purple storm front. The wind is strong, carrying the scent of sage and sandy soil. The sage is tart in my nose. The earth seems to tilt upward toward the west; the tilted land has dips, swells, ridges. The wind is frightening, chills run across my body in waves. I begin to chuckle. I'm crazy alone and I'm alive.

The pickup truck returns. They must have had visions of me blowing across Nebraska on the front of the storm. The vastness and emptiness of the land, the wind, the coming storm has frightened them, and so they think I must be frightened. They drive me into Sidney, then hurriedly turn around. When was it written into their conscience- they must return for me?

Sidney has trees along the streets. I ask a high school girl twirling her baton in her front yard, dreaming of the big game, where I might camp. She calls to her family, bathed in light, gathered around the dining room table. Brother comes out and gives me directions to a campsite outside of town by the fairgrounds. I walk through the business district; ranch girls in pickups whistle and holler at me. I walk past a one-story building with a big storefront window. Fiddles and banjos are playing, people square dancing.

A scrawny teenager from Arkansas invites me into a bar for a drink. He is traveling without purpose, his car broke down. I sense he's an all-right kid, probably from a divorced home, probably had some minor trouble with the law in his hometown, just wanting an adventure, needing a friend. Darkness has come, I want to set my tent and sleep. I tell him maybe I'll be back, knowing I'll probably never return.

I am walking a deserted road; between the racing black clouds are glimpses of the moon. The white wooden buildings and fences of the fairground seem ghostly. A tree by the road is almost bent double, the

The Silver Cord

wind strips the branches of leaves. I sleep on top of my tent after the wind blows it over. Late at night a car pulls up, occupants: a man in his thirties and a sheep. The back of the car is caged. I think this odd. I don't want to believe what I am thinking when, in the night, I hear the sheep bleating.

The next day as I am walking past a used-car lot, I feel eyes staring at me. A loud voice, tinged with disgust, a voice of contempt and ugliness, bellows at me. "That's a hell of a way to travel. Who would want to travel like that?" Maybe that was his sales strategy—taunt me into buying a clunker. He couldn't hear his own frustrated, bitter life in his words. I suppose to him I was a derelict, jobless, against all that he was for. If he had been happy with what he was, he would not have been agitated by me. I was happy at the time and felt no need to say anything; there is nothing to say to such people.

I am in Scottsbluff, I tour the national monument, from the bluff I look out at the dry plains and meager Platte. I watch the swallows careen, glide, cut, dive—the sky, their never-ending dinner plate. In Scottsbluff I sit on the curb and apply moleskin to a blister, on the advice of the previous ride. I walk out of town; churches are leaving out. I wait two hours for a ride. A girl, eighteen, and her sister, fourteen, stop. I say to them, "Two beautiful women! What luck. Wonderful. I'm glad you stopped." As I am looking at them, they are smiling back, glowing. I am happy, confident; and they have caught the happiness.

They are beautiful to me. The young girl has long, fine, brown hair, her rounded ears stick out unaffectedly, pleasingly. She has dark, thick eyebrows and black-rimmed glasses, a thin body but not frail. The woman driving has the same hair, only shorter, to her shoulders. She has a lean frame, a tight waist, a straight back. Her eyes are the clearest, cleanest blue. She is wearing a slightly faded, silky, blue dress that clings to her yet does not confine. I know the dress feels good against her skin. A trace of soft perfume lingers in the car.

The woman driving has the dark eyebrows, both have the clear white skin. They are sisters. They can't take me far, ten minutes out of town. I say that is enough. Are they bored with Scottsbluff on a Sunday? Or was the lesson in church on "love thy neighbor as thyself"? The driver and I steal glances at each other when little sister is preoccupied with her words. Little sister is leaning over the front seat, talking to me as if she's known me her entire life.

The day is hot; outside of town the plains undulate, the grasses are whitish-green. Along the berm of the road, where the runoff is caught, yellow daisies bloom in profusion. We pass an irrigation canal with high cement walls, green water; a pumping station sits back from the road. There is nothing else in sight, just a canal on the vast plains.

Little sister tells me of a boy who drowned recently in the canal. I say, "No! " This releases from her a gossipy torrent in a tone of whispered confidentiality. She is excited, pleased to inform me and yet not forgetting the tragedy. There is sadness and melancholy for an unfulfilled life. Her tone seems to say, "Here are the facts; take them to your heart."

They drop me off on the top of a swell so that I can delight in the breadth of the rolling plains. I wonder now: What if I had remained in Scottsbluff, courted older sister, married her, leaned upon her goodness, delighted in her being, felt her passion for life, had sons and daughters with her. The thought trails away. Cattle are spread on the land—brown specks, so far away. Somewhere are the ranches. The road is a black band, I see fragments of it in the distance, miles away. I lose sense of time as the wind sounds hollowly past my ears, as the sun squints my eyes.

In time a pickup hauling a piece of weaving farm machinery passes by. I see an older man and a younger—father and son, is my guess. They stop when they are well past me; I run to them. I sense they did not stop for me but to check the hitch to the towed machinery. They wear faded jean jackets, John Deere baseball caps. They consent to give me a lift. At 15 miles per hour, propped against my pack, I watch the land roll by and think of the past, of buffalo and plains Indians.

I am standing on the plains by the road when a small pickup pulls over. The bed has a canvas roof like a prairie schooner. The bed is crammed with furniture. The tall, blond man makes room for my pack; he is determined to give me a ride, for the furniture is stubborn. I sit with the man and his wife. She is a blonde, has a wholesomeness and beauty. They are going to Chadron, where there is a college. He is an assistant professor and will teach biology.

As we drive, the country changes from rolling, barren plains to ridges and scattered pine trees. I have not seen so many trees since the Platte. I ask why there are suddenly trees. He has never thought of why there are suddenly trees. I had not passed by the trees so many times that my mind ignored their presence.

The smell of the pines is strong in the intense heat. That he is a biology professor and doesn't know why the pines grow here disturbs his confidence, his competency. He teaches others; he should have the answer. He is a wise man for I have learned self-doubt is the beginning of wisdom.

I said, "Is the soil different here than on the plains? Maybe we rose in elevation so that the land gets more moisture? Perhaps the ridges protect the seedlings from the wind? The Black Hills are nearby; perhaps they spill some of their water here?" So there it is: we ask questions about life. You can stop the questions anywhere you like, or not ask at all, or you can go till you have no more questions left.

My head is reeling from a pleasant dizziness caused by the movement, my tiredness. My stomach is empty and seems to sink down into the seat, and the sensation is good. The wind rushing through the window plays in my ears. The engine hums, singing like the patterns of my brain's waves. My body wants sleep. The warmth in the cab melts concentration. My mind wants to remain awake. I do not wish to miss life.

I trust the people beside me. They are honest, friendly, caring. What makes them that way? I wonder where I will be that night. I trust that wherever it is, it will be good. Life is an adventure. The sun pulls the smell of dust and vinyl from the dashboard. The smell of pines is good, the green soothing to the eyes. Dry pines, blasted by plains winds, dry pines spaced apart in their search for moisture, sucking the ground like straws in an empty cup. The wind is like fire and as destructively lonesome. There are clouds in the sky, and shadows pass.

CHAPTER 6

To me the Black Hills are: the scent of pine and spruce upon the heat of grasslands or within the coolness of ravines and creek beds. Turkeys gobbling, running through the woods. Antelope, sitting upon the plains, in the shade of a lone tree. Antelope bounding on taut legs, moving at blurring speed. Prairie-dog towns of shrill voiced, alert residents. Wild burros, the descendants of long-dead pack animals of prospectors, taking a bemused interest in two-legged beasts.

Herds of buffalo sprawl over bare hills or are tucked into forest hidden meadows. Buffalo wallow in mudholes, snort, stare malevolently or with indifference. Prairie debris hangs upon them, twigs, grasses, plates of mud. The old bulls have rheumy, bloodshot eyes, move like an old black man who works two manual-labor jobs to feed his children. The light-brown youngsters frolic, learning of their muscular coordination. Mothers watch.

The Black Hills are gushing brooks wedged between trees and cliffs; trout streams of deep water, amber, green, meandering through meadows. High in the mountains, streams race through lush meadows where the grass is cool and thick. The aspen leaves turn their pale undersides against the wind, and the clouds are etched into the sky like a woodcut. Bare stone upthrusts rise above the forests.

The Silver Cord

Black Elk Peak towers above this Garden of Eden, seven thousand feet of gray stone looking down upon the rugged land. The wind upon the summit pummels the body. I feel an affinity with the wind, I travel as the wind travels, I know what the wind knows. The sky moves like a living thing. Gray-black, water-carrying clouds roll, skid upon the icy air; tickling, cool showers fall. The wind sweeps the clouds from sight; more clouds come, never ending.

I came west for such a place. I live like the first man, camp in the pines, sit by the fire, and wonder at creation. To walk the land, be amazed by the profusion of plants and animals, is why I exist. I came to feel fear when the buffalo bull walks toward me, snorting. I came to fish unknown pools, to stalk deer and antelope. I wish to run across this land till the earth is dizzy beneath me, the vast sky lifts me up. A man could sit in a library for a lifetime and learn what is under, upon, over the land. I have told you little of the Black Hills, just that I was there, and it was good.

I leave the Black Hills and go east to the Badlands. I have been told to see the Badlands, the misshapen earth, earth that is different from other earth. The difference holds men's interest. I was told since a child to go see the strange earth. Told in books of geography, told by elementary-school teachers with their summer-trip slides. Told by their excited voices, remembering the time outside the machine, in their summers of fun.

In the Badlands, I hitch a ride with two guys from Michigan. They are on vacation, decided to tour the west. They show me two bags of fluffy, green marijuana they found on a picnic table at their last campsite. We ride in the cab of their pickup. The wind coming through the open windows is hot and dry. We stop at all the educational signs; we walk the trails. Far in the distance, to the south, is the White River; beyond the river is the continuation of the land we stand upon, all that is missing between is called erosion. I tell you to see the Badlands, see the colors in the soil, the wide-open land.

I go back to the Black Hills. I want to see Mount Rushmore. The road is heavy with traffic, but these tourists don't have room or time to stop for me. I walk until my body and spirit give up. A car stops. The man and woman are nervous about picking up a hitchhiker. They want to help, think the best of a person, yet know that hitchhikers can be thieves, psychos, murderers; I thank them for taking a chance.

Because of them I stand before Mount Rushmore. Tourists surround me, Japanese, Austrians, Germans, Americans. Mount Rushmore is like the pictures you've seen. The pictures are so much like Mount Rushmore that there seems no reason to see Mount Rushmore. Unless you become aware of the size of those faces. I return to the visitor center, where I have left my pack.

Uniformed rangers are standing by my earthly belongings, filling out forms, poking, commenting. They tell me there have been bomb threats made against Mount Rushmore by left-wing radicals. I allow, encourage them to peer inside. When they are finished, they smile at me and say, "Have a good day." I leave with no ill feelings. A country western singer and his wife give me a ride out of the heavy traffic.

Of Rapid City, I remember some dirty, dusty streets, mines in full production, trucks and their exhaust. I eat at a fast-food restaurant. I sit at the outdoor tables even though they are sticky from spilt sodas, dripping catsup. The restaurant is swarming with people. By the way people glance at me, I understand that I am a novelty, a part of the vacation adventure. They will talk of me between themselves, speculate, make good and evil comments.

A couple approaches me. The man is in his twenties, long hair, medium height, slightly bowed back. He has the flabby skin of a man who has lost considerable weight rapidly.

His eyes are bloodshot; the pupils, wide. Is he on speed? The woman might be twenty-one or twenty-two, her hair is dark, stringy, snaky. She wears shorts, a tight shirt. She has a tan, her body is wiry, sexy. Her stomach bulges slightly, almost unnoticeably; I think there is a child within. She has a little girl trailing behind her. The two-year-old is naked except for a diaper. The kid is snot-nosed, dirty, shoeless.

John has been fasting for five days. Life is enhanced through fasting. Last night he watched the moon rise, and it was good. The woman

The Silver Cord

interjects that he gave in to a box of doughnuts one night. He isn't perfect. The woman has a pleasing face, the smile in her eyes says she likes me.

John wants to start a commune somewhere in the Hills. The Black Hills are sufficiently rugged and vast to hide a commune. John can't get the effort organized; friends vacillate. He says he admires me because I am doing, not talking. I have the drive to live fully. To me, the idea has merit. Leave the machine people behind. Hunt, fish, trap, garden, build a home, maybe find a part-time job. Find a woman with a kind heart and love her through the nights. A year in the Black Hills would be good.

I want to know if John is a dreamer with the conviction to make the dream reality. I talk about hard work, feeling trees, gathering stones for a fireplace and foundation, building a cabin, planting crops. Where would we locate our commune? What crops can be grown? What of Forest Service intervention? Can we find private land? As I continue talking, the woman, Jan, hangs on every word; her eyes glitter with desire. She likes the depth of understanding, the pragmatism. She thinks I am a man she could lean on, depend upon. I talk about cold, hunger, medicine, money, jobs so that staples can be bought. I see John's enthusiasm fade.

I could have talked him back into the idea, him and his friends. But if they have to be talked into it then they were never meant to do it. If you want something, do it—don't ask for encouragement or help. If others follow or help, fine. This has always been my philosophy.

Jan is a temptation, but I don't allow my lust to control my mind. Who is the father of the two-year-old? The kid is dirty, runs barefoot in a parking lot that has broken glass strewn about. Jan has a part-time job. Is she sleeping with the fasting friend? She doesn't have her present life in order. Why would it be different in the Hills? I thank them for their talk, wish them luck, walk to the road, and stick my thumb to the wind.

I go west into Wyoming to see Devils Tower, a volcanic plug rising above the land. I have rides with servicemen, construction workers, ranch hands. I run into rain, sleet, numbing cold, deserted roads. The soil has a red within it that reminds me of hot tomato soup. The sky is thick with speeding clouds, scraping the dark-green pine and spruce hills. I think that I must be easy for God to see, a lone being in an empty land. He sees even the sparrow fall. I wonder what will happen to me. I smell the wet earth, the sage, the pines, and I begin to sing.

I make up a song about love, peace, people being good to each other, pure thoughts and lives. My song is sweet, joyful, sad. I sing it as dusk comes and I begin to walk. I see lights in a far valley, I stumble across a national-forest campground. I build a fire from stump and squaw wood, cook my emergency food supplies, sleep contentedly. Within me, I want to say thank you, I want to talk to someone. I suppose it is God I wish to converse with. He knows what you are thinking, right? So, I do not speak, but I talk. The next day I get a ride out, without reaching Devils Tower, with two high school kids going to a rodeo.

I am in Belle Fourche, South Dakota. Belle Fourche is pronounced *Bell Foosh*. I am standing by railroad tracks as a train streams past me, boxcars of green, blue, orange, rusty red, black. The towering, gliding cars wobble a few paces from me, the smooth glide broken by a sunken tie. I hear the metal groan, creak as the wheels run upon the rails.

Now come coal cars, grain cars, chemical cars, flat-bedded cars. The rails are clacking, couplings squeak, ties crack and buckle like popping knuckles. I smell the air of train odors, diesel exhaust, chemicals, dust, chafe, cinders, oil and tar. Cinders smack into me, I squint my eyes. The wind from the train carries a heat. The train speeding by me has enough weight to crush me a million times over. My body is tense.

I turn my eyes to the empty brick buildings with western facades. Weeds grow through the sidewalks before the buildings. The names of the companies on the boxcars have a romantic quality—the names come from far places. The steel cars are wanderers like me. This country is rich and vast. Lettuce from California is moving to the East Coast; the apples of Washington, to where apples aren't plentiful; and so it goes. The cars are built to carry and to give.

I stand in the silence, watch the train glide to the east. Across the tracks I walk, up a hill, out of the old town, along the newly widened road where banks, supermarkets, malls are being built. People stare at me. A police car passes in the other lane. The young woman in the car behind

The Silver Cord

the police car smiles. I return the smile; we both know the police car will turn around and stop. For a moment she thinks of stopping and picking me up before the police arrive. But she doesn't.

The police car does turn around, stops short of me. I wait for them to come to me...I don't wish to hurry them. I know the image I must project, college kid, searching for America. I have my baseball cap, my fishing pole sticking out of my pack, my college ID in my wallet. I'm tan, lean; I'm on the road, but I'm no bum. They say little, they take my social security number and add it to a list. They say many drifters come through Belle Fourche; some are found dead along the tracks or in an alley, if not in this town, then somewhere else.

It's true. I've met these drifters, talked to some of them. Some you can't talk to—they're too far gone. Gone because they came from brutal homes, were never loved, touched, never taught right from wrong, never had the power to rise above the pain. Some were born evil, some gave in to evil; they are sullen, harboring grudges, hates; they are liars, thieves, killers, perverts unconcerned with what others feel.

The police run a check on my number; they say, "Good luck." I like them; they treated me with respect, even friendliness.

A pickup with two women and a young boy stops; a big black dog rides in the bed. They are attractive women in their thirties. Both have short blond hair, dried and bleached by the sun and wind. They have tanned faces, dry skin. Their jeans fit snugly around the curves of their hips. There is a healthy musculature underneath the tight jeans and windbreakers that comes from a strenuous life upon the ranch. They have the tiredness that creeps up on women in their thirties, a physical tiredness in the posture, a mental tiredness as much from boredom as worldliness. In some women, the tiredness appears as a calm.

The woman nearest me has a strained expression upon her face, as if there is something inside of her that wants out. I know she is divorced, or her husband or lover is away, has been away a long time. I know that is why they stopped for me. I don't want to play the game of being what she wants me to be. Finding what she likes and presenting that side of me. Then I must allow her to know that I know what she wants but pretend that I don't know. Compliment her on her appearance, subtly hint as to what her flesh does to my mind.

Is it because I have the road that I don't play the game? Is it because I know nothing lasting will come from the experience? I say, "It's crowded up front. I'll ride in the bed." The woman who I think has an interest in me looks at the woman who is driving, and with her eyes says, "How long must I wait?" For an instant I am torn. I don't like to see people hurting; it is a lonely world. She wants loved; we all do. Few truly are loved. She needs loved so badly that she is willing to pretend, to gamble in her need.

I can give her what she seeks. I know how to enter a woman's mind, talk, touch, understand. I see the hurt vanish. She'll find some cowboy, some railroad man, some store clerk. She has already forgotten me. The woman driving says it will be cold in the bed. I tell her I like the cold. I hop in with the black dog, pull my sleeping bag out. We head north into the plains.

The ride will be long, approximately 170 miles, taking me into North Dakota to Interstate 94. I can relax, no waiting for rides, no lifting of the pack, no walking, no tension from meeting new people. I'm safe for a while. I'm cold and haven't eaten since sometime in the early morning, and it's one or two in the afternoon. The sky is cold gray, the wind strong, rain is coming, I think of the blonde in the front seat. What if she only wanted a friend? What if I had been wrong about her need?

What if...?

I'm on US 85 north, no windows, no roof, just a bed of cold metal and an unfriendly dog that can't be coaxed into warming my legs. He has no interest in me; he stares out into the sage brush, looking for rabbits and antelope. In the distance are buttes, brown, majestic. The land is newly wetted so that the pale sandy earth of yellow-browns, gray-whites, browns, reds, is dimpled by the rain. The scent of the clean earth is in the wind. A cool, sandy dirt smell with just a tinge of blanched paperlike cow dung and sage.

The sage is pale green, whitened as if bloating from the water spilled upon it. The sage smell comes powerfully, cleaning out the deepest

The Silver Cord

corners of my sinuses. The tires hum frantically on the wet road. The plains are vast. I watch four different thunderstorms at the same time. Each storm is separated by clear sky, gray clouds, and sun beams.

The sun beams slant, become thicker or thinner. The light touches the buttes. Pines are sprinkled on the brown buttes. The clouds give their rain, the water slants down through the light. The clouds move, and the rain sweeps behind like the bristles of a paintbrush. Where the rain has passed the earth is dark, rich in color, as if the rain were under the hand of an artist. The brush has not passed over the land evenly; dryness, faded colors stand beside wet, beaded sage, mist, deep color.

By luck we miss passing under the thunderstorms. The feeling of intense happiness comes upon me. I know there is a God who made all this beauty for me. I thank Him. I love the cold, the wind that slaps my windbreaker hood around my ears. The smell of sage is burned into my senses. I want to take the leaves, the branches, rub them into my dry skin till the juices soak into my pores, enter my bloodstream, tingle in my lungs and within my stomach; I love the vast sky, the open unending land.

Then God gives me two rainbows, side by side, almost touching. The rainbows must be miles in width, miles of arcing colors over the plains. Every color has integrity; none is crowded or smeared, every color seeming fluorescent. The sunlight is shining golden yellow. The beams of light seem like columns, pillars. Around the rainbows, between the columns, are the dark storm clouds, flashing lightning and rolling thunder into my innermost being. Silver rain falls, lit by the sunlight. My body tingles with the cold and the beauty.

The ride ends in the stone parking lot of a restaurant near I-94. The wind is blowing hard, the sky is solid gray. Droplets of rain fall. I'm shaking from the cold. All my clothes are upon my body. I enter, the waitresses stare. One asks me if I have the money to pay. I see them gather, talking about me. I order hot coffee, French fries, a deluxe cheeseburger, warm blueberry pie. I order seconds; the coffee washes the food down, focuses my mind. In seconds, the food is spreading energy and warmth throughout my body. I feel as if I have been given a new life.

I watch the waitresses, wonder about them. Where do they live? What distant ranches gave up their daughters to this restaurant? What do these girl-women do with their time in this empty, beautiful land? What are their dreams? I leave a generous tip just because they wondered if I could pay.

I stand by the interstate, look to the east, at the rolling concrete on the rolling land. Snow flurries brush by my eyes, then hard sleet. The cars coming from the east begin as small dots. I see them on the rises, lose them in the dips. Headlights are on. The cars hurtle by me. You hear the wind screaming from some rough edge of metal, you hear the tires whine, the pistons wild in the block of metal, then the sound is gone.

One car does not pass. A big man steps out, six foot three, wide, over 225 pounds. He has a hard, aggressive handshake, a deep voice, looks me directly in the eye. He wants to establish who is boss. I sense he does this from anxiousness and not aggressiveness. It is not a simple thing to let a stranger into your car. He wants to help but he doesn't need trouble. I understand. We place my pack in the trunk, enter the car. He offers me sandwiches, soda or beer. He is traveling two hundred miles to see his girlfriend.

The road is wet, rain and mist come. Four coyotes tumble down from the hills, gray, formless in the mist. The driver tells me he once shot coyotes from a plane. He says this wondering if I will think his actions right or wrong. I don't judge; I encourage his conversation. A rancher paid for the ammunition and the plane's fuel. The ranchers in that particular area could take no more damage to their herds. I can sympathize; and shooting coyotes from a plane might be enjoyable—to the shooter. Yet, there should always be a place where coyotes roam free and unmolested. No one disagrees with this last statement. The problem becomes complicated when you ask how much land should coyotes have and where?

We are in Medora. I am exiting, and the big man is continuing west. He is not satisfied to leave me out on the highway. He exits, takes me the distance to the entrance of Theodore Roosevelt National Park. In the west, the clouds are breaking apart, the yellow of the sun is shining on the clouds like glaze on pottery. I see the setting sun. I unroll my

The Silver Cord

sleeping bag under a picnic table, on cement, in a deserted picnic area. The cement is too hard, I move to the earth. At dusk, a group of teenage cowboys pulls up in their cars and pickups. They are wearing their dress hats; clean, ironed shirts; untorn jeans. They are whooping and hollering, drinking beer and a pint of hard stuff. When the bottle has been passed, the cowboys leave.

In the park, I become first man. From four-hundred-foot bluffs I watch deer play on the sandy shores and sandbars of the Little Missouri. I stalk herds of buffalo. I walk up deep arroyos, whose banks tower over my head and crumble as I walk. I wonder at the profusion of bones sticking out of the banks, lying on the bed. Skulls, antlers, femurs, scapula. I walk the open plains; the sun dehydrates me, tans me; life is good.

I camp with the recreation vehicles in the shade of cottonwoods. All I need is upon my back. My neighbors need tons of steel and gadgetry. When night comes, there is not one campfire among the metal. They do not see the stars, smell the wind, hear the beaver tails slap the water. My neighbors are inside, blinded to the night by their electrical lights. They are playing cards or attempting to fix the faucet or some other piece of gadgetry. They're doing whatever they do at home, only now they do it in the park.

I suppose there is a tinge of loathing in my thoughts. My health won't last forever, and then I'll need the machine. Someday there might be a time when I have only so many days of vacation. The machine may capture me, my health may break. Yet there is truth in what I think; I let the loathing float out of my head. I'm thankful that I'm strong, hardy, tough; that I'm nature's child. It is not the machine I need—I belong to life.

The park is good; in time, the road calls. A garbage truck stops, I throw my pack in the rear, where the scoop sweeps the garbage into the bin. I hop into the cab with a positive, friendly guy who admires what I'm doing. Outside the park, I walk to a commercial campground, hoping to take a shower, talk to someone just for the sake of talking.

I go into the main building thinking I will be charged a few cents, maybe a dollar. I ask the older man behind the counter for the price of a shower. He says showers come with the campsite. I will have to pay for a campsite. I tell him I don't need a campsite, just a shower. He repeats his first statement. The price is high for a shower. A young kid, who I assume is the man's helper, is listening.

The man says, "We don't want your kind here."

I ask, "What kind am I?"

He doesn't answer. He doesn't know me. What has he assumed about me? If he truly knew who I was, what I thought, and he didn't want me at his campground, then I could live with that. A rage comes. I wonder why I bothered to come out of the wild land. A buffalo has more humanness than this man. I curse the man. I wish that I hadn't. He brought me down to his level. I see the kid watching and feel as if I have failed in a responsibility to him. I knew he was on my side.

I leave angry. I don't allow my mind to say, "He might have had his reasons." Perhaps a hitchhiker had treated him wrong, stolen from him. Perhaps he had pressing bills to pay, or a wife in the hospital and really needed the money. Some people can't handle the pressures of life. Should I curse them because I am in control of my life (though I am not)? The code within me says to treat everyone with respect, even when your life isn't pleasant or good, even when it is crumbling around you. My anger quickly fades as I stand beside the interstate.

CHAPTER 7

I am not by the highway for more than five minutes before a Volkswagen bug pulls over. My ride is a serviceman, US Air Force security. He's about my age, from Vermont. It is an easy meeting; servicemen as a rule have learned to make friends quickly. They know how to judge, how to get along. I know he is as straight as an arrow and just doesn't want his adventure alone. He has two weeks' leave. He's going to Yellowstone to fish, then to the Black Hills. As we ride I interest him in the Custer battlefield. He wasn't planning to go, but since it is on the way, why not?

Wyoming begins as hills, plains covered in grass, monotony, broken only once by the sight of cowboys pushing some steers. Cowboy hats, handkerchiefs around their necks, lariats coiled on their saddle horns, blue jeans under chaps. Somewhere we make a wrong turn, the road is gravel; we see deserted ranches, working ranches, meadows, pines, rock outcrops. A Native American reservation, alfalfa and irrigation pipes, a river hidden in trees. We see distant mountains, long and rolling. The bright slopes hold pockets of snow. The sky is clear blue, the plains grasses green; wildflowers paint the land in swaths of yellow and orange.

We are on the battlefield. We follow the strategy of the campaign using the visitor center map. Custer wanted to find Indians, and he

The Silver Cord

did—thousands, camped beside the peaceful Little Big Horn River. A river with a flat plain on one side, bluffs, hills on the other. Custer came through the hills, leaving his main force behind. He wanted to pinch the Indian encampment between his forces, never realizing the size of the encampment. On the hills sloping down to the river, he was surrounded. White stone markers show where the bodies of the Seventh Cavalry fell. The hilly earth still holds the impression of trenches where the main force, which could have supported Custer, bogged down, harassed by Indians and perhaps the fears, timidity, or cowardice of the officers.

It is strange and sad to walk where so many men died. The Native Americans said the land was theirs because they had possession first. They were warlike people, they raided their neighbors, killed, enjoyed torturing, practiced slavery, slew women and children on occasion. They constantly challenged the borders of neighboring tribes. The white man was warlike long before he met the Indians. His superior technology gave him an arms advantage in war. His armies could be on campaign indefinitely, soldiers not burdened by the needs of their families. The problem that is war is many times the clouded vision of opposing desires.

I have read books about the battle and the men who fought—immigrants, ne'er-do-wells who didn't die well. The soldiers had rifles that jammed; they panicked, shot into each other, ran. Some died like men, fighting. You see the lonely marker far from the others and wonder what went through that man's head. What is it like to die alone, so far from your friends? What is it like to die with your brothers and nephews by your side? After the battle, the Indian squaws plundered the dead, mutilated the bodies. Some of the men were only feigning death. The women took their knives to those men.

I feel the hopelessness of the doomed, the presence of fear, the absence of strength, thought, reason. I am about to die. I shoot but don't aim, distracted by too many targets. The enemy on foot, moving through tall grasses. A swirling mass of horses of every natural color, painted and feathered, carries warriors, leaning low, or behind the horseflesh. My gun jams, horses are coming, I hear yelling. The horses are upon me, the barrel of a repeating rifle slams into my head even as the trigger is pulled. I am just flesh now, falling to the earth; the remnant of a mind hears gunshots, yells, feels the jolt of the earth. I am dead, the leap has ended. Where do men go? Into nothingness? Heaven? Hell?

The soldiers died knowing there was no hope. Or did they believe their comrades would come to rescue them? The Indians knew the battle was won but a way of life was dead. Both sides had angry men, both sides had men who did not want conflict, both sides had relatives—sisters, mothers, sons, fathers—empty of hope, of companionship taken, grieving. The people who cried for the dead are dead now, and someone cried for them. On and on it goes.

The car is moving toward Yellowstone; it is night, we see light, a waving haziness, a vaporous aura, in the sky. Rightly or wrongly, we conclude we have seen the northern lights. Sleep comes at a gravel pullover where other vehicles have gathered to spend the night. We express the strangeness of sleeping in a car with a total stranger. This wariness assures us we are safe. The sleep is a catnap; the cold and discomfort prod us to wakefulness.

In the early morning, we are in the Rockies. The road carries us up a valley with sides so steep I cannot see the sky. The sky is directly above the roof of the car, a narrow sliver of blue. I can only see the sky because I put my head out the window and look straight up. We come to a road that switchbacks up a mountain. Barriers say the road is closed because of snow.

Air Force goes through the barriers. We leave the tree line; rock slides are on the road; one forces us to the edge. I look down hundreds, if not thousands, of feet to a rocky valley. At the summit the road is snow-covered, the wind howls, the snow is driven, clouds are ripping, tearing around us.

There is complete silence in the car, as the car shakes, buffeted by the wind. The snow driving against the metal sounds like sand, a hissing, slapping sound. The wind streaming through the car makes a sound as if it is blown out of a conch shell. The cold air streams, flows into the car, between doors, windows, up through the gear box. Two hours in this cold and wind and we will be dead.

The Silver Cord

I have my first awareness that I am nothing to the Rocky Mountains. Nature, once my friend, doesn't love me. Break her rules, and death will come. What if the engine stops? We are the only ones on the mountain. The clouds thicken, a snow squall comes with the clouds. I am dizzy with the speed of the clouds. I am shivering though the heater is on. The hollow sound is rushing through the car. We turn around and cautiously creep back down the switchbacks.

For three days in June, we are in Yellowstone National Park. The temperature hovers around freezing, as rain, sleet, snow fall. Clouds blanket the sky, no sunshine, no color except the dull-green uniformity of fields, meadows, trees; the dull-gray uniformity of sky, rocks, water. I wear all my clothing, shiver even when moving. Air Force fishes till the cold, the weather blunt his desires.

We leave, pass hot springs, geysers, Yellowstone Lake, go east into Cody, Wyoming. I say good-bye to Air Force. He is going to the Black Hills. I check into a rundown motel that allows tents on the lawns behind the units. I take my first shower in two weeks. The shower stall has two inches of backed-up water on the floor, but I don't care. After cleaning up, I walk into town, eat at a fast-food restaurant. Coming back to the motel, I see a guy standing by the road with a sign that says, "Yellowstone." He carries a huge backpack; a seabag four feet long and solidly packed, and an overnight bag are at his feet. I stop to talk.

He's from Philadelphia, flew the entire distance to Cody. On the local flight into Cody, he met a rancher and his wife, who invited him to their ranch his first night of arrival. Philly works for a large corporation; his job is to keep people happy. He's about twenty-five or twenty-six, above medium height, wiry; his skin tends toward olive. He doesn't seem interested in talking about his work, and what he does say he keeps vague. He is intelligent, perhaps with the ability to be cunning. He took time off from his job; not vacation time, just time off.

I want to go back to Yellowstone, see the park in the sun, in relative warmth, and backpack some of the trails. Would Philly make a good backpacking partner? You need a partner backpacking. There are dangers; sickness, broken bones from falls, sudden snow storms, swollen streams that must be crossed, bear attacks, avalanches. I tell him that if he doesn't get a ride into the park today—the day was late—to come back to my camp and we'll talk. I leave it like that, giving him time to decide.

Not soon after I am back at my tent, Philly comes along. We talk. He has a vibrant attitude, doesn't seem to be a complainer, has that desire to have other people like him, says he's not queer. We decide to travel together. I wonder if he can keep up with me; he has done no running or walking prior to the trip.

He has too much gear, little first-aid kits, various-sized canteens, exotic dehydrated foods, little containers full of clever tools, fire-making ingredients, foods of all kinds. He says he thought he could find a central location, drop off the unwanted gear, and take only what he needed for his backpacking. I tell him he'll never get to a central location because people will only pick you up if it is convenient, easy; all that gear is troublesome to a driver. Even if you get to a central location, who is going to guard what you leave behind? I sort through his gear and explain to him what is unnecessary. I don't want to make him appear foolish, or me superior. He doesn't become defensive at my advice.

We go into Cody together, to the post office, to ship half his gear home. I still think he has too much, but everyone has his own idea on what is necessary and what is not. In the post office, a woman comes up to us. She saw we were hitchhikers and has a proposition. She will take us anywhere we want to go if we will pay half the gas cost. I can't believe our good fortune. She is our way into the park, we will be able to see the main sights, have her drop us off at a trailhead. Without her, life would have been miserable. There is no hitchhiking allowed in the park; the cars are so crowded no one stops anyway.

Her name is Laura. She is twenty-three or twenty-four; short, honey-blond hair, unkempt, greasy; her frame leans toward pudginess. She is not beautiful, nor is she homely. She wears no makeup, hasn't bathed in a while. She is nervous. She is traveling in a pickup with a camper, the license says California. She is vague about her past. She has seven brothers, grew up on a ranch.

The Silver Cord

Her brothers are a "bunch of savages." She shows us a picture of bare chested/tanned, long-haired, wild-eyed boy-men. They appear crude, unfeeling, undisciplined, living for the next beer party or sexual adventure. She has nothing good to say about them. She shows us a picture of a bearded man bent over a microscope. This is her boyfriend; she has borrowed his truck. I am skeptical of this boyfriend loaning a truck to this girlfriend but keep the thought to myself.

She talks about the Peace Corps and a book. The book deals with the problems within the Peace Crops—bureaucratic red tape lousing things up; confused, ignorant natives; even more confused Peace Corpsmen. She is either writing such a book or had read such a book. I sense Laura is confused, depressed, that she is taking this trip to straighten out her thinking. She is lonely, her mind is numb, and she is hoping one of us has the answer.

We gather up our gear, tank up, split the cost—three people who hadn't known each other a few hours ago—and head for Yellowstone. Philly begins talking. He wants or needs Laura to like him. I begin to believe Philly doesn't have the line. There is a line I will not step across to be what someone wants me to be. I think Philly would be anything. Another difference appears as he talks of his work. He is talking of Las Vegas, the entertainment industry. He refers to a once-prominent actor as "one of them." The tone is of disgust. I discover somewhat obliquely that "one of them" means a Christian. What could Philly have against a person who has morals, knows right and wrong? This actor-comedian had spent most of his funds on a hospital for disabled kids. How can you dislike someone who does good unless you are not good? I suppose that is my line—morality, right and wrong.

The rain and snow are gone from Yellowstone. Golden sunlight creates an entirely new park for me. We tour all the major sites—waterfalls, canyons, geysers, lakes, gorges, elk, bear, buffalo. The foreign tourists are in abundance as well as the American variety. The foreigners always seem to be trying to glean some immutable truth from you about this place called America. The American variety astounds me with its bad manners—they do everything that common sense and the signs say not to do. Throw your trash to the wind! Mutilate trees, rocks! Shake hands with bears as you feed them potato chips! I wonder how many more

Americans want to do these things or worse and are silently awaiting their chance.

Buses clog the roads as well as cars. Motor homes lumber along and are like dueling jousters when passing in opposite lanes, their extended mirrors acting as lances. Usually, the motor homes flinch before contact, swerve to the shoulders, send bicyclists flying. When the tour is complete, Laura drops off Philly and me at a trailhead. We become backpackers.

We find an elk calf in deep grass, all knees, legs, panting in fright. We startle moose in a sparkling pond, heads buried underwater, the antlers rising. The moose thrash through the water, crash through the pines. On the gentle slope of a hill, covered in pines and dewy grass, a bear roots and explores. The sunlight is pristine, tinging his coat. His nose catches our scent and in a two-legged gait, he gallops down into a thicket. Herds of elk bound through the trees. Coyotes yip and whine through the freezing nights, their tracks beside our tent. The evening sun bathes cold rock peaks. We tramp across snowfields and drink the meltwater.

I climb a mountain peak alone. I see for miles. Forest is laid in the creases of the virgin land. Rugged upheavals of rock rise to a sky so close and vast that clouds catch upon the peaks. I see streams sparkling, bloated by the work of beaver dams. Here on this desolate peak, I find two elkhorns locked together. I cannot pull the horns apart. I see in my mind two elk upon this cold pinnacle, necks thick with passion, eyes glazed, breath streaming, muscles tensed, quivering, fighting for a cow.

I come down from the pinnacle because my body shakes from cold, and I see a grizzly track twice the size of my boot. The clouds pull together, coagulate, darken the sky. The wind shrieks through boulders. Snow whips past my face. I fear the grizzly, and I hope some unseen force, God, will protect me from harm. In time the trail ends, we ford a stream of ice-cold water, stand beside the road in wet jeans, and wait. That is the end of Yellowstone.

A woman picks us up, a college girl, with long, fine silver-blond hair. A big shaggy dog rides with her, a wolfhound. She and the wolfhound are built the same, long, lean, but not thin or frail. The dog is nervous, flighty like the woman. A dog that was bred to run must run, or the unexpended energy corrodes the spirit. The woman drives us into Bozeman, Montana, tells us where we can get a room for four dollars a night. She tells us of a bar; we make plans to meet her there in the evening.

Philly and I feel like mountain men at the rendezvous. We eat at a fast-food restaurant till we can eat no more. We walk down the streets boldly, for we have proven ourselves in the mountains; the pride of accomplishment walks with us. People are now a pleasure, for so long they weren't seen. If people are not good to us, with a boldness that vacillates between good-naturedness and indignation, we will find the reason why. As darkness falls, we find ourselves in the bar. Our woman is here with a friend who has no interest in me. I drink two beers, say to myself, "That is life." I melt into my chair, enjoying the heat; think of my travels and wonder at the future.

The next day we find a thrift store, and I buy a blanket, long underwear, a sweatshirt that advertises a Christian camp/ranch. The sweatshirt has a cross upon it in black ink, and the word *Christian* in bold lettering. Philly makes a face of amusement and disgust upon seeing the cross. I say, "Yeah, this is the sweatshirt for me," in a positive, aggressive tone. I don't think God is such a bad character, and Jesus dying on the cross—who should object? I don't understand. I know if the sweatshirt had advertised a nudist ranch, Philly—and most people—would have thought that cute. I'm enjoying the life God gave me; the recriminations of my childhood and youth are forgotten. He was with me in the mountains. He has followed me on this trip. Life is good.

We walk through town, thumbs out. I'm ready for the mountains, ready to leave civilization behind. We are going to Glacier National Park, Montana.

A man in his late twenties picks us up. A scar runs from his neck to his forehead, passing over the bridge of the nose. The scar is not ugly to me. I always look at a person's spirit, personality; the flesh is just a container. I see the man wince as we make eye contact with him. In the West and Midwest the farm and ranch machinery take their toll. Wheels spin so fast they aren't visible. Belts move so quickly, quietly, smoothly they appear still. The sounds of the machine are so soothing the mind loses its concentration. The machine has its tricks.

I think the machine and the flesh are in a conspiracy. They want the soul of a man to hurt long after the machine has done its damage. There is a segment of society—some would argue many and some, few—who call the scars ugly, make painful jokes at the ones who carry the scar. People who are always elevating themselves, even if it means hurting another. The ride isn't long, but we are out of town. The driver is a good man; we are on the highway again.

Sunny day, clear sky, temperatures in the seventies; green wheat fields surround the highway. The wind swirls through the wheat. A navy radar technician picks us up. He's bearded, has a big stomach, quiet demeanor; a family man. I let Philly do the talking; he's overflowing with the excitement of the trip. The man says that we are traveling through the greatest wheat-producing area in the country and probably the world. This family man, who seems to carry responsibilities, says good-bye.

I remember little of this part of the journey. Helena is just a name on a map. Of Great Falls, I remember a few smokestacks, row homes on hillsides, and an airport. I remember a jeep stopping. The driver is small, five feet; thin; with reddish hair, military cut. He is in the air force, security. I sit and see in the back seat a pistol in a holster, a target peppered with holes.

Our driver likes survival camping in the most primitive areas of the Rockies. He goes into the mountains with a flint, a knife, some fishing line, perhaps a pistol, then lives. He likes to read of mountain men and of the history of the old West. I think a part of his personality is of the little guy who feels he has to prove his manhood, to show that he measures up in heart. This standard of manhood, which goads every man, is an agitation, a sore spot rubbed raw. As I come to this awareness, whether true or not, the ride ends.

We are deposited on the gravel of a restaurant parking lot. A few houses are scattered along the road past the restaurant. I tell Philly that if we don't get a ride, we can sleep in the field across the highway. The thought frightens Philly. I go into the empty restaurant for a fast cheeseburger. One girl works the counter, does the cooking. Outside, with full stomachs, we watch the motor homes pass. A motor home roars by, the horn is sounding, we wave. I see people in the cab peering

The Silver Cord

down at us. The motor home stops up the road, turns around and comes back to us. A man in his late forties or early fifties asks gruffly, "Do you want a ride?"

We get in. As we talk, he and his wife, Philly and I, in the cab, his two kids in the back, we find we have interrupted a battle of the sexes. He said he'd stop for good-looking females. His wife then wanted to know why she couldn't stop for handsome men. She made him turn around. They're from Oklahoma. He works in the post office and is in the Air National Guard. Philly takes a liking to our driver, they talk. He seems to have a distrust of me. Philly gets this guy talking about his life, his job, his family, his vacation. I watch the country pass.

I like the family, and they like us; even Dad eventually warms up to me. Food and drink are offered. I climb back into the camper. Daughter, seventeen, not unattractive, shows me where she and brother watch the world pass. I lie on a thin mattress above the cab, looking out a window at the road. You can't see the truck's hood or the edges of the road. The top sways in the wind. Daughter has the radio playing; the music is, by coincidence, about traveling. The music melds me to the high, rolling land of green, irrigated wheat squares and circles; plowed fields of brown earth; yellow-stubbled fields. The colors follow the contour plowing or the stripes, circles of wheeled irrigation pipes. The sky is clear and faded blue. White grain elevators and silos dot the land. I think of our good fortune—first Laura, and now the Okies. Life is good.

CHAPTER 8

We are in Glacier National Park, with the Okies, driving upon a road called Going-to-the-Sun Road, but we are going to sleet, snow, fog, clouds. The mountains are jagged, perpendicular walls. I am in awe of their size, their thrusting brutality. My head rests upon my back, and still the mountains rise. The clouds are moving at incredible speeds, being raked over the jagged rock peaks, spilling their innards of moisture.

Some clouds are pushed through gaps, shoved against rock; some mill at the gaps; they are like cattle moving to the slaughterhouse chutes. Up in the torn, milling clouds, the fog banks, and the perpendicular gray rock are white specks. I think them patches of snow until they move. Goats! Entire families perched on sheer rock walls. "Incredible!" I say to myself as the wind sounds hollowly in my ears. The sound of the wind seems to always be in my ears, as if I am inside a vast tunnel.

This is our initial introduction to Glacier. But Glacier is also sunlight, glistening peaks, deep-blue, cold lakes, crystal air that is like a clear white wine. There are roaring falls, pummeling winds that a body must lean into, forests of lushness, huge lodges of immense

The Silver Cord

timbers, grizzly bears in campsites, harried rangers, college students manning the motels and hotels.

On the second day, Philly and I walk into Saint Mary, directly outside the east entrance to the park. Saint Mary consists of a gas station, a convenience store—heavy on camping supplies—a hotel with cabins for the employees, a native american crafts building, two bars, and up the road is a restaurant. We ask two female employees of the motel where we can take showers.

The blonde, long fine yellow hair, is eager to talk. She is wiry, with prominent round cheek bones that give a sexiness, straight white teeth, laughing eyes. She has a vibrancy, a positive attitude. She is one of those people who is never daunted, who can only go through problems. She is from Wisconsin, her named is Lana. Her companion, Dawn, is from a ranch in Wyoming. She has shoulder-length brown hair, large brown eyes that make you feel calm when you look into them. Her calmness is self-possession. She is every bit as desirable as Lana. Lana says we may shower in their cabin.

In the evening, a group of female employees is in Lana's room, collecting one of Lana's roommates for a Bible study being held in another cabin. I am asked if I would like to attend. I want to go. I want to see and hear what they think. What do they know about God? Perhaps I will hear something I don't know. Perhaps God will give me the answer I am seeking. Who else can have the answer? But Lana and Dawn are not going, and so I don't go.

Philly makes his appearance, and the four of us talk. Lana says she and Dawn are planning to quit their jobs as motel maids and hitchhike to the coast. I tell them the trip will be dangerous; they should go with a man. At the same time, three people are unlikely to get many rides. They talk on, I become sleepy. I want to talk, want Lana to know me. I would like to travel with a woman like her. But what is there to know about me? Even then I was in the leap called life.

Lana tells us how she and Dawn and another girl climbed the mountain nearest the park entrance. She tells of boulders falling, avalanches, fatigue, cold, the girl who began crying, a grizzly bear rustling through the brush. They made the climb in sneakers, in one day. My mind recalls the image of the mountain, towering, bare rock, perpendicular sides. The feat seems impossible without climbing gear, ropes. I don't doubt that she climbed the mountain.

I take my shower. Lana says we should stick around Saint Mary for a while. I know if I stay, get to know her, the chances are good she would travel with me. But I don't stick around a few days. Months later, she sends me a postcard from Oregon. She says there have been no problems, and she adds, "So there!"

I wonder about her often now. Where is she? What is she doing? Does she have a husband, children? I think of her as the type who travels—Vail in the winter, or the Yucatan; Europe in the summer. We both wanted life, adventure; searched for it, lived it. I was searching for the answer, the idea behind life, what this means to a man's actions. Lana did not need to know who she was, what life was for; her search was out there. She would react to the world presented to her. My search is within. If I find that answer, maybe I will shape life—not simply react to what is cast upon me.

Philly and I spend an evening at the motel's bar. A blue grass band is playing, the room is packed. We listen to the sounds of the Appalachian hills, the nasal sounds that vibrate within, the lyrics of lovers, unrequited love, horses, hounds, foxes, poverty, coal mines, mountains, sad laments, yearnings. I meet a girl named Mary, from Chicago, who is working as a motel maid for the summer.

She is one of those people who seems to have been born with a natural amphetamine in her blood. The mind is always racing, grabbing hold of another thought even before it is done with the thought that it has, as if all thought is meant to overlap. Her thoughts entertain her and don't necessarily need to be understood by those listening. Make believe, fantasy is in the words, but the listener listens because the words are spoken with enthusiasm and pleasure.

She talks of the book *On the Road* by Jack Kerouac. She loves the book, uses phrases and words from the book. She has ingested the book, and it is part of her dream mind that moves at Mach speed. A person such as she sometimes is fleeing the real world, so that a book is like a glove through which the real world may be touched, secondhand. She may touch the world through Jack Kerouac but not through Mary. I remember what I learned of the book through the ride outside Omaha.

She has an interest in us, likes us, because we are like the characters in the book. Philly takes an interest in her as do I. I've been on the road longer than Philly, and I use this to my advantage. I am the worldly one, the true traveler, the true Jack Kerouac. What a fool I am. What do you want from her? I ask myself. Nothing really, except I'm supposed to pursue her, make it with her; isn't that what a man does with women? The game I refused to play with the woman in South Dakota is being played. She is skittish, I back off. I give her the piece of me she will like.

I know I don't know who I am. That is why I am uncomfortable, afraid someone will find out that I am totally lost. Yet, I admit this readily to myself and to God. Is that why I call meeting a woman a game? Because I am hiding from myself and hiding from her? If I knew who I was, I would simply state who I was, let them like me or not. What would it matter if I were rejected?

Mary begins to talk about the Rainbow Gathering near Choteau, which isn't far away. I have met some of the people coming and going to the gathering on the streets of Saint Mary. They say supplies are scarce; they seek fully stocked stores. Rainbow people are people who have left the machine. They travel in converted buses or vans, they thumb, they drive conventional vehicles. Some are back-to-the-land types; some have craft skills; some have part-time jobs; some, full-time. They come in all types, but they dress rakishly, gypsy like. Some who hang on the fringe have less-rigid rules of conduct and morality—sometimes.

At the apex of the rainbow scale might be a man who owns land, lives partially from it, who has a craftsman's skills, a converted bus, a family. The tail of the rainbow would be some hitchhiker who works menial jobs all over the country, does a few more drugs than are good for him, and steals when he has the need. They meet every year at a different location, make new friends, converse with old friends. They tell of the things they have done or exchange information—on how to build a cabin, buy land, or feed a family from a garden. Mary plans to go to Choteau.

Mary begins talking of the book again; she has the book in her purse. She reads a passage, about the sad, sweet, blue smell of lilacs on a Denver Street in June. Another passage is about black people living sadder, sweeter, more intense lives. She believes this to be true. A part of me wants to say Kerouac is right; I know what he is feeling. Sadness does give life a sweetness; life should be lived intensely. Because I feel his melancholy, his statement becomes truth?

I think of real black people, the ones I have seen, gone to school with, know—not the black people seen through the eyes of another man. I see too many children—no fathers, mothers without enough love to cover them all—growing up wild. Beatings, incest, drugs. Self-esteem stripped away. Men and women scraping for everything. The black man, the actor, pretending to control life, when he is only a bruised child whose soul is scarred from tension, fear, anxiety; who wonders which white man will call him *nigger*, never judging him on the content of his character.

I try to tell Mary the truth, that such a life is not to be sought. You will lose your character, you will return hate for love, the soul will be bitter. If such a life has any sweetness, it's because a man looks past the rough times to some better vision. The lilacs will smell just as sweet sitting on the porch of the home you own, after a hard day of work. I don't think that I get through to her. I am not trying to convince her the words are false. I want her to see there is more to what the words say. Don't buy into someone's feelings until you search them out for truth.

We drop the topic. We leave the warm building, walk back to my tent. The night is cold, crisp; the sky is black. Millions of planets, stars thicken the sky in clusters, bands. We walk down the middle of the road. The night is still except for the coming wind, which rushes through the high grasses in the fields beside the road. Then there is quiet again. The vast sky pulls my eyes upward.

My mind passes amazement and settles upon reverence; I wonder if God made other worlds, other peoples. The sky is vast, space is vast. The God who made it all is unlimited. He is a God of power. I am a very small thing. Something inside wants to fight the smallness. Pride?

The Silver Cord

This something has no strength. I am small, puny, made by God; I will never be God's equal. Peace comes to me; strangely, my smallness pleases me. I think that if God is my master, then I owe my allegiance to no man.

Mary is in my tent. We are on my sleeping bag, clothes on. We talk. Her story is this: Her parents are divorced. She spent most of her life in a Catholic boarding school. Her parents seemed to have no interest in her. She doesn't think they really wanted a child—she was an accident. Her father is an executive-type salesman, interested in getting ahead. She shows me a picture of him—crew cut, plaid jacket, lean face. From her expression I know she wanted to be loved by him and never was. Her mother's interests were dressing right and attending parties.

Mary is one of the few people who senses she is in the leap. Cut lose from parents, a homelife, love; receiving nothing but discipline and knowledge from boarding school; she senses the leap. She is attractive, intelligent, educated, and she has nothing. She wants something to hold onto, even if it is only a book. She wants to forget the absence of love.

Her life is without purpose, she has no anchor. She is searching for an idea to live by but can't see out of her humanness, her hurts. No one can see out of their humanness; we are limited, confused; we can't be objective; all have been mangled by life. Only a perfect man could give us the wisdom we need. Only he would understand life. Even if he told us what was wrong, where would we get the power to untangle our lives, thoughts, and live as we should? Some say the man is Jesus. Some say He has the power.

The words stop. I kiss her. She doesn't return the kiss, nor does she fight the attempt. For a brief moment, Mary becomes the symbol of what life is to me. Only a part of me wants the kiss returned. If life won't return love, then I don't want life. I need life to want me. I think life would say, "Hey, I don't want you—never have. You are alive; you think, speak, act, and now you're trying to take. If you are looking for a sign from me, forget it. If you're hungry enough, mean enough, and you want it, take it. You better want it; because I'm not helping." For some men that is enough—they will take. Taking leaves me empty inside. I want life to want me; I want to do it right. I think I'm saying I want God to want me. He did make life, didn't He? He allows life to go on even when it is ugly and not so kind. Or maybe I'm responding to a cold tent, a tired body, and a woman who doesn't know what she wants.

The next morning, Mary gives me the book to read and to keep. I am headed into the wilds with Philly. Mary has decided to quit her job and see the Rainbow celebration in Choteau. She is gone when I come down from the mountains. We meet again thousands of miles away, a year later.

Philly and I go into the mountains, some days we walk fifteen miles. I catch two nice trout and we eat them for dinner. We pass waterfalls, forests, lush jungles of undergrowth, wide white-capped lakes. We walk trails rutted from years of hiking; we walk trails covered in vegetation, absent of footprints. We walk switchbacks up bare stone cliffs; we walk across snowfields. The lungs breathe deeply, desperate for oxygen.

We gain the pass between two solid-rock valleys, both valleys bored by lakes of ice water. Still the bare rock towers over us, the home of goats and marmots. The clouds move fast, are torn on the peaks. There is nothing kind in the clouds. If you were able to touch them, they would burn you like frigid metal; they would stick to your skin, pull your skin away if you moved. That is what I think of the clouds. The wind howls, the wind is clean; you are dirt, sweat, filth. When the wind roars through your body, you are clean.

I stand between the valleys, listening to the avalanches. One lake is milky-white-blue from cascading snow; the other, a deeper blue. Both lakes have no shoreline, just the sheer sides of the mountains. The sun is a cold rose tint on the horizon. Supper is eaten, a pot of the hottest, blackest coffee tingles within. I study the bare rock peaks above me, stretching around the valley. The recesses are filled with black shadows, blacker than the night, more lonesome, desolate than the void between the stars. The unseen sun is shining golden-yellow on the rock peaks. I am such a puny thing; the earth turns away from me. I am dizzy with my smallness. I am fatigued, starved even after eating. I am high on the air, the coffee. The beauty has raptured me. I jump from boulder to boulder, boulders the size of cars. I run up a ledge, the goats are waiting for me.

The Silver Cord

They have watched us all day, dads, moms, kids, babes. Black horns protrude from their heads like daggers of obsidian. The babies have pure-white fur. The oldsters range in color from pure white to the yellowness of a cigarette filter. The goats move with a deliberateness; time means something different to them. Their minds never go beyond the step they are taking. They have no past and no future. Their feet touch the rock as a magnet to metal.

They stare at me; we are only feet away. I look into their eyes and realize they see me as another goat. Dogs, cats, deer see a man as a man, superior. Not these goats. A male lowers his head. Within my mind, I say that I am a man; the thought is communicated to the goat, his head rises in acknowledgment. Their pupils have an odd shape, a deadness is in their eyes. I talk to them, but they pretend not to hear. I walk away and stand on a boulder. I watch the last of the light leaving the mountain peaks.

A sense of accomplishment wells up. I have beaten the mountains, the cold, hunger, fatigue. I have dared to live. I have conquered the stranglehold of my parents, the people of the machine. I exalt in the incredible beauty of the mountains. God is good—He made these mountains.

I have held the earth, creation in the leap called life. That is what I gathered close to my soul since a child—since watching the summer storms from my bedroom window. I sing and I dance. I am first man. It has been the sweet sadness, this love. Sad because I have no other place to turn. Sweet because I have become one with her, nature; she is what I am. I am in the faded light within the cold rock. I am the jagged mountains in the high air—sighing, shrieking. I am in the trees, the earth, all living things. I am in the cold purity of the snowfields.

The dance dies—the flesh cannot dance forever, and even the passion has an end. The song stops. I have a melancholy. I know that you cannot love her twice, I know this instinctively. The wind is lonesome on my soul. My body is heavy. The mountains are just rock, stone. My imagination and my need have made them more than what they are. I made nature something she isn't. I jump from boulder to boulder; the goats follow slowly. They knew before I did. They know what they walk upon, what they are. Their minds hold no illusions.

It was over then, but I didn't want to see it. The earth is dead. The earth changes, mountains are raised, they crumble; animals are born, and they die; seasons follow their cycles. The wind has the smell of snow, the wind carries the perfume of summer. The earth changes, moves, transforms, but it has no passion. Only man has the passion. We are of the earth, scooped up from the earth by God. We are saltwater and minerals, but we are more. On the mountain, with the goats, the truth of my illusion was revealed. My emptiness, my desire burned me into the earth, so we seemed to be one. But she is futility, a wound clock repeating the same hours through the ages.

In the leap called life, I grabbed the earth and hugged her dearly; she was my security, my blanket. She spoke to me of God also, for He made her. How long have I held her even after I knew her dead? I kept her memory alive—a woman's hair becomes one with the leaves of a tree. God is still here—He made the earth. But I can longer hold the earth in the leap called life.

The next day we leave the mountains. My pack straps have been eaten by ground squirrels. The salty, sweat-stained canvas must have been delightful eating. I rig straps with twine, the twine cuts through my bulky clothing into my shoulders. We walk through dense fog, over avalanche fields, where trees have been snapped in half, where deep crevices await the unwary. We find a lodge, a restaurant in the mountains. A tiny meal is served. I don't like being with people. I want to go back to the solitude. I have never found any consistency in people. The earth is steadfast. People are mercury bound in flesh.

That I paid so much and got so little was a spur in my side, a "welcome back!" from the machine. Someone seemed to be saying, "You're a fool, and there is nothing you can do about it." The food at the restaurant had to come by horse. Horses are expensive forms of transportation and don't carry much of a payload. This is true, I should have been thankful for anything. But I couldn't make myself believe this. I suppose I wanted to feel bitter. I am mercury bound in flesh.

Then it is back down into the world. The elevation decreases, the clothing is peeled off, the jacket, sweatshirt, long underwear. Mosquitoes are in the air, sweat on the skin. The sunlight is hot. Tourists come up the trail, puffing, panting. A group of guys is attempting to carry coolers of beer to the mountain's top. At the bottom of the trail are three high-school teachers from California. We hustle a ride into Saint Mary.

Only one of them seems to know who she is, has character. Who would allow the other two to teach? They are like children themselves, not role models, not people to respect. But this is vacation not the classroom, so why do I judge? We find we are just about out of gas. The engine is turned off, and we roll down Going-to-the-Sun Road. I need to urinate. They won't stop. My bladder is bursting. When you don't own the machine, you can't tell it when to stop. I am at their mercy—or lack thereof.

In Saint Mary, the ride ends. Philly wants to go to Calgary for the annual Stampede, I want to go west until there is no west. We part company. He was a good traveling companion—never complained, always positive. I think we both have some apprehension, he more than I, for he hasn't hitchhiked alone as I have. Being alone is good too; it is honest, it is how we come into the world. You may share time with people, they can know you for a while, but they will never know you. My life is larger, more complex, full of memories, more debates and battles than I could ever reveal to someone. Someone knows all of me, God. There are moments when I know, feel Him watching. That is what I think as I am alone again.

CHAPTER 9

I am in Browning. I remember the homes of the Indian Reservation, wooden-box homes sitting on cinder blocks, reminding me of military barracks. No grass, no pavement, no concrete streets, just brown dust. Indian girls, young, thin, built like newborn colts—long, knobby legs and small bodies, with black, shining manes—play with a lopsided ball. They wear: dresses, some pink, some blue, between knee and thigh; white anklets; the hand-me-down, too big jackets of their brothers. Some girls wear bell bottoms that rise well above their ankles.

If they were my daughters, I would give them green grass to play upon, new clothes, warm homes. I would give them hope, keep them chaste, sober, with clean minds that know no bitterness or hate. If I could.

On the highway carloads of Native Americans pass me, most in low-slung, rusted, crowded cars; some in new pickups. An elderly native man, his face weathered, brown as dust, gives me a ride. He works for the government. He says no more, nor do I. It is a good silence. We pass the dusty streets, the worn homes, moving toward the mountains of high rock, clean pine forests. I say thank you to the elder, and he is gone.

The Silver Cord

Road construction is taking place. Burly Indians on graders, front-end loaders; behind transits do the work. I hitch a ride in the bed of a pickup. Light is sparkling from snow-covered peaks; pine forests press against the road. The road is called the Hi-line, Highway 2, the most northern east-west route in the nation, though it curves south in Idaho. Light slants down between the pines, light and dark shade jitters over my eyes like a silent film.

Outside of Kalispell there are fields of hay, alfalfa, cows, barns; but it is lumber that is the big crop. Sawmills, logging trucks imprint upon my mind. Then I am in Libby. A quiet town when I pass through, perhaps always a quiet town. I see lumberyards down the side streets, I hear the buzzing of saws. In Sandpoint, Idaho, I find an army surplus store. I buy parachute webbing, rig straps for my pack to replace the temporary cord. I stay at a campsite near a lake. I think upon my rides, a man and his young son, a bar owner in a Cadillac, a cowboy who says, "Stick around and I'll show you how to ride a bronco." A driver of a logging truck, a back-to-the-land couple in a beat car, a grandmother with bleach-blond hair, a forest service employee.

The next day I pass the Priest River, wide and blue. I remember gentle, wooded hills of pine and spruce; flat valleys with thick hay smelling sweet. In the fields are dairy cows, black and white with big, heavy milk bags. The first dairy cows seen since Wisconsin. I find myself on a highway ramp in or near Spokane, Washington. Spokane is pronounced minus the *e*.

I'm standing beside a superhighway, ramps and lanes rise, loop and twist. The temperature is in the nineties; car exhaust sticks to my skin, is in my lungs. I have the heat you get when you've been moving all day, when you haven't eaten, when you're in strange surroundings and have an anxiousness. The mouth is dry, the feet are blazing, the skin feels dirty. People stare as they pass. A serviceman gives me a short ride out near Fairchild Air Force Base.

I leave my pack by the road, scramble down an embankment, change into a pair of shorts. When I return, a car is stopped by my pack. A young guy, seventeen to eighteen, sharp eyes, thin body, bandanna around his head, is driving. He has two girls with him, both around his age. One is his girlfriend, she has long black hair; the other girl is a friend, her hair has a silvery-gold hue. They are both attractive girls. The kid is friendly, acts mature because he knows two women are watching him, depending upon him.

He says hop in. They are going to the apple and cherry orchards, going where the Grand Coulee Dam gave the desert life. They are on an adventure, and I am part of the adventure. He says it is easy to find work; stay as long as you like, then move on. Most of the orchards have bunkhouses or places to pitch tents. His girl puts her arm around him. He's not wearing a shirt, this excites her. It's a scrawny chest, but it belongs to the man she loves, and she likes it. Volcanic mountains rise in the distance, naked, brown and gray. Between the road and the mountains is sand with sage or mesquite. Rising from the flat sands are black volcanic rocks. Where there is irrigation, patches of yellow wheat grow—wheat so dry that it seems a touch would shatter the stalks to dust. The kid says the land is called scablands, dry streambeds or steep-walled ravines are called coulees. He feels good about giving the information, something from high school finally came to be useful. I feel good about hearing the information. We pass through some small towns—a few deserted buildings, barren downtowns, no people on the streets, few parked cars, no shade, just intense sun and heat.

The kid and his girl talk, then they coax the quiet girl into talking. She has a voice that sometimes has tones of childishness, sometimes the tone of a woman. The woman's voice is playful, fun-loving; the child's voice is sensitive, shy. If you weren't listening closely you might think her words of no importance. She is one of those people who has a quavering tone, of the soul wanting to come out, to love and understand life. She wants to be an artist, a painter, someone who is creative. But the other half of her says no, be a mother with plenty of children, flow with life and what is expected from you. She pauses often because she wants to choose the right words, tell what she really feels. There comes a point when she thinks her words aren't saying anything at all and no one is listening, so she stops.

I know she has something deep inside that makes her different, special. She senses she has a soul, an inner voice. I tell you; few people know they have a soul. She senses this soul and doesn't know if it is good or bad. She studies those around her and sees no one is like herself. She dreams her dreams, talks to herself when it is God she talks to. She is

The Silver Cord

talking for me, she likes me, and I know she thinks I am not listening. This hurts, and I hear a sigh. I turn around and say, "Keep talking. I'm listening" in a tone that says, "I care about what you think." I see her soul smile; the eyes smile only slightly, but the soul smiles.

The land becomes drier, now there is only sage and brown plateaus. We are outside of the town of Grand Coulee. They leave me off at a store. I feel the girl wants to come with me. I wonder why I am leaving her. I would give her soul rest; I would hide it within me, nurture it. What would life have been like with her? Perhaps she was the connection I missed. I missed something somewhere, and perhaps she was it. They wanted me to remain; they said, "Are you sure you want to go?" And the fool said, "Yes."

I am given a ride to a road that leads to a camping area. I begin walking. A pickup truck stops. The older man driving is the one who wants to pick me up; the younger man, in his late thirties, does not want to give me a ride. That is what I sense. The campsite is run by the government. The Grand Coulee's lake is called Lake Roosevelt, it is one boundary of the campsite. The man in uniform charges me nothing to camp. The campground is crowded with vacationers in motor homes or pulling camping trailers. I pitch my tent, gather my wood from the load dumped from the back of a government truck. Some of my fellow campers bring their power saws.

After splitting my wood, I walk down to the deep, long lake. The water is gray. Brown cliffs fall straight into the water on the not-too-far shore. Huge logs float in the water, strays from the logging upstream in the mountains. That night, the man who gave me a ride into camp invites me over for watermelon. The son-in-law and his wife are there and a daughter with her husband. I am uncomfortable; no one wants my presence but the man. I read into the tension; there is stress between the older man and the son. Here is what I find. The older man has a business, took a lifetime to build, carpentry; now none of his family members, particularly his son, has a desire to continue the business. This is an affront to him and makes him feel as if his life achievement is worthless. I thank him for the watermelon and go my own way.

The next day I am on my way to see the Grand Coulee Dam when some high school kids give me a lift. They are on a mission—to paint the class rock outside of town. They are in a hurry because some unauthorized classmates are attempting to get there first. These kids are the sons and daughters of the men who operate the plant. One kid tells me there are miles of tunnel inside the dam.

I view the dam. Like Mount Rushmore, the dam is so much like the pictures that I am not impressed. I go into the building beside the dam where the generators are housed. Three generators in an empty, antiseptic tile room. The generators hum. I have this information written down: The dam irrigates an area three-fourths the size of Rhode Island. Six turbines, two reverse. The lake is one hundred and fifty miles long, four hundred feet deep. The dam is three hundred feet high, built on granite. Work began in 1934.

Quite an achievement. I am impressed. The machine people must have some pride. One man could not have built the dam, he could not comprehend or store all the fragments of knowledge that were brought together. The dam seems bigger, better than a man.

But one man did build it—one man and his needs. The first man born knew he needed food in his stomach, light in the darkness, warmth in the cold. The first man hunted and gathered, picked fruit from the trees. His light came from flint or friction, his warmth from fire. Thousands of years later, he is doing the same thing, filling the same needs. Now the fruit trees grow in rows, are sprayed with chemicals. His light comes from a light bulb, his warmth from electric heat.

How man meets his needs has changed. Life is like a continual play with the same script, same plot; only the stage props change. The props are called progress. The props are better—there is no doubt. The sad thought is that people think the world has changed, the actors are better, the props better; they convince themselves that even the plot has changed. It is good there is a Grand Coulee Dam. People need the food from the irrigated fields and orchards, they need electricity, but it is all meaningless if you don't know the script.

I sleep outside of Brewster, Washington, down a dirt road, by the Columbia River. Orchards are everywhere, some have old mature trees, and many have young, waist-high trees just planted. The land is green as far as the pipes stretch, then the land has squares of yellow wheat, then sage and brown cliffs.

The Silver Cord

In the ninety-degree heat of the morning, I wait by the State Agriculture Department trailer. The woman asks for identification, asks me how long I want to work. I show her my college ID and say a couple of weeks. She seems to like me—no doubt, the college ID—and I know she will find me a good employer. She tells me to wait on the bench, and my boss will pick me up. Another man waits on the bench under the trailer's awning.

He is old, in his sixties, thin, fine featured. He is old but spry, limber, with the constitution of a forty-year-old. He is clean shaven, his skin darkened by the sun. His clothes are worn, but neat, clean. He has his bedroll wrapped up tight, a worn travel bag, a blue bleach bottle with a rope strap as a canteen. He sits with his legs crossed almost daintily. He is at that age where the sap barely flows. He travels the rails, works the fruit orchards. He is a hobo and no bum. He speaks concisely, slowly. We talk about riding trains. He says grain cars are the best; hide in the overhang where you are protected from wind and rain. He talks of other railcars, their disadvantages; he talks of cars no longer made. He understands I'm thinking about hopping a train. He says jumping aboard a moving train is dangerous. He tells of people who were hurt, a friend lost his heel. He believes he has a responsibility to show me the dark side of the hobo life. Where did this hobo get his feeling of responsibility? What misfortune, character flaw makes a man a hobo?

We talk about working in the orchards, the relative merits of cherry picking over apple thinning, the advantages and disadvantages of boarding houses. Another hobo comes along. An Indian, small, old, big chested—or rather, a wide rib cage, shrinking flesh on a once-robust build. His clothes are ragged. His eyes say that he likes to drink. His voice is raw from sleeping in cold places, smoking and drinking. He says to the hobo that Mexican Sam went up to the shacks and caused trouble, found a woman, but was discovered sleeping outside in the morning. The shacks are up over the hill from us, a little rural slum hidden from view. The Indian laughs as phlegm gurgles in his throat.

The Indian and I talk, and I find he's been to Madison—that is the farthest east he's been. He tells me he once rode straight through Madison in an open boxcar. I remember the tracks through Madison, some I used as shortcuts to classes. The only street name he could remember was State Street.

My boss drives up in a pickup. He's short, with big beefy forearms, stubby hands, a protruding stomach. The salivated stub of a cigar is trapped in the corner of his mouth. A straw cowboy hat completes the picture. He picks up other new hires then stops at a small, one-room store in an old lady's house. He gives a draw on the worker's salary to anyone who needs it. I have plenty of money in traveler's checks. He is surprised I don't want a draw—most people come to him broke.

We turn up a dirt road, pass a white, wooden farmhouse that could be from the Midwest. Huge, thick, shade trees surround the home. His daughters are on the porch, and two big German shepherds are in the yard, no doubt to protect the daughters. We pass another farmhouse in need of paint and curtains; there are no trees here. Married workers live in the house. We pass a low, one-story barn and a long garage-type building, and then there is a row of cinder-block rooms, side by side, sharing a common roof. About six rooms in all. Each room has bunkbeds, stove, refrigerator, table, chairs.

Around the cluster of buildings are the orchards of apple trees. The leaves are waxy green; high, sparse grasses grow underneath the trees; sprinklers flick on and off. Behind the workers' quarters, high cliffs rise, covered skimpily in sage. Occasionally a stand of birches is found in depressions where rainwater is collected. In the other direction, across the road from the farmhouse, across more orchards, is the river. Behind the hidden river, I see cliffs rising; some have plateaus that are barren and brown, others hold yellow wheat shining in the sun.

I make a cinder-block room my home. I don't know why I stop traveling. Perhaps I am tired, or want a routine, or see this as part of the adventure. Maybe deep down I realize the Rocky Mountains were the apex, there would be no experience greater, no natural wonder more splendid. I work two weeks, six days a week, nine hours a day, minimum wage.

I am up at six-thirty, eat breakfast; the heat is already intense. Seven o'clock the workers gather by the long, knee-high trailer that carries us and our step ladders into the orchards. Our foreman's tractor pulls us through the orchard to the yet unthinned trees. The trees have been sprayed until there is no natural smell, only a powdery, waxy odor. The ladders go up. The apples grow like clusters of grapes and must be thinned

The Silver Cord

so that an apple hangs every five inches. The finger and the thumb snap off the unwanted apples, which fall to the ground. You are supposed to snap the apple off from the stem, not the stem from the branch.

In the relative coolness of the morning, there is bantering between the workers, high-school kids clown—throw apples—until the foreman yells. The heat asserts its presence, the voices are silent. You hear the snapping of an apple from the stem when it is plucked, the leaves shushing as a branch returns to its place, discarded apples thudding to the ground, branches shaken by men leaning from their ladders, the creak of wooden ladders as men climb and descend.

Ten fifteen in the morning, water break, everyone has a water container. It is ten fifteen, and it seems a lifetime that you've been working, and you wonder how you will make it to four thirty. The fifteen-minute break is over, back up the ladders. Lunchtime comes—half an hour—back to the cinder-block room, eat, back to the orchard. Four-thirty comes, ladders are loaded onto the trailer, everyone sits wearily. The tractor pulls us down the dusty road, between the spraying of the sprinklers.

After supper, the boss sometimes makes a beer run. The workers sit on the common cement slab porch and drink, watch the sunlight fade. No one gets drunk or causes trouble, because then the boss would make no more beer runs. The beer tastes too good after sweating all day in the sun. No one has the money to drink every night; people sleep, read magazines, paperbacks, papers. One night the high school kids decide to climb the cliffs. I go halfway and lose interest.

These are the people I worked with: high school kids, freshmen, who had never had a job, didn't know that sweating wasn't an abnormality of the body, who thought throwing apples at each other would be tolerated by the foreman. One kid bunked with me for a while; the foreman was trying to break up the group. The kid wanted to smoke a joint. I said I didn't care if he did, but the foreman's room was beside ours, and smoke travels. The entire idea seemed immature and unnecessary. The kid smoked; the foreman smelled the smoke. A day or two later the high school kids were fired, for goofing off, for smoking marijuana. Later, I was given a ride by the kids and their parents. Dad asked me why the kids were fired; I said I didn't know.

Zip is an Indian, short, wiry build, stringy long hair, wide mouth, always smiling. It might seem a sly smile if you don't know him. He was a Ranger in the army, a field radio man. He was planning to go up to Canada for the winter. He knew an old Cree who had a trap line. Zip had trapped the area before, used a mule to carry his traps. Zip tells the story of going to an Indian gathering and unknowingly eating dog.

Zip is traveling with Dave, thirties, tall, thin, slow of speech. Dave has the voice of a man straining to survive life; some inner sadness is eating him away. His last job was as a building supervisor in Seattle. He is withdrawn, a man of thoughts, a homespun philosopher. Somewhere in life he missed the connection, the spark. Sometimes he plays the harmonica and then all the pent-up passion, all the brooding sadness, all the pain comes out.

Another worker is Red. He is in his twenties, broad shouldered, well proportioned, strong jawed, and, of course, has red hair. He rode a boxcar in from North Dakota. I look into his eyes and know that he is disturbed, haunted, perhaps paranoid, at the least distrustful. He is defensive. The first day he walked into my room I sensed the aggression clinging to him.

He opens up to me, tells me of his US Air Force experiences in Alaska, a group of blacks that picked on him. They made his life miserable. Red has a simple mind, one a person could bait and string along; a mind that takes cruel words, insults to the heart; is even foolish enough to believe the words have truth in them. I tell him that insults tell a man more about the speaker's mind than the condition of his own soul. I picture the smirking faces, the stifled chuckles, the humiliating confrontations as his tormentors watch and enjoy the pain on Red's face.

Later, I hear that Red and some others went into town on a Saturday night. Red started a barroom fight for apparently no reason. I know where Red's mind is at and what alcohol can do—distort, twist, magnify. I am not surprised. They say it was a real barroom brawl, bottles over heads, flying chairs. Frank, another worker, has a black eye the next day.

Frank travels with Mike. Frank is forty-five, a five-foot-six man, dark hair, muscular, running away from alimony payments. I sense a bully, a manipulator. Anything he can do to increase his power, he will do. I think there is a touch of perverseness in him, but he hides it well. Mike is in his

The Silver Cord

middle twenties, wears black, sturdy-framed glasses, has short curly hair that gives the appearance of having been worn much longer. He is easygoing, likes to read, sends money to his sister. Mike and Frank have traveled for some time. They have worked in foundries in New England, making wood stoves; in Butte, making bricks; in the fruit orchards. I wonder why they haven't saved enough money to buy a car. I wonder why two men of disparate ages travel together. I wonder why they haven't drifted apart and settled somewhere. Some are born to perpetually drift.

Another worker is John, twenty-one, college student, six feet, one eighty. He's never done manual production work. Slow as they come on the ladder, though he can handle the heat. He seems to want to be alone. He's like Zip in his desire for nature's solitude. He is like Dave with the passion of the philosopher. He is like Red in his distaste of the cruel and unkind. He is like Mike in his reading and kindness. He has nothing of Frank within him. John hails from Pennsylvania.

Jim is our foreman. He is forty and some, tall—six three or above—thin, with sad eyes that have the world figured out, and the world is simpler than other men believe. He wears an old felt hat, 1940's style. He moves slowly, talks calmly. The long arms have taut muscle hiding under the skin. He is the kind of man who means what he says; there is no humor, satire, sarcasm, cynicism. He means what he says, and there is a kindness in his voice. He is the type of man people might think they could take advantage of, say something crude or impolite to, and they would find themselves flat on the ground before they knew what happened. He doesn't have a temper, he would endure insult and foolishness, yet he seems to have the uncanny ability to perceive decisive moments when tolerance becomes foolishness. Jim sees the bully in Frank and never allows an ugly word from Frank's lips.

Jim knew his job down to the smallest detail. He knew how to talk to his workers, how to make the job easier. The first day of work, he asked me if I had ever used a ladder. I said a little. He says, "Get that ladder and follow me." He watched me pick the ladder up, struggle to find a point of balance as I walked. He stopped me, knowing I hadn't carried many ladders, showed me the ladder was balanced where the identification number was printed on the side. No doubt he had stamped the number on the ladder. Let a person speak, then quietly see if it was true; that was

Jim. If a person needed help, or knowledge, you could depend on Jim to give it to you kindly.

Jim had a wife, in her thirties. She loved him. I saw her once after work massaging his shoulders as he sat on the porch reading the Bible. She wore an old, faded dress. She was my idea of a farm girl from Arkansas, vintage faded dress, as right and proper in the 1930s as now. I saw love in her eyes when she rubbed his back, the type of love that says, "We're in it together, babe. I'll never run out on you when life gets tough. My dreams are your dreams, your sorrows my sorrows." You don't get a woman like that unless you're the real thing yourself. Jim lived up to his responsibilities. When it is all said and done, perhaps that is all a man has.

Jim and his wife are time travelers, they come from our country's past. From that time when men worked hard, knew their jobs—however humble—inside and out and were glad for any job they could get. They have a desire for excellence, honesty, patience; respect for even the most worthless, lowliest man. Jim drives the tractor slowly so we won't shake and bounce. He waits for the sprinkler to turn away before driving through. He never forgets us. He's no machine man, he is made for a lifetime. He has character. If a man wants to know Jim, he has to watch him, not ask him who he is. Today you sell yourself, boast, tell lies, bend to other men's perceptions; that is how you fit into the machine.

Jim was holding onto something in the leap that I had never seen anyone hold onto. I see this now; back then, I only saw the sadness that hung upon him. A man in a nowhere job, getting old, waiting for a break. I only saw a hick family. I was on the road, had hope; life was still good. I was trying to be a good person. He had something time and circumstance couldn't destroy, and I'd accept a little sadness to have character through the leap. You can call me a hick. If that is the price of character, I'll pay it. What was Jim holding onto? Where did he get his character? From God?

CHAPTER 10

I left the orchards, couldn't take any more of the mindless work, the routine, the stagnation. I wasn't good at it—my mind wanders—I couldn't concentrate on being machinelike for prolonged periods of time. I made as much money as I had spent on the entire trip. I had to see the Pacific Ocean, the end of the land, the place where the sun sets. I walked away from the quiet, green orchards; the hot, brown land beyond the irrigation pipes.

Caught a ride with an insurance salesman, past Lake Chelan, down close to Wenatchee, then up Highway 2, heading into the Cascades. I remember clear skies, brown land, then pines, mountains, a climb into fog, mist, cold. Coming down the west side of the mountains, there is more traffic and fewer rides; people seem less friendly, suspicious, harried, rushed. The land is green and lush.

I am on the outskirts of Seattle; I can feel the giant sprawl of concrete, brick, stone, macadam, cement. I can smell the city, car exhaust, chemicals, industry's odors, fast-food restaurants' grease. I hear car horns, grinding gears, curses. This is desert to first man, a teeming desert, where he can't sleep on the ground or build a fire, hear the wind play over the land. The desert is thick with vultures. I wander around in a daze, in a

The Silver Cord

maze, walk the streets till I find signs leading to Interstate 5. I am picked up; I am gone from the city.

I am waiting for a ferry to take me across the Puget Sound. The sky is dark gray, the clouds hard and ridged. It is cold. I want to talk to the people waiting for the ferry, but they eye me distrustfully. I sense it is soon over, I am in the machine. The huge ferry comes, I cross the gray water. I walk through a town that is an artist community. A small town with little shops and restaurants with poetic names. In the pubs, women wear bandannas, macrame belts, tight jeans, expensive sweaters. Gaslights line the streets. Dusk has come, I am ready to call it a day. I ask for a room at a small, unpretentious motel. I watch the proprietor's placid face distort into anger; he says he doesn't want my kind at his place. I wonder what kind I am. I walk away chuckling.

I keep walking, through the dusk, down the straight road lined by forest and occasional clearings littered with brush and stumps. A woman stops, she wears a nurse's uniform. She thought I was someone she knows; fear is upon her face when she sees that I am not that person. She looks in her rearview mirror, back down the straight, deserted road, and her fear increases. I tell her she doesn't have to give me a ride. Angrily, she says, "Get in."

I don't know where I slept, but I know the day is bright and I am happy. Through mountains, fog, dense forests of huge cedar trees, sawmill towns and past lumber trucks carrying one huge log—three at most—I come to the Pacific. I don't smell salt or sulfur—that rotting smell that clings to the Atlantic. The wind is clean, the water blue, the beaches have pebbles, rocks, jumbles of huge cedar logs. The gigantic logs roll in from the sea. Press your nose against a bleached, barkless giant and smell the cedar smell. In the forests back from the ocean, the stumps of logs harvested a hundred years ago sit, surrounded by new growth, towering trees.

I camp at a state park, in a thicket of a plant resembling the eastern laurel. These shrubs rise above a man's head, trails wander through the thickets. I go through the thicket, down a cliff, to the beach. The surf sparkles in the sunlight; the beach is pebbled by the cliffs, sandy by the water, wide and open. Single, billowy clouds float across the sky, coming from the west, like sailing ships. Log piles are heaped back from the shore. The gray sand by the water collects sand dollars, seaweed, beached fish. I take my shoes off and run, sprint, till my body can't continue. I have touched the waters of the Pacific. The elation is followed by a sudden urge to return home.

I know my parents want me home. I made the mistake of calling them. In the leap called life, my mother holds her children in her arms. Her love is enslaving, not freeing. She would protect her offspring even if it meant killing their souls. Dad says mother is not well. She has never been well, but I swallow the bait. I want to go back to tell others, my friends what I have experienced. I want to tell someone of my victory, my adventure. I want to go back with the new attitude I have about life. Maybe, I want to go home because I know it is over, the magic is fading. I came to the end of my yellow-brick road. Whatever my reasons, I decide to make a game of going home. How quickly can I traverse a nation hitchhiking? From the Olympic Peninsula, the shores of the Pacific, to the East Coast, Harrisburg, Pennsylvania.

First ride, a park ranger back from three days of trail inspection. He gives me his remaining granola bars. An electrician in a panel truck picks me up. He likes working with his hands, doing his own home repairs. Two high school kids in a vintage forties roadster with power under the hood. Out of the forest, from behind the logging trucks, past the sawmills I see Olympia at the end of an inlet. A drug addict on speeders, little guy in a big car, sends the car speedometer over 90 miles per hour. He has a radar detector on the dash. He hopes I will crack. He wishes to frighten me. He watches me look at the speedometer and then says, "What's the matter?" But his tone says, "Are you frightened yet?"

I say, "You might get stopped for speeding. That airplane could be monitoring traffic." He looks up at the airplane that seems to hover over the highway. I say, "I don't care how fast you drive; you seem to be in control." I lied but it was what he wanted to hear. He thought I cared about him getting a ticket and a heavy fine. I am not frightened; maybe I don't care if I live or die, or maybe deep down I know it isn't my time.

The land is flat and open toward the east. In the distance, rising from the flatness, are triangular mountains, snow-covered peaks with cloud

The Silver Cord

halos wrapped around them. The mountains appear blue-gray. With sane drivers, I pass through some sawmill, cedar-shingle towns of smokestacks. I'm in Kelso, two thirty-plus newlyweds give me a lift, play their tapes for me, ask me about Pennsylvania. I'm in Vancouver in ninety-degree heat, by a maze of ramps, standing on a narrow shoulder. The cars almost brush me as they pass. I begin walking, pass two other hitchhikers. A car slows down to stop, all three of us run to it and catch a ride.

I'm on I-84, a road that hums even in the night, even on the most deserted stretch. I step into the car of an old couple—so old their hair is white, and I must speak loudly. They barely drive the minimum speed. They are looking for their fourteen-year-old grandson, who was supposedly hitchhiking to them for a visit. He never arrived. Have I seen him? They are worried, have been driving the highway for days.

This old couple is vulnerable, trusting, and should not be picking up hitchhikers. Someone will con, use, or steal from them. I wish I could help them. Was the trip to the grandparents a pretext to run away from home? What parents would let a fourteen-year-old boy hitchhike? Did he imagine how he would hurt his grandparents? He at least owed them a phone call. Another thought says his body is lying in a ditch somewhere.

The land is flat, barren except for the bluffs along the Columbia River, where scattered trees grow. The traffic has thinned. The heat is intense, my body feels as if it is melting. As I stand by the road, two construction types, my age, in hardhats, pass in a pickup. The one driving gives me the finger. I suppose he had a hard day; something is bothering him; perhaps he imagines me to be someone he dislikes. I give the finger back because I'm tired, hot, and deserve some respect—the respect to be left alone, ignored. He is ready to turn around and come back, but his friend is talking to him, convincing him to let it slide. It's strange, because I wanted him to come back, wanted to flatten him.

My next ride is from a man in his thirties, weathered face, short sandy hair, average height. He has a female companion in her twenties. She is beautiful, natural orange-red, silky hair, lipstick to match, cool green eyes, flawless white skin. They don't speak to each other much, and I wonder what they are to each other. She looks at me with promising eyes. She wears a green, silky dress that is the color of her eyes, and within the green are wisps of color matching her hair. She's dressed, and the guy is in grungy work clothes.

On a near desolate stretch of highway the guy pulls into a motel parking lot and separates from her without a word. She says she must use a restroom, in her friend's room, and then the ride will continue. She says come along. There is a man in the room as she goes into the bathroom. He runs the motel, is retired from the army—the Eighty-Second Airborne. Pictures of his platoons and companies adorn flat surfaces. I ask him if he is proud of his time in the service, and he answers yes. I tell him every man on the photos appears proud—good men. The woman comes out of the bathroom, looks at me, and then leaves before I can follow. Finally, I catch on something isn't right. The manager tells me the steaks are good at the nearby restaurant. I say thanks and move quickly to the door. I do go to the restaurant, and the steak is good. The restaurant owner comes up to me and asks if I enjoyed the meal. I must be his kind of people. I say yes, very good.

I stand by the road, gaze into the sage flats, watch the glass-like heat rising from the concrete. I wonder about what just happened. The attractive, dressed-up woman with the grungy driver who seemed to be strangers. Was the woman delivering me to the room? I decide to think the best—think innocently and let it drop. I can see the cars coming for miles, shimmers on the flatness like splinters of glass. A guy picks me up; he looks normal but talks as if he wants something from me. He says, "Why do you think I picked you up?" as he glances at my crotch.

I say, "Like everyone else—from the goodness of your heart, because I needed a ride. If that isn't the reason for picking me up, I'll get out right here."

He hesitates, says there is nothing but desert here.

I say I like the desert. He pulls over in the middle of the desert, and I get out.

A ceramic salesman picks me up. He's going six hundred miles. He buys me lunch, partly because he's a good person, needs company to keep him awake; partly because he doesn't want to leave me by his car

The Silver Cord

while he's inside. Sometime after lunch, we are in the Rockies. The mountains are high, rolling hills of burnt grass and sparse pines. I try to get this guy talking, but he seems happier to remain quiet.

I am riding with two construction workers in a van. They have a cooler of beer between them and are drinking steadily. They are overseas construction workers; they've been to the Virgin Islands, Guam, Japan, South America. When they aren't working, they are getting high or drunk, or whoring. They are big men, in their late twenties or early thirties, long hair, earrings, a wild look in their eyes. They have no line within them. I don't fully trust them even though they offer me a beer. I imagine them as the type who, on a whim, might start something, kick me out, steal what little I have. The conversation between them reveals childish minds, unpredictable. Their wildness doesn't come from a desire for freedom but from a lack of discipline and purpose.

In the middle of the night, they leave me out in or near Salt Lake City, on one of those roads of gas stations, all-night convenience stores, banks, businesses. I sit on the cement curb outside the cash register/office room of a twenty-four/seven gas station. I want to make the connection with Interstate 80, which will take me into Pennsylvania. My familiar highway, my road that once took me west. The guy working doesn't seem bothered I am there. I ask if I can pick up a ride at his place. We talk a little; he says no problem. He has second thoughts about my presence the few times he puts money in the cash register. I see his nervousness. What if I rob the place while he's on duty?

Two young women drive in for gas. The guy says, "Maybe you can hitch a ride with them; they have Wyoming plates." I go over and begin talking, ask for a ride. The one girl is frightened of me. She says she has a gun, and she will shoot me if I get out of line. She pulls a thirty-eight from her purse to give me a quick glimpse. The other girl is calm. She sees who I am. She has brothers, and I am just brother's friend, asking for a ride. Interstate 80 is their road. They give me a ride.

I am on I-80, the highway to home. It is strange that the girl with the gun never thought to deny me a ride. I climb into the back of their station wagon and sleep. Early in the morning we eat breakfast together, the one girl still watches me warily.

I'm in Wyoming, the highway is almost empty of traffic; sage brush sits on the faded-red soil. The occasional breeze is as hot as the sunbaked earth. The traffic picks up—all families, tourists with out-of-state license plates. I wait hours for a ride. I leave the road for a line of railroad tracks. I'm thinking of catching a freight train east. A shed sits by the tracks with telephone lines going into it. Two men are inside. I ask if there are any trains going east. They say the mail train but not for a couple of hours. I go back up to the road and walk into Laramie, find a bus station. On the sidewalk before the bus station are Japanese tourists; city blacks, seeming more out of place than the Japanese tourists; old spinster ladies. I buy a ticket to Omaha, thinking this will carry me over the ride-less area I know is ahead. We stop in Cheyenne; I eat at a nearby fast-food restaurant. Back on the bus, we roll into Nebraska, stop at Sidney. Two guys my age get on while the sheriff watches. They sit in back of me. This is their story: They went to Las Vegas, made thousands of dollars, lost it all. They were hitchhiking back to the East Coast, penniless or almost—they had enough for food. The sheriff caught them hitchhiking through Sidney and made them spend the last of their money on bus tickets out of town. We settle back into our seats, the diesel whines, we float over the land.

I am in the Omaha bus station at three on a summer's morning. I step into a taxi and say, "Take me to the interstate." He does and charges me nothing. I stand by the highway. The highway, raised above other lanes, loops. I watch the janitors, night watchmen, nurses, the partyers going to home or work. I see an all-night doughnut/bakery shop and walk down, buy some doughnuts and a cup of coffee. I go back to the highway and watch the city; the tall buildings of downtown, to the west of me, come to life. The coming sun puts an orange-rose stain in the sky. The tall buildings catch the color. I don't think there is any sight grander than the sun rising on tall buildings, except the sun rising on mountains and hills. A dirty brick building, a meat-processing plant, is nearby. I smell the odors. I see men at a loading dock, dressed in white, staring out at the new day on their break. Even the meat-processing plant is good—for this is Omaha, in the heart of beef and pork country.

The day comes softly, so smoothly over the city. The air is one moment cool and the next, hot as midafternoon, like summer mornings sometimes are. The air is humid, the dampness collects the smells of the awakening

The Silver Cord

city. The air has only a trace of exhaust, has the smell of the bakery and a bread factory, the slaughterhouse. The slight wind that comes from the flat land that surrounds the city carries the scent of corn and cleanness. The day will be hot. The humidity soaks up the rays of the sun. The humidity tells me I am going back home. Out west, there is no humidity, no smell of green fields.

A woman picks me up, then a guy who has just been picking cherries. Cherries are my breakfast. I ride with a woman and her three-year-old daughter. The cornfields stretch, the land is green again, rides are plentiful. I meet another hitchhiker, Joe. He's going to Chicago to visit his girlfriend. She is blind; he shows me her picture, she is beautiful. He says, "Why don't you come along?" I say no thanks; I'm homeward bound. He wants me to use his name if I ever write a book of my travels. A van stops as we are talking by the highway.

Two women, middle thirties, hillbilly accents, new clothes, sunglasses, floppy hats; one has dark hair, one is a blonde. They say they are running away from their husbands. The dark-haired one says she was beaten by her husband. She took his van, his credit cards; they bought themselves new clothes and hit the road. If they are not telling the truth, then they are two prostitutes running from a pimp. I sense anything goes with them, that they have been liberated from all moral restraints. I see them talking; I can't hear over the radio, but I assume they decide we're not their types. Somewhere near Chicago, Joe gets out. On the eastern edge of Chi-town, the ride ends for me.

Toll gates are thirty yards away; this is good, the traffic slows down, has time to judge you, plenty of space to pull over. There is another hitchhiker at the same location. He's twenty-one; long hair tied in a ponytail, covered by a baseball hat. He's going to New York City, where his sister was given an apartment. She is a delegate to the Democratic National Convention. She has plenty of room for him. He is holding up a hubcap that has an *E* written on it in Magic Marker. *E* meaning east. I make a sign from a cardboard box found along the road and my Magic Marker.

No one is interested in hitchhikers that day; the day drags into early evening. This guy has two baseball gloves and a hard ball in his pack, we begin throwing. The lights by the tollbooths go on, we continue throwing—a night game. The cars pass our signs propped against our packs; we are unconcerned, absorbed in our game. As we are throwing, another hitchhiker comes walking up the middle of the ramp, cursing, thrusting a sign at every car that passes. After the car passes, he gives the occupants the finger. His sign says "PENA," which he had mistakenly heard was the abbreviation for Pennsylvania. His face and neck are red from his anger. His curses seem to come from down deep in his soul, where some demon lives. I know there is a medical condition that causes cursing; I don't know if that is his problem. I do know I think him a danger.

Another group of hitchhikers gathers farther from the tollbooth. They are ragged, wearing castoffs, unkempt, not even hobos or bums; derelicts might be the word. One passes me while I am eating doughnuts I had stashed in my pack. His clothes smell. He looks at the tollbooths then turns to go back to his friends.

I give him what is left of the box of doughnuts. He says nothing; I suppose he is in disbelief. His eyes are glassy but not from drugs. I say, "Share them with your buddies down there." He keeps walking without answering. He looks back at me like a hunted, wary animal when he is halfway to the others. Then he stuffs every powder-coated doughnut into his mouth until his cheeks are bulging, crumbs hang from his lips. He throws the empty box over the guardrail well before reaching his friends.

Evening comes; the ballplayer finds his ride, tries to talk the driver into taking me, but no deal. The group of castoffs, five or six in number, head into a low field toward a thick tangle of trees. I suppose they plan to spend the night in the thicket. The mosquitoes will be thick; the land is swampy looking. I move closer to the tollbooths, put my sweatshirt on. I lean against a concrete guardrail. The bright lights protect me from ambush from the group in the thicket. A wind picks up, not strongly. In the cool of the night and with a touch of dampness, the wind causes the flesh to shiver.

I will never forget that night, it's just one of those memories that never is lost. The night is a midwestern and eastern summer's night. I've been away so long that I reexperience what was common. The western nights are gone—dry, cold, windy; sage, pine, sand smells. I smell the dampness that is caught in fields of weeds, corn, tangles of woods. The soil

The Silver Cord

smells heavily of humus. Exhaust lingers in the air; warmth mingles with coolness yet is separate as it touches me in waves. Up high, around the lights, insects cluster in a pulsing circle. A bat works the mass, cutting through the insects happily. The lights hum; the light is blurred, softened by the humid air. The women manning the tollbooths talk across the concrete to each other. I listen to the trucks coming.

Trucks are all that pass, mostly tractors without trailers. The trucks are separated by long stretches of silence. The concrete before the booths shines from the slickness of countless vehicles. Tractor trailers roll up the ramp, the air brakes hissing and trumpeting, diesel exhaust a cloud around the truck. The high sides of the trailers press me against the cement barrier at my back. The dull-gray road dirt sometimes carries the message, "Wash me" written by some unknown comedian. The big wheels turn directly before my eyes, the wheels tower over my sitting form. The woman in the booth hands out cards; sometimes words are exchanged, asking for direction or just because the man in the machine is lonely, needs the voice of another person. Then the truck slides through the booths, and he's on the open road, bound for Pittsburgh, New York, Boston, somewhere he knows, and I can only guess.

The tractors with no trailers play a game. They must come from a terminal somewhere nearby. They come to the tollbooths like racehorses to the starting gate. When the driver is handed his ticket, that is the bell. No, the bell is the boredom within the driver's head. To force life to give him pleasure, release from boredom, he makes the diesel roar.

The driver digs into the gears with his concentration; the tractor arches, rises, then lunges as the power is taken through the gears. The lunges come farther between, smoother; the truck is gone into the night. That is what the terminal drivers do to make the night pass. My entertainment is to watch the tractors lurch, judge the skill of the driver.

Four in the morning, I'm half asleep. A guy with a gauze-bandaged hand stops. He's so dopey from lack of sleep he can barely make coherent sentences. I get in; he says his hand is swollen from a bee sting. He is from Wyoming, going to New York City to a maritime college. His dad got him the appointment. He is trying to make a deadline. He drives to Cleveland then must pull over for sleep.

I step out beside the road. A Volkswagen bug, with elk horns strapped to the roof and Maine plates, stops. A huge man emerges, six foot six, broad, massive bones, no flab. I feel like a child standing beside him. It seems a miracle that the small car can hold his size and weight. He says he is a cabinetmaker. He has huge hands thick with muscle. He is coming from Calgary. He's been mountain climbing in the Canadian Rockies. He said his last hitchhiker slept the entire distance, ate his food without a thank-you, didn't offer to pay for gas. I know what is expected.

We slowly gain momentum as we pull onto the highway. People stare at the antlers and at his foot sticking out the window; he feels cramped otherwise. He talks of his trip. The climbs weren't too rough, not challenging enough. The elk horns were taken from an arch made of elk racks by a motel. He justifies his theft by saying the arch wasn't used and was deteriorating. He thought someone should get some use from the racks. Which sounds reasonable, but did he ask the motel owner for the rack? He describes the Calgary Stampede. I briefly think of Philly passing this guy in the street and think life is strange. He was drinking with his climbing buddies; one was thrown into jail for smoking marijuana. He wasn't smoking but ended up in jail. He said the experience was frightening. He was given no chance to call a lawyer, was never told of the charges against him. He was interrogated roughly, spent the night with puking drunks. He saw a fight outside of a bar where an Indian got his face smashed in by other Indians. He said blood was everywhere; the guy's face was really pounded. He took the guy to the hospital.

His wife is a social worker, works with hardcore juvenile delinquents. He thinks she is wasting her time—once kids are raised wrong, programmed to trouble, they can't be changed. How can a person raised to perceive life one way suddenly see it another way? How can one person tell another that he or she is living wrong and then have that person not only believe, but have the power to alter his or her life? I don't want to believe a person can't change. If people can't change, then there is no hope for the world.

We are in Pennsylvania; the realization jolts me. The mountains close in on the road like velvet, green pillows. The scent of the forest is upon the air. The sky is no longer spreading and vast, but tamed. For a moment I can't remember the ride between the West and the East. I have had very

The Silver Cord

little sleep in three days. One minute there is sage; clean, dry air; sandy soil; open skies; rocky, towering mountains; and then there is the soft velvet land, greenness, lushness, moisture, humidity to carry the scent like a misty perfume. A soft world bursting with life.

I'm hitchhiking down the Susquehanna, and the river's breadth and the mountains that flank the river and are cut by the river have a grandeur. The river and the road seemed wedged into this fertile land. The road and the houses—so many houses—seem crowded between the tall trees that are bursting in lushness. The greenness is in my eyes, ears, mouth, lying on my skin.

I am across the river from Harrisburg. The river is crowded with bridges. The city sits on the low bank. Back from the riverfront homes and offices, the few high buildings rise. North of the city, the long line of a mountain is broken by the river. The river reflects the city. A flock of ducks sits contentedly on the water behind a great weed bed. The islands of the river float above the water, pulled up from the water by the ballooning trees.

This was my home, but it isn't my home now. I've seen so many cities, towns, mountains, rivers that this city has nothing to do with me, my past. It is a city of the land, the nation. It is a special city now, unique, with possibilities, promise. I am free to see this city in a new way; I am a stranger to this place, and it is very good.

CHAPTER 11

I stand before the family house in the suburbs of Harrisburg. The house hasn't changed, it is always frozen in time. I see the huge, spreading sycamore, a picture-perfect tree, trimmed professionally every six or seven years; the cut lawn, which seems a golf-course green. The house sits solidly, no curtains blow in the breeze. The day is still, hot, humid. No voices echo from the windows, no movement is seen inside. Nothing moves, no traffic on the street, no pedestrian on the sidewalk. Not one leaf of the sycamore tree moves. It is a dollhouse, stamped out by the machine, and I sense I have made a mistake by returning.

My family is glad to see me for a few minutes, then the novelty of my presence wears off. It isn't me they love, but the machine part named *son*, who works with the machine part named *family*. In time I meet my few friends; they are the same. They know no more of life than when I left. Moe wrecked his car. Phil is engaged. Jerry is working for a truck terminal. So it goes. I try to tell them of what I have seen and done. That I was truly alive for the first time in my life. They listen but are not enthused. Yet, I am a zero hero of sorts; I'm someone they talk about in idle moments, while sitting in a bar drinking.

The Silver Cord

Within a month I have a job; I am in the machine. The machine makes it difficult to get back in; the machine knows what a danger it is for people to escape. Penalties are placed on people who escape; on the form it is called Past Work History. Don't say, "I've been traveling. I've thinned apples in Washington." The machine knows you aren't fully machined, you might fall out again—a loose nut. This piece still has life in it; it isn't dead yet. Finally, you get in, in a job that doesn't need finely honed pieces.

My part in the machine is to clean aluminum siding at an apartment complex. Lug around a generator, stand on ladders, scrub siding with a long-handled brush, rinse with a high-pressure hose. I enjoy the work. When this job is completed, I am shifted to a construction site as a laborer. I also work in concrete, really just lug around forms for the curbing and sidewalk of the development. The work is good. I'm outside. I'm learning what goes into a housing development. My physical strength is surging ahead to new levels. It is a real job; streets need curbs, people need homes.

The work is good, and I say to myself, "I don't have to be a machine person. I'll live within the machine but be separate from it." I am friendly where once I was aloof. I find humor in situations that once brought recrimination and anger. I choose to only see good in people as I did on the road. I will not let their ugliness become my ugliness. I will walk away from the rude, the unkind, and not think the worst of humanity. I feel as if I am beginning life with a clean slate.

I will keep searching for the knowledge that will make every day an adventure, that will make rising every day worthwhile. I will find truth and live it. If work becomes stale, I will have my weekends. I will camp, hunt, fish, hike, revive my soul with these things. This is what I say to myself.

I think about my trip in odd moments; the memories bring joy, bolster my confidence. I see the city, the countryside with a new perspective. I'll look up to the skyline and see the mountains and say to myself, "I never realized I could see the mountains from this street." Or "Look at the beauty of the mountains!" Or I'll be stopped at a city traffic light, glance at an old building, and wonder what the city was like when that building was constructed. Who worked within? What were the times like? Sometimes I hear a voice in a store, or market, or gas station and the voice will have an oddness. I'll realize the Pennsylvania German in the voice or perhaps a Pennsylvania backwoods, country pronunciation, and say to myself, "Isn't this a strange part of the country?"

Within three months, I am a machine man. It goes like this: Our foreman has borderline psychiatric problems; he is mercury bound in flesh. He has pressures from the main office, he hands them down to us. He will go into wild fits for no apparent reason or for the smallest reason. His directions are vague, always confusing. He is happiest when thinking of the lower anatomy of the female form; then he smiles, bubbles of saliva come to his lips. He is both an irritation and a joke, yet deep down he does know his job.

The game being played by the other employees is called, "Cover your ass." Behind the back, insults and viciousness; smiles to your face. Mistakes abound, no one will own up to them because everyone is afraid of getting fired. Everyone is blaming someone else. Everyone has his own idea of how to do the job. They balk when their way is not used. There are people who don't want to work and would rather waste time. Stealing from the company, misappropriations, discrepancies on hours worked occur.

I try to remain apart from the situation, be an honest person with only good to say. I might have been able to succeed, but no one wants my success. They don't consciously wish my failure, but a part of them wants me to be as ugly as they are. The foreman says, "Put an extra hour down for yourself." Someone will say, "What do you think of X and the way he's working?" I make mistakes and get chewed out. Behind my back, they talk of my stupidity. Then the main office hands me a paycheck that is short, and I must prove my hours. We run into hard shale, the work slows, we get behind. Or I'll be with my partner on the truck, making a run, and he'll decide he wants to stop at McDonald's or his old high school instead of going where we're supposed to go.

I am in a rut. Up each morning at the same time. I drive the same roads. I know the road by heart. I know when to shift gears, not by the engine, but by signs, potholes, homes, trees. After work I lift some light weights,

The Silver Cord

then go to a bar and drink with my friends. My head is empty, I sit in a pleasant daze, and times passes. When I go to the bank with my paycheck, or for a haircut, or to the gas station, it seems I am always waiting. The machine lets everyone loose at the same time, on the machine's schedule. I am irritated as I hear the seconds, minutes tick from my life.

Everyone I meet, everyone I deal with seems harassed, angry, with an attitude, even if only of indifference. People behind the counters, people in their cars, people in bars, no one seems to be truly happy. I try to talk to people. On the road I talked to everyone, but in the machine, if you talk to a stranger, he or she looks at you as if you're diseased, simple, a homosexual, or on a con. I give up, and I begin to give them what they give me.

My own heart is not pure. I am a mass of insecurities, paranoia, anxieties, some reaching back into my childhood. I have my moments of anger, belligerence; I am always wronged. I can never say, "I'm sorry," or "It was my fault." I give people the finger, I swear. I look at people as if they are odd when they talk to me. I am not friendly. I cannot find a woman, and this goads at my spirit. There is something within me that isn't right, but I don't want to see it, admit that it is there.

My weekends fizzle. I am too tired to live on the weekends. Organizing a weekend takes thought, planning, effort. You've got to interest people, bend your schedule to theirs, gather the fishing equipment, buy the bait, food, load the boat, till it seems you are organizing an African safari. Hunting! The land is privately owned with NO TRESPASSING signs. Every field seems to have a suburban home upon it. The good hunting land is a long drive away. Camping degenerates into beer parties. Hikes turn to boring walks. Sometimes there are no free weekends, the car needs repaired, you need a haircut, and on it goes. Those things I thought would revive my soul weigh me down or, if the experiences are good, seem to mock my present life.

In the suburban dollhouse, all is not well. Parents continually harp at son to take on responsibility, insurance, home, wife. *Finish your education, get a steady job with security, pension, health care.* I hear them enslaving me to a system, a life that cringes my soul. All the while, mother manipulates her son with her moods, despondencies. *I will love you when you do as I say. I will take my love away when you disobey.*

I ask them why. I look at their lives and see nothing good. I see a woman pent up in her dollhouse, unsatisfied, wanting more than she has. Her housework is a burden; she cooks, washes, never laughs; only complaints come from her. She can't tell me why I am alive, what life means, because she doesn't know herself.

My father doesn't know the answer. He brings home reams of paperwork from the office. Is his mind slipping, or is the company unfair? He is underpaid. The company wants men like him out, the older men, who have put their lives into the company. These older men don't work fast enough, these older men have pensions coming to them. The machine doesn't give a damn about my father. He comes home weary, numb, never a positive word from his mouth. He has no pleasure in life, nothing that excites him.

I see my sisters, who have bought the machine heart and soul, who never ask why. Yet they are better than I am; they don't need to ask why, they think the best of people, they like their studying or their work. They want a good life, but they have never had to ask what life means. It could all be so comical, this dollhouse family, if I didn't love them. Not that I could ever say it. Perhaps I am the comedy. I am the problem.

In February work is slacking off, and the boss doesn't mind if I take some time off without pay. I decide to go south. I'm hoping the road will give me back life. That is what I hope. My soul is on empty, I leave just to be gone. I could be responsible if there were something worth giving my life to.

I stand beside Interstate 81 South. Snow still hides behind rocks and trees like shrunken white shadows. The raw air and the car exhaust mix in my lungs. The shoulder of the road is littered with cinders, hubcaps, exhaust pipes, air filters, shredded tires. Plastic cups, fast-food restaurant bags, someone's old plaid shirt plastered into the stones complete the scene. The ground is frozen beneath the mud. The food I have eaten is a cold lump in my stomach. My cold hands grip a sign that says, "South."

A pack of homeless dogs scrounges in the bent stubble of a cornfield across the highway, poking into brush, gullies. The dogs are gaunt, starving. Cars hurtle down the cement, making a sound as if they feel the

The Silver Cord

coldness of the air, a sucking-in-of-the-breath sound. It is I who is cold, but I make the cars cold so that I am less lonely. I want the metal to suffer with me. The people inside the metal are warm.

A refrigerated delivery truck passes, the man looks at me; I know I have a ride. I hear the gears downshift, see the brake lights stutter; the truck weaves stiffly backward. The driver's name is Ike, black hair trimmed to a stubble, flabby white skin, an unhinged jaw that is like a snake swallowing an egg when he talks. His words and the hum of the engine mix, I am not listening. I hear the word *niggers*, I tune in.

"I get a pain in my gut when I see niggers. It feels like when you haven't eaten and your stomach's churning. This nigger pulled up across from me at a red light in a big fancy car. I stared over at him until he looked, then I called him a nigger. Boy, they hate that! He was steaming but he didn't come over. I have a club behind my seat. He'd a been sorry."

I wonder if it was a good, decent man that received such treatment, or a scumbag of a man. Either way, he didn't deserve such treatment. Why do people act that way? I melt into the heat, the drone of the engine, the sound of the tires on the road till the Chambersburg exit.

I stand beside mounds of piled snow; the wind has died; the sun is bright. A jeep stops, a young college kid is driving, going back to his Virginia college. We smoke a joint, and I space out, lose track of time; my mind is blank, I don't know how long I am like that. The kid says to me, "Are you all right?"

I say, "Yes, I'm all right." But I am not. I'm running from something, not searching; I feel unclean, stupid for smoking.

I watch the land, but it holds no real interest for me; I see an old farmhouse, two-story, orange-red brick, shuttered windows, double chimneys, a house made of windows. A woman lifts her arms to a line of clothing. It is cold outside. Her figure is outlined against a sheet. Then I am gone as the jeep thumps over the cement slabs laid like dominoes, back to back. I remember a field overgrown with sumac and a rotting hewn-log house with the same sumac growing within. Within the sumac trees, I saw apple trees long neglected; bitter, rotting fruit hanging, good for nothing but deer and mice.

Somewhere I leave the jeep and hitch a ride with a fifty-five-year-old woman. Her voice goes on and on, and it is witchcraft and astrology that gives her life taste and direction. Spells work; there is a world behind this one that is manipulated by Ouija boards, incantations, rituals of darkness from antiquity. She says there are good witches and bad witches but declines to say which she is. The mountains are in the distance, the trees bare, dustings of snow on the high elevations. The mountains run like one solid, continuous wall, only wind gaps break the straight edge. In time the ridge breaks, becomes like wave crests, churning into peaks. By the road are brown hills patched with snow, stitched with leafless, squat apple and cherry trees. Farms with long poultry sheds behind the barns are scattered over the land. Cattle graze in the fields by broken bales of hay—Hereford cattle—looking warm in their fuzzy brown coats. The grazed fields have young hemlocks growing, scattered as if deliberately by an errant landscape gardener.

The sky is gray; the earth cold and damp, bare; the traces of snow are gone. I leave the witchcraft lady, stand under the gray sky, which seems to press against me. Snow flurries, sleet rake across the land. A rusted, patched, backfiring, oil-smoking station wagon stops before me. The man driving is in his forties; short hair, worn work clothes, wire-rimmed glasses, square jutting jaw, gray-blue eyes that sparkle but are in another world. The sparkle is like that of superiority, but it isn't; it is like when you know something good that another doesn't know. Joy, maybe.

The heater in the car is not working; the man drives with a smile on his face, thinking of some inward thing. He hesitates for a moment, then speaks. "Have you experienced Jesus Christ as your Lord and Savior?"

I say, "No." I know who Christ is, or I think I do. I know he died for my sins, though I didn't ask him to. I haven't experienced Christ and can't begin to imagine what that means. I say, "Tell me about it."

I know people who wouldn't want to hear about the Christian God; they become bitter, angry, cynical. These people who don't want to hear will listen to any other subject thrown their way—Buddha, Marx, sex, drugs—any topic, just for the sake of conversation. I listen. Why couldn't Christ be the final truth, the only truth? What is there to fear from this man's conversation?

    A tent revival came to his hometown. He went more from curiosity than a pressing need. The tent was crowded, people packed shoulder to shoulder. He said a warmth, a love, was in that tent, in the hearts of the people and in a presence separate from the people. The preacher began to speak, and everything he said struck home. Every word rested on the Bible. An electric feeling ran through the audience, a power, a presence, the Holy Spirit. The preacher asked people to accept Jesus Christ into their hearts. He said that Christ loved you and all you had do was reach for His outstretched arms. My driver went down to the front, got on his knees, and began to cry. The Holy Spirit was within him. He has been a changed man since that time.

    I know that he did experience something and that he still has what he experienced. I wonder if it wasn't his own loneliness, failings, need for love that broke him down. I ask myself why his state of mind should make any difference as far as truth is concerned. Men are more susceptible to help, outside influences, even their own imaginations when they are in despair or need; but that doesn't mean what they experience isn't the truth. Truth even for those who think they are in control of their lives—if you can be in control without knowing the final truth. I wonder if what he has now will be in evidence five years from now.

    He tells me his wife and children have noticed the change. There is no more arguing, fighting; they talk, there is understanding. He told them how much he loved them. They go to church together; for the first time they are a family. I am happy for him. I have never told my family that I love them.

    He tells me he used to work in an apple orchard for minimum wage, his trailer home was in disrepair. His yard looked like a dump because he didn't care and didn't know better. He is studying to be a mechanic now, his home has been made livable, his yard is clean—all the junk hauled away. He will raise himself out of his poverty and ignorance with the help of the Lord. His wife and children are behind him 100 percent. Someday he will live in a real home.

I like this man. I like what God has done for him. He turns to me, looks into my eyes, asks me who I think Jesus Christ is. I don't remember anyone asking that question before. I say I believe he is the son of God, though he did things I wouldn't expect the son of God to do. He said things I don't understand, and which sometimes don't sound loving. There seem to be lots of gaps in the Bible, and we're left to fill them in for ourselves. How can you love a God you don't understand?

He wants examples of the gaps I mentioned.

I say what of turning the other cheek? Does that mean toward thieves? Certainly not murderers. You could turn the other cheek to people with a conscience; they would feel guilt, and this might spur change, an apology, restitution. There are people who, if you turned the other cheek, would feel nothing but contempt for you, and they would continue taking from you until you are dead.

God knows what kind of men live upon this earth. He knows there are men who would abuse His mercy. Could I be wiser than God, who made me? Maybe my problem is that I don't know when to turn the other cheek and when to stand firm. Maybe that is my complaint. Maybe it is that I feel no power or presence, no Holy Spirit within me. My driver smiles faintly in agreement, shrugs his shoulders. His eyes are momentarily lost, then they harden in resolve. He has found something to hold onto in the leap, and he isn't going to lose God by doubting Him.

Somewhere near Harrisonburg, Virginia, my ride ends. To the north, the sky is a light-gray band; underneath the band of solid clouds is another band of blue-black rain clouds. The dark rain clouds are hard in texture because the air is cold; I think sleet will fall. Across the fields a single tree stands. It is one of those field trees that was left standing to give the cows shade, and the cows, in their kindness, manured the tree to bushy greenness. The tree grew tall and wide, and then the insects ate the life out of it, lightning blasted it. The dead tree stands against the cold sky.

Two Virginia boys and their woman companion pick me up. The men, in their middle twenties, are tanned in the face, wear checker-patterned hunting shirts, faded jeans, torn and patched. Their hair is almost long, grown out of a conservative clipping, so that it isn't so much long and

The Silver Cord

rebellious as ignored. It gives a rough, wild look that they like, but not so much so that the older men they work with can't understand. These Virginia boys have calloused hands and lines of grease under their fingernails. They work at a little of everything—mechanic, carpenter, bricklayer's helper—until they get that steady blue-collar job that is so elusive.

The woman is a wife or live-in girlfriend. She is younger than the men, but southern women get married early and divorced early. This woman-girl's hair is long, stringy; she didn't have time to run a comb through. Her clothes seem neglected, not ironed. She is thin but physically tough; yet when it comes to love, she is vulnerable and doesn't seem to understand it at all. That is who I think they are. They aren't inclined to talk; they just wanted to give me a ride.

The forest touches the road and smells of wet oak leaves. In the west, yellow sun bursts from the clouds. I am in the bed of a small pickup with an Irish setter. The driver seems concerned about me and stops at a backwoods store so that I can pick up some food. Near dusk I knock on the window, and the truck stops.

I climb a barbed-wire fence, then a hill spotted with cow dung. On the crest of the hill, where the forest begins, I pitch my tent. An oak, hemlock fire cooks my watery soup. I am tired of jumping in and out of cars, of standing in the cold. A part of me wants to be home, sitting in a comfortable chair after a home-cooked meal. My mind is empty; a guilt comes and goes.

I look into the fire, and it is just a fire. The magic is going from life, or whatever it is that binds your soul with the experiences of life. No remembrances of other fires that were good, no sense that I am on a journey, a quest. I tell myself tomorrow will be warm, tomorrow the sun will shine.

I have a clear view of the highway. Car lights are blinking on; I hear the sound of the highway. The lights delineate the highway; the lights curve around hills, go up and down hills, then are lost in the misty darkness. One band of light is white, the other red; traffic is heavy. My mind tries to make something deep and mysterious of the moment but cannot. The string of lights has beauty, but there is no truth to be found within.

These people have a destination. I stare into the fire, and my mind is blank. I have no destination even as I plan to go to Florida. I come to think about fate. Fate is such a kind idea to a man who has nothing. Whatever happens is meant to happen, and it is beyond my control. I don't think of God being involved in fate or in my life. I think about my rides and what they might be doing. Ike, the truck driver, is sitting in front of TV with a beer and a snack in his hands, watching a jiggly show designed to appeal to a thirteen-year-old boy. The college kid is trying to score with a college girl, telling her lies, playing mind games, plying her with marijuana. The witchcraft lady is putting a spell on someone or searching for the ghost of someone dead. The Virginia boys are in a cold garage, working on their car or drinking whiskey or bourbon at home. The born-again Christian is studying the Bible or his mechanic's book or praying to the God who made him. Or is he playing with his children?

I climb into my sleeping bag feeling so alone. I say the prayer I once prayed as a kid before bedtime. *Now I lay me down to sleep; I pray the Lord my soul to keep; if I should die before I wake, I pray the Lord my soul to take. God bless:* I name mother, father, sisters, grandparents, and then finish with all my friends and folks. *Amen.* I think God has given up on me and I, on Him.

CHAPTER 12

I awake stiff and sore. The cold of the ground has entered into my bones. I cannot shake the cold; my focus is not upon the quest; my mind sinks broodingly back to my body. The clouds are rippled, the smell of moisture hangs in the air. The mind catalogues the smell of moisture from past times and says hard pellets of frozen rain will come.

The trucks pass, few and far between. The men sitting high in the trucks are on their CBs, talking about me. I know I am the conversation because there is nothing else upon the road. One trucker has an evil smile. He brushes close to the shoulder in an attempt to frighten me. Cinders, exhaust blow into me. I sense he is trouble.

In a few minutes, a state police car is pulling violently off the cement on the other side of the highway. I know the trucker has reported my presence, complained. I can hear the conversation. "Why don't the state police ever help a trucker out when he needs it? Instead of making life miserable for a working man. I got a hitchhiker, here, obstructing traffic, close to the road." The state policeman sits in his car and stares at me.

He is studying me, my clothes, the look in my eyes, my stance, even where I am on the stretch of highway. His head is working. Where did

The Silver Cord

this hitchhiker come from? Is he a bum, college kid, drug user, drifter, fugitive? If a fugitive, does he have a gun cocked, ready to blow me into the next world?

He should be thinking like this—God help him if he is not. He is on the highway alone, the sole representative of the law. He deals with ordinary honest folk, smart asses, simpletons, law breakers, liars, thieves, killers. He has seen mangled bodies in twisted steel, blood, and gore. He must be the man in charge—the man in control.

His tone may say, "I ask the questions, you answer politely. I need no jokes, no levity, no cynicism." His tone may be courteous. "Are you aware that you were breaking the law?" Or his tone may say, "You broke the law, fool, and I take it personally." Hands on hips, disgust, impatience in the snarl. I will take whatever he gives because I know we, our nation, need him, and he has seen too much.

He gets out of his car with a loudspeaker in his hands. My empty, hurting eyes look at him and say, "Why don't you leave me alone?" He is studying my size, musculature. I am bigger than he is, lean in the waist. My eyes have a trace of meanness within because I'm cold, going to Florida, and there is nothing in Florida for me. I just want to be left alone. For a brief second, I see apprehension in the trooper. In that moment, he is someone's husband, someone's father, someone's son; he is not an enemy, just a man in a difficult job.

He tells me to come over. I go to him. His voice is firm, businesslike. He wants a driver's license. I use the old trick and let the cards unfold. I see him glance at them rapidly. He asks me where I am going.

I say, "South to Florida to look for a job." He writes out a ticket and says I must appear in court on a certain date or mail the fine money in. He says he gives tickets to those he thinks will pay, and those he knows can't or won't, he will take to jail. The subtle threat angers me, but I hide the anger. I tell him I'll pay. He looks at me hard, judging. I don't like being given the ticket. I don't see any crime in what I am doing. I lie to myself.

He drives me to a country exit, one of those that sees one or two cars a day, and he leaves me out as it begins to rain. The ice bounces, makes a ticking sound as it strikes the stiff poncho. I shuffle my feet, wiggle my toes. I make three signs from discarded cardboard boxes and wave them at every car and truck; I am so far from the road that most drivers do not see me. I inch closer to the highway. A van stops.

The two men in the van are in their late twenties or early thirties; they talk with thick southern drawls, softly to each other. One has a black ledger book; they are determining who owes them money. The smoothness of their voices gives a feminine quality to the tone. I see no indication the van is used in a business. Is it drugs they sell? They take me into Tennessee. They never ask who I am, what I am doing on the road.

I stand by the road as rain comes. The mountains are high, rugged. The wind is cold. Two other hitchhikers walk up to me. They are going to the Mardi Gras, New Orleans. They offer me a swig of whiskey, I decline. They are from Vermont. They continue walking. I see a car stop for them.

A car pulls up to me, fifties model, rusted, streaked with red mud, the windows have a thick coating of grime. A black, apprehensive face leans over the passenger seat as I open the door. The face says, "You want a ride don't you?" I had taken my thumb down because my arm had tired just as he had come into view. The face says, "You'll take a ride from a black person, right?" I feel he has made a connection between my arm going down and him. I am correct, for he says, "You do need a ride?" I say, "Yes."

I get in, the car pulls out, the seat tilts back, begins to slide into the rear. I'm momentarily frightened, till I realize there is no plan to this—just a falling-apart car. The car is filthy, thick with dirt in corners, on the dash; greasy newspapers, trash everywhere. I can barely see through the grime on the windshield. The driver smells of stale, greasy cooking odors; cigarettes; perspiration. He has not bathed for some time. When he talks, I can barely understand him. His words are heavy with his blackness. I nod in agreement to whatever he says.

He has an old CB radio, which he reaches for hesitantly. We hear truckers talking about what bridge to take over the Delaware to Newark, New Jersey. My driver lived in Newark before coming south, traveled across the bridge a thousand times. My driver picks up the CB; keeping

The Silver Cord

his voice white, he tells the white trucker what exit, what bridge, the highway number. The words float over the concrete like the sound of the tires. My driver wants to be a part of the highway's song. But his voice isn't white enough, and somewhere out there, a white voice, in a southern drawl says, "Why doesn't that nigger get off the air?"

I see my driver's chest sink as his soul collapses, as the air is expelled in a resigned sigh of utter despair and pain. His eyes become soft, the face drops into a lifeless mask. Why does a stranger hate him, want to hurt him? Why is evil returned for good?

His car is filthy, he smells. I can't understand half the words from his mouth. I sense he knows these things. I sense a light in his eyes that is intelligence. I understand the pain. You don't need to be black to know that men are hateful, cruel, unkind. They hate you like they were hated, hurt, made to feel small, ugly, inferior. If you hate in return, then there is no more man, only a machine man made from the dead earth.

A tear comes to his eye, and there is nothing I can do except pretend I don't see him in his pain. I want to tell him he is no different than me, that I respect him as a person, even love him in the brotherly sense. I want to tell him that God loves him. I don't know what that means except that it is true and good. I don't understand.

I know black people who are the scum of the earth, like the white bigot on the CB—kindness, goodness are lacking, nonexistent. Why do people judge by skin color, speech, the quality of clothes on a person's back, by job, or possessions? If you must dislike a man, hate him, do it for the goodness lacking in his heart. I don't understand…and I do.

The ride ends; I say thank you for the ride, for the kindness given. That is all I can say.

A Corvair van stops. The driver is in his early thirties, gangling, stooped slightly at the shoulders; straight prominent nose, slightly receding chin under a beard. His eyes are thoughtful and suffering. The suffering is hidden, not an outward painful look. A look of doubt and hope, an inner searching for something to hold onto and thinking it may not exist. The van, never made for the open road, is loaded to the ceiling with the family's belongings, most of which are vinyl record albums and clothing. When he opens the rear door to put in my pack, possessions come tumbling out.

His wife is short, flabby, with a kind, naive face and eyes of childish vacantness. A kind of childishness that doesn't concern itself with the world because the world can't be understood. Thinking would only ruin the contentedness. She isn't aware that she thinks in this way. She only knows what she likes, and what she likes hasn't altered much from her first remembrances of what brought pleasure to her. She gladly speaks when spoken to but never volunteers conversation.

This man, who I will call Bob, facially and bodily reminds me of Abraham Lincoln, but with a dream mind, not the keen mind of a lawyer. This man and his kindly faced wife together have produced a child named Mikey. Mikey is eight, undernourished, thin, undersized—more like a five-year-old, with a mouthful of rotting teeth—rotted brown stumps for teeth. He has a sugar habit that makes him hyperactive, squirming, uncontrollable.

Father has left the care and discipline to mother, kind of shrugged off his duty as if he never had any part in the creating of the child. Mother looks at her son with an expression of vacantness, childishness that says, "Where did this creature come from?" As if it had never spent nine months in her womb, to emerge from her body. Mother and Father are overwhelmed by the child, the child rules them. They can't say, "No," and make it stick. It is much easier to give the kid his sugar. When Mikey gets his soda pop or candy, there are periods of respite. It is when I meet such people that I wonder about life in these United States.

Bob and his family are moving from upstate New York to Texarkana, Arkansas. His wife's brother says there are plenty of jobs in Texarkana. Bob has no special skills or knowledge. He will work in a factory, pump gas, whatever it takes; he will survive. The work will be no different than it was in New York, but there is work. He believes, hopes Texarkana is the promised land. He is from the country's past, a drifter, moving along the frontier, always thinking the grass is greener over there. I drive for Bob, something I don't normally do. The man needs help, needs someone to take part of the responsibility. Soon as I touch the steering wheel

The Silver Cord

I know the van is dangerously overloaded, the van is frail, the weight heavy. For all the negatives I see, I still like Bob and his family. They aren't perfect, they have gaps in their knowledge, they have their failings. But so do I, so does everyone. Bob and his wife do have kindness. To me, kindness is the greatest of virtues.

Somewhere in the cold dusk, somewhere in the Tennessee mountains, we exit the highway, drive into a small town that has a gas station, a restaurant, a motel. The motel was built in the time when the two-lane highway that connects the small towns was *the* highway. Now the roller-coaster road, made for Sunday drives, milk deliveries, the farmer's hay wagon is, like the town, in the backwash of progress.

I take a room in the motel beside Bob and his family. We eat together at a rundown, aluminum-bodied restaurant built whenever those airplane fuselage-shaped restaurants were built, back in the fifties, I think. Old men with ear-flapped hats are drinking coffee at the counter. Ladies with gray hair piled high on their heads, glasses with chains, bitter mouths heavy with red lipstick, give us the once over and begin their whispered appraisals. The waitress has thick makeup. Her hair is the way she wore it when she was a young woman; the color hasn't changed.

She says there is no water; the reservoir is polluted downstream, so we must order drinks that cost money. I wonder how the dishes are cleaned if there is no water. She gives us the news of the reservoir with a certain amount of happiness because this event will mark the month, if not the year. Maybe years from now, the polluted reservoir will be mentioned in conversation, tied to some more personal event, such as the time the neighbor kicked his wife out of the house, or the grandson broke his arm.

The plates of food served us are skimpy, embarrassing, but not to our waitress. I look to the locals sitting beside us, their plates are heaped with food. Mikey tries a spoonful of potatoes, but they aren't sweet enough, so he spits them out. He bugs Daddy, and Daddy gives him money for a gumball machine. The candy and the plastic spider in the plastic bubble make Mikey happy. Then Mikey drinks two Cokes. That is all the kid has for supper.

In the morning Bob asks me to drive to the interstate. The overloaded van stalls three times before we reach the gas station. We fill up. I turn the ignition, the battery grinds like a dentist drill deep in a tooth. The engines catches then stalls. We play this game three more times. The fourth time, I put the gears in drive, gently give the engine gas. Bang! Metal is thumping underneath our feet; the differential couldn't take the strain and so it broke.

The gas station attendant, who has swarthy skin, rotting teeth, says that his brother owns a garage and has a tow truck. He smiles—I suppose partly to be friendly and partly because in a dying town, money is welcome even from the hardships of others. Sometimes I forget that most of America is small towns, and money comes directly from other people and not in a weekly, monthly check from a corporation.

In the cinder-block garage, surrounded by a junkyard of old cars and car parts, I wait with Bob. A mangy-looking coon dog with a hanging head, chained to a piece of worn and pitted ground, lounges. The inside smell is of grease, oil, gas, tires. Broken windows are covered by cardboard. Tools are sloppily laid on a long table.

Above the table, on a calendar, a naked beauty from another time, her feet tucked under her, her back arched, shows her breasts. Her red lips are pulled open and between half-parted teeth, a tongue curls out. I suppose she is there to drag the lust up out of a man if his mind is at peace. That is what she does to me.

The brother who owns the garage says the part will be hard to find. Bob and his family will have to stay in town. I feel responsible for Bob's setback. I offer money. I look into his eyes and for a moment think that he will snap under the uncertainties, the responsibility. The repair will cost money and so will a motel room. He refuses the money, doesn't say an unkind word to me. Instead, he says, "Maybe this is where I'm supposed to end up."

As I walk out of town the air is clear, the sky blue, the morning is crisp. Church bells are ringing. Uncharacteristically, I shrug off the incident with Bob's van, no self-condemnation. A young family, going home from early church and Sunday school, gives me a ride. I sit in the back seat with a little girl of red hair, dressed in her clean, neat Sunday clothes. She shows me her crayon-on-manila paper drawings done in

The Silver Cord

Sunday school and blushes as I tell her how good they are. I am thankful families like this one exist in America. If I had kids, church would be a part of their lives. I say that even as I don't understand God. I suppose that means that I believe I've gotten more good from knowing Him than bad.

The next ride is in a long, wide, plush, black car. In the corner of the windshield is a sticker picturing a cross, around the cross are Latin words. A smiling man, dressed in black, with a white collar—preacher, pastor, father, whatever name, whatever denomination—offers me a ride. He is of medium height, portly; he has a common face, a firm voice, which nonetheless contains a false gaiety, an insincere concern. Perhaps I think all gaiety is false because man is a part of an anguished world. Perhaps this man has been forced to act continually happy, radiant, confident, concerned, by people who can't let him be anything else without feeling they didn't get their money's worth. Maybe he is the real deal.

He gives me the hitchhiker story, which he uses on all the hitchhikers he picks up. "I don't often pick up hitchhikers, but you look honest. I once picked up a man, in his thirties, dirty ragged clothes. Hadn't shaved. Didn't really have a destination. I gave him a few dollars so he could get something to eat. He said, 'You know, I made myself a promise that the next car that stopped for me, I would rob the driver and steal the car.' He pulled out a gun from the waist of his pants. 'I was tempted to do all I had promised myself,' he said, 'but I am going to leave you go.' Since that incident I'm careful who I pick up."

That is his story, so smooth and polished I know he has told it many times. Why shouldn't he tell it? Am I bitter, or is he a phony? I think of him as a man who will return to his book-lined study and sip sherry from a sparkling glass. He is not the pastor in the church but the man up the ladder to whom religion is a business. Budgets, expenditures, expansions, assets, credits, debits, meetings, parties, politicians to meet, vacations in church-owned homes in the Bahamas.

He says, "Tell me about yourself." Is he hoping for a moving story to tell at the next party? I hesitate, and I can tell my silence is irritating him. I begin with college. He knows his anthropology, has read all the heavy works, ones I have not read. The books we have in common, I remember as being tedious—authors lost in their own conceit. Men who possess no answers to life and don't really want answers. He mentions other titles and says I should have read these works, being an anthropology major. But I have not read these books.

I attempt to speak but my mind is dull, my tongue thick. I can't remember the nail-hard facts of anthropology, the facts that when repeated make one sound intelligent; the pieces have turned to dust. There is no sparkle in my conversation. I'm not concerned if this man likes me or even believes me. I say, "I just had the basic stuff," knowing how this would sound to an educated ear.

He says, "I see." And I see too, that he likes sharp, witty people, and I am a bumpkin. He is silent.

The wide black car rubs the white line and the road's shoulder through fields, over hills. The black car with the cross decal speeds through glens of cool shade. We skirt a lake, the reservoir, empty, save for pools of water in the mud and silver specks like aluminum cans in the sun—the bellies of dead fish. Tennessee Valley Authority Reservoir.

The Smokies rise ahead, naked, except for bare trees that rise like porcupine quills. The black car comes to an intersection outside of some crossroads, hick town. "You take that road," he says impatiently.

I say, "How far to the interstate?"

He says, "You'll see signs," a slight anger in the voice.

Before I can say thank you, the black car is gone.

I am at the bottom of a steep hill. I have no energy, no desire. I compare the preacher to the Virginia orchard laborer. The preacher did not tell me about Christ, did not mentioned his name. The preacher left me without giving hope, without giving an encouraging word. The preacher's reason for living is for position, for the power knowledge brings The Virginia laborer lives for Christ. One man knows Christ; the other knows the ritual, the book learning. I would rather know Christ.

The Silver Cord

The hill is pulling out my strength. When there is no place you want to go, the hills get higher. Traveling no longer seems an adventure, just a flight into an unknown land. At the top of the hill is a new church, a loudspeaker broadcasts music from the church. Beside the church are wood shacks, unpainted. The boards have wide cracks between them. The shacks sit on cinder blocks and have tin roofs. The yards are dirt, the curtains torn. The clotheslines are hung with cheap, faded clothes. I know the cold spring air comes through the floor boards as well as the winter winds. That the shacks sit so close to the new church seems to say something. The people in the shacks must hear the music. I hope the people of the church help the people in the shacks, like the Virginia laborer was helped.

I remember feeling like a fool walking along the road as traffic increases and people stare.

CHAPTER 13

I am on Interstate 40 when a faded-green Rambler stops. The woman driving has gray eyes that say, "I would like to know who you are." Her voice is soft, her southern accent half womanly artfulness and half innocence. She smells clean like the fragrance of a flowery soap. A delicate bracelet is upon her wrist. Her brother or friend is in the seat beside her. I enter into the back seat saying, "Thanks." She says, "I can take you a little ways" as she pulls onto the road.

I know she is intrigued by me because I am a loner; a rebel, in a sense. Southern women like their rebels. I am outside society just like the South is outside the country, even as the South is within this nation. A man is respected for being a rebel, receives a grudging respect, as long as he has a certain dignity and extends respect to others. You can be a drifter, change jobs every year, drink too much, marry seven times, lose your life's savings on a horse, dare death in a fast car—as long as you do it with a certain dignity toward others.

The highway descends down a seam in the mountains. I can see beyond the piedmont to the flatness that is the coastal plain. It seems the whole southland is below me. A spring haze hangs over the land, trees are budding, the temperature is rising. She pulls the car onto the shoulder.

The Silver Cord

We look each other dead in the eye long and hard. We are both going to speak. But we don't, and I open the door and stand along the road and watch her pull into the traffic.

I hitch a number of short rides on Interstate 26 till a station wagon filled with Koreans pulls over. Father, mother, grandmother, children—girls in their teens. Dad works for the government, has engineering degrees that would make him welcome in any country in the world. He thought I was a soldier; that is why he stopped. American soldiers rate highly—they saved his country. We talk.

The purpose of life is to work hard, make money, get ahead; that is a man's job. Marry, have children, instill the work ethic in your offspring, help them succeed. Life is simple when you have come from poverty. I don't have the goad of poverty. I do not think that even poverty could goad me into life, the machine. I need the answer.

I sleep in rows of pine trees a short distance from the highway. In the morning, the wind is warm, the earth has that awakening smell of spring. I stand by the side of Interstate 95. I see no local traffic, no delivery trucks, no people going to work. The interstate seems to be expressly made to take Yankees to the sun and warmth, then back home again. Tractor trailers are on the road, but they are on every road, going the distance, filling the shelves, making the country run.

Swoosh, swoosh, swoosh, the vacationers are rolling. The license plates say Quebec, Ontario, Maine, New York, Connecticut, New Jersey, even Michigan, Illinois. The plush sedans are usually from New York, guzzling the gas, a carload of friends, the kids raised, silver-gray-haired distinguished Jews or Italian-Americans. Wasp America comes in their motor homes; gregarious men, playing cards in the back, drinking scotch and waters. You can see college kids cramped in small cars, surfboards on the roof. Average Americans are in the station wagons, Scouts, SUVs piled high with beach chairs, beach umbrellas, charcoal grills as canvas blows from loose ends. All are going to Florida for sun, warmth, tans, ocean surf, fishing, beach walking, sailing, surfboarding, or just to be there—where it is happening.

A car is on the shoulder, coming at me with great speed. I grab my pack, jump into the drainage ditch. The car skids past me, stones flying.

The man's eyes are wide in fear, wonderment. The car stops. The driver, early twenties, laughs embarrassingly as he apologizes. He is coming from DC, where he has partied all weekend. The amphetamines are wearing off. His hair is combed neatly, he's well dressed. College student, Gainesville, Florida. His eyelids seem propped open.

Gainesville to Washington and back, he does the trip often. He says to visit friends and to make money. Jamaican grass, Columbian coke. The radio says a frontal system is moving over the land, rain will come. The college kid looks out at the sky and says it won't rain. Meteorology is the fragment he studies in college. The land streams by. I see a corner of Savannah, Georgia; smokestacks, warehouses, rails, a rank odor in the air. A sign out on an empty plain says, "Jacksonville City Limits."

In time I am in Jacksonville, the college kid is gone, the sun is setting, the cumulus clouds are piled high, the exhaust is thick, the traffic whizzes by me, staring. My eyes are sullen, my face mean and hurt. I know that is how I appear, but I can't change. If I were sitting in a car driving by, I would not pick me up.

Palm trees; wooden, rickety, one-story houses with screened porches littered streets. A school busload of pubescent black girls unloads; their mouths wear that cynical half snarl between pudgy cheeks that seems a trademark. A naked doll lies in the street. A Hispanic passes along the road, emaciated, short, with darting black eyes, an acne-scarred face. The black eyes show hate, paranoia.

A toll bridge, traffic bumper to bumper, not moving. They stare at me. I look out at the water. I see the city sprawled out along the side of the river. Finally, a scrawny guy, who calls himself a construction laborer, picks me up. He talks about topless bars and wet T-shirt contests. He drives me to Highway 1. I walk past used-car lots, slummy apartments once motels, and motels from the fifties—motor courts—still in use. I see no place to sleep, no clean fields, no stands of trees, just vacant lots full of rusting refrigerators or decaying sofas. I must sleep in a motel room.

An old motor court has a neon sign in the office that says, "Vacancy." A man comes to the counter, he looks me over and says, "No vacancy." I see his hand reach for a switch under the counter. He says, "Go look at the sign." His face is seething in hate. I know he has just changed the sign; I leave. I must have a skid-row-bum's face, at least to this man. As I am leaving, he says, "Try down the road, the place with the tall white columns; they take your kind." My mind doesn't want to hear the "your kind," so it doesn't. I hear the advice and think the man might not be as evil as he first appears.

I come to the place with the tall white columns. The building sits back from the road, the yard contains sparse grass and blooming tropical bushes. An iron fence surrounds the grounds, a driveway loops up to the wide porch beneath the columns. The porch has iron chairs.

On the chairs are a collection of lunatics, mentally infirm women. Old women with hair nets and shower caps on their heads. A woman with massive calves covered in blue bruises, rocks gently. The old ladies have flabby, fat arms; the flesh seems to hang from the bones. Some ladies are emaciated, every bone shows as they swat nonexistent flies or knit air sweaters. One woman has no teeth, her lips are sucked into the gap, the jaw juts. They are a sight; to some, they are crazy; that is why they were put in the mansion of white. To me, they're someone's mother, sister, aunt.

The man who ran the motel got the last laugh on me. He must have enjoyed that. He mistook me for someone I wasn't; I don't mind. We all have to judge sometimes; you save yourself a lot of trouble sometimes. But the man had no kindness, no respect, nothing good within him. I would have rather stayed in the white-columned mansion than in that man's motel.

An old junked-up car stops. The driver is dressed in laborer's clothes. He works for a landscaping company where he is paid the minimum wage. He says he steals when he has the chance. The majority of people talk in such a cynical way—half truth, half sarcasm—that you don't know if they're serious or joking. People like this guy can tell you the truth, and you don't really believe it. The cynical, sarcastic way of speaking protects people, hides their confusion. This guy isn't confused; he's a thief. His truthfulness makes him appear an honest guy and opens you up. He wouldn't steal from me, you might think. He would. I don't worry; I have nothing of value.

He says I can stay at his house; his roommates are gone. I ask him if he is a homosexual. It seems strange that you need to ask such a question. He says, no, he is not.

We are in his house. I go into the bathroom. In the magazine rack are magazines of nude men. He says they belonged to his one roommate's girlfriend. I don't believe him. It is night. I don't know where I am, in some suburb of rundown homes. I want to leave, but where would I go? I stay in the empty house. I have a nightmare that this guy is standing over me. I leave before sunrise. I feel filthy for having stayed within the house. I should have slept in the gutter or walked until dawn.

I wait an entire morning before a ride takes me into Saint Augustine, oldest city in the United States. I sleep in a state park where the raccoons are thick by trash receptacles, the paws of armadillos clatter on the road at night, the temperature hovers near freezing. In the morning I attempt to leave Saint Augustine. I stand near a retirement village; the old people look at me with fright and apprehension. I walk back to Saint Augustine, buy a bus ticket to Miami.

From Saint Augustine to Miami, this is what I remember. Small towns with shady streets and old homes; spinster ladies boarding at each stop; a town with a beautiful lake, water-skiers; the white walls of the Daytona Speedway. Fields of tropical grasses, cattle grazing, the land perfectly flat, ragged trees on the horizon, armadillos along the road as common as groundhogs in Pennsylvania. Small, rolling hills stitched with row upon row of orange trees; between the rows, smudge pots.

Congested areas, rows of slum houses, hot in the steamy air; palm trees illuminated by streetlights—the light hazy, fuzzy circles that people and cars enter and exit. Deserted streets, cars only parked under the lights; a group of Cubans under a streetlight, a man walking, warily glancing over his shoulder. A young black man sitting close to the black bus driver because he is lonely, afraid he'll miss his stop.

A bus station with vending machines smeared with stickiness and grime. Dirty rest rooms smelling heavily of ammonia, urine, urinal fresheners. One sexual deviate, or drug seller, waiting for a sign, eyeing me. The smell of bus exhaust in the hot, humid air. A change of buses. I see

The Silver Cord

a Miami of beachfront hotels; posh restaurants; expensive cars; tanned women in evening gowns, looking so clean and rich.

I am gone from Miami on a narrow road that has no shoulder, the bus continually slides off the concrete when traffic fills the opposite lane. The odor of marijuana comes from the back of the bus. The drivers states, over the intercom, that he can have those people arrested who are smoking. It is obvious he has dealt with the problem before. The odors die as giggles and sniggers begin.

The fat bus, like a bullet down the barrel of the road, aims us, targeted, for the Keys. The engine growls and screams like a whining cat shot in the guts. Diesel exhaust lingers in the mind, the toilet door bangs, people talk in low voices, coughing; the smell of someone's sandwich or orange, body odor. Prop your head against the window, feel the cold air coming through, your head thumps on the glass as the tires on the cement thump.

Outside you see a person who sees the bus. They read the destination, the city, lit above the black windshield, the label that is like a brag when the distance is great. The bus brags of the hundreds of miles it will cover, the importance of the city, the city's size. The bus says the people are connected to the destination; they are important too. Not celebrity-famous-important people, but people with lives, with a purpose somewhere else. You look at the person outside looking at the bus, and you want to make eye contact just for a second, just so you can speculate upon them, their life in that place that is only a fleeting second in your life.

I am in the Keys—coral and mangrove lying flat on metallic-colored water. I am at the entrance of John Pennekamp Coral Reef State Park at three in the morning. Two high school kids from the bus, with bikes and gear, are at the closed entrance with me. I will call them Jack and Larry. As we wait for morning, a figure comes down the dark road—long hair, one leg swinging in a leg cast, hobbling on a crutch.

Dave is his name, from New Jersey. Unlike Jack and Larry, he's lived in Florida for some time; was in a motorcycle accident, hospitalized in Naples. He received a large insurance settlement. Now he's enjoying his freedom. Dave appears to be the partying, marijuana-smoking, beer-drinking free spirit. But I sense he has the line within him, he can be trusted; there is no viciousness within. He talks about his bike, the freedom of riding; yet the bike isn't what he holds onto in the leap called life. Later, he tells me he doesn't want to live as he's been living, with wild partyers in Naples, working a crummy job. He wants a white-collar job, CPA, and a family.

The four of us decide to share a campsite—this will save money and assure us of getting a site, as others are on a waiting list. Jack and Larry get their sleeping bags out. I lean against a rock, and Dave sits against the entrance booth. I make an appraisal of Jack and Larry. Larry is the leader, probably a good student. He put the trip together; others were to come, they backed out. Larry wants to make something of himself. Jack is short, looks like Joe E. Brown, a comedian from the thirties, long dead. His voice is incredibly deep, rich. His words are slow, but his mind is not. His words have a seriousness, which is probably caution.

Through the night, other campers come to the closed gates. They reverse, pull off the road, form a line. In the morning, we are the first to enter. The park isn't what I expected. It is small, the campsites are close. There is a docking area for glass-bottomed sightseeing boats, tour boats for snorkelers, a small manmade beach. I decide the place isn't worth more than a week. I'll stay a week and see what develops. Here are some of the people I meet, some of the things I see and do.

CHAPTER 14

I meet the owner of a sailboat-rental concession. He's in his forties, retired, more or less. He was a newspaper reporter at one time, in Los Angeles or San Francisco. He dropped out of the grind, the rat race, the machine. He found a niche no one else had exploited; that is the way he described his business. Now he is set, makes some money, relaxes in a tropical climate.

He once traveled like me, bummed around in his college days in California. He met an older woman, whose husband was a doctor; she put her young college student in a beachfront home hideaway for an extramarital affair. I suppose the story was meant to send shivers of delight up my spine, but it leaves me cold. He comes across as a sneak, a user instead of an adventurer and an upright guy.

He gives me a ride on a Hobie craft, a small catamaran. I tack perfectly, which astounds him and me, though I don't let on. Later, I watch the place while he is gone for an hour. I know I could work for him if I wanted. He's restless, not the kind of guy to sit around all day. I think he wants to give someone a chance to live and work in the Keys. That is a good attitude—sharing a good thing, an opportunity.

The Silver Cord

The campsite has two Canadian women, both traveling alone. One is from Saskatchewan. She is tall, big, built like a Venus figurine, blond hair, fair skin burned ruddy, beautiful face, kind personality, ponderous chest that needs a child to complete her. She wears a long, print skirt, sturdy hiking shoes, gray socks, a blouse, and a big straw hat. She has been gone from her Canadian home one year. Her dad drives a truck; the family is large. Her parents want her home. She traveled from her western home, through Canada to Nova Scotia, where she lived awhile, at a fishing village. The village was quiet, the people friendly. She won't go home until she has found what she is looking for. She doesn't know what it is, but she knows it's out there.

We talk about what we are looking for, in that pseudo-intellectual jargon of the lost, using pieces of book philosophies and the mysteries of our own vagueness. We fit the little scraps and pieces of philosophy, knowledge gained from books, teachers, television, experiences into what we see or think we see in the world around us. We are vague because the pieces just don't fit; they have no beginning and no end; they just hang in our conversation, in our minds. As soon as our thoughts wander from these pieces, they crash to the ground. They have no real substance, they don't have body, they don't energize. You cannot live by them. They are just words.

I have no idea what this woman wants after having talked to her, and I know she has no idea of what I want—for I don't even know. I think maybe in the end, all she wants is a husband to love her. Would that be enough? Who is she? How can you love someone without form and substance? I listen to my own words, and they make no sense. Why can't I fit into the machine and be happy? Why is there nothing in life I want to do, become?

She reassures me that there is something, some answer. Her hope, her strength, is deceiving. Humankind always does that—you're down, so the other person who is up gives you hope. Then they're down, and you give them hope. A seesaw, a mutual ride, with compassion, self-interest, kindness that takes you nowhere, just up and down. At this moment, she has strength.

The other Canadian woman is of medium height and build, with short, close-cropped hair. Her face seems to be leaving pubescence, the baby fat just melting away, the nose still without adult definition, though she is in her mid twenties. She is from Ontario or Quebec. She came to Miami, Florida, to find and board a boat to Mexico. She wears her shirt unbuttoned low, has that look in her eyes that says I could travel with her if things go right. Go right meaning I fulfill the qualities of her dream man. I can also picture her dumping me in Mexico for another guy who is nearer her dream. She speaks Spanish, I don't.

It strikes me that a woman is no answer in the leap. It wouldn't even help to have someone sympathetic, understanding as you search for whatever it is that will make life whole and good. Strain and tension would be the only result. You would try to find the answer in that person, and they could not give you what you need. Then they would seem a burden, making demands you could not fulfill. To become involved before the answer is found is foolishness.

One day, Dave and I go down to the store outside the park, on the main road. Sitting on a crate in the parking lot is a man. He's in his late thirties, maybe forties, white, shirtless, with a thin, wiry build. He wears baggy, army fatigue pants, sandals. His hair is tied in a ponytail. His face is long, creased in vertical furrows, bearing a similarity to a worn-out workhorse like you might see in a forties cartoon. His back is slightly bowed from the load carried.

He is Harmonica Dan. In the sack by his feet are harmonicas of all types and keys. He plays, asks for donations. The donations buy beer, marijuana, or food. I don't know if he has a room to sleep in at night. He sips from his beer. When he plays, saliva covers the harmonica like it is food. His horsey lips touch the harmonica gently, then he plays the blues.

The blues is music that is sad sweet. Sad because life has turned on you, something good has been taken away. Life has betrayed you with such speed and vehemence that the situation almost seems comical, unbelievable. The sweetness comes because even in the pain there is defiance, hope, pride. Pride in being alive when it would be easier not to be. Defiance is in the ability to sing, to play, to mock that pain and the people or situation that caused it. The hope comes when you have the blues song in your mind; you are still alive, the good times will come again. Pain only wins when you don't feel anything at all. When you can no longer feel, that is called despair, and it is worse than death.

The blues is private, for the individual. In the pain, I once thought I would rise back up, perhaps on anger, hate, joy, or life itself. The blues is a temporary fix—nothing but the pride of man worshipping his own pain because it is his pain. The blues has no answer. I listen to Harmonica Dan play and feel nothing. I am in despair, and Harmonica Dan may be a burned-out flower child of the sixties who has drunk too much beer, smoked too much dope, dropped too many tabs of acid. Harmonica Dan feels nothing as he plays the blues. Or has he felt so much his nerves are deadened to the pain?

One night Dave and I borrow a rowboat and venture into the quiet pocket of water that is the harbor. Sailboats are anchored in the smooth water like a flock of ducks sitting. Some boats are monohulls, others are catamarans. There is one huge trimaran, jade-green in color, looking like a stingray up from the depths. Every night there is a light in the cabin. We row out to the trimaran.

The temperature is in the seventies; the breeze smells of salt, tropical ocean. The boats rock gently at their anchors; the water laps the hulls, slaps the fiberglass; wires rattle against aluminum masts. Safety lights glow dully from the boats. We hail the skipper; no answer. We board; a shadow passes over the light; a French-accented voice calls out, tells us to come below. In the cramped cabin, among shelves of books, is Jacques, a tall, lean Frenchman. Jacques's English is halting. He is unaccustomed to company; his mind is dull to the sensation of the human voice and face. He wants company because he is lonely; the ocean swallows up the mind. He doesn't want company because dealing with people is work, stress. The sea has done this—the looking inward too long. He must think carefully before he speaks. I glance at the books; they are philosophy, except for a few sailing manuals. The philosophy books are not of the self-help, everyman fare, they are of college text grade.

He has sailed from France alone. I cannot learn how he earned the money to buy such a boat. He talks sailing, the different types of boats in the harbor. We drink a beer together, realizing his English has been exhausted, then say good-bye. Later we see him on shore, in loose baggy pants, looking like a Moroccan pirate, or Sinbad. He is a laborer to the men building a concession stand.

They hired him because he asked for work; this is America. They have a story to tell at the bar. They must explain everything to him; he doesn't know the ins and outs of construction, can't think ahead in the process of building, doesn't know what is expected of him. He can only respond to orders, and even responding is difficult when you don't understand the language.

We meet a guy named Sam. Sam comes gliding through the mangrove swamps on a thirty-foot monohull and docks beside one of the glass-bottomed boats. Sam has thin, brown-blond hair tied in a stubby ponytail. A red bandanna is folded, tied over his head. He is tall, six four or better; lanky; thick-boned; tanned. His long, sinewy arms swing loose at his sides. The arms swing as if ready to uncoil, unleash the huge, bony fists that he carries like suitcases. His skull is compact, bony, like you could bang it against concrete and watch the cement chips fly.

Sam is an ex-motorcycle gang member from outside of Chi-town. He prefers bridge construction, working with steel beams and girders, welding, when he needs to work. That is how he made the money for his sailboat. He comes into port to shower, buy food, pick up women. Sam has that wild look in his eyes, that movement to his body that is violence barely constrained. Or maybe it is aggressive hopefulness, a desire to seize life.

He tells us, Dave and me, of his barroom fights. "Hey, I'll tell ya." He speaks with pride or as if talking to an understudy about the great fights of the past. The last fight was near the Marine Corps Base in Quantico, North Carolina. Those in the bar didn't like his looks, didn't like the idea he was jobless, a vagabond of the sea. He had to retreat because he was outnumbered, but he held his own. Once Sam has respect, he doesn't push for fawning or worship. He doesn't belittle. He has been at sea; he wants company, people to admire his lonely life, his adventures.

Later in the day, Dave and I walk down to the beach with Sam. Sam boldly walks through the hundreds of sunbathers, studying every group of women, taking his time. He finds the women he's been searching for, three attractive twenty-one-year-olds from Ottawa, Canada. He must have said something like, "Would you like to take a sail on my boat?" They answer yes. Then he says, "Why don't you buy some beer and food for the party? I'm broke." They say okay.

They want an adventure. He has the sailboat, they bring the food; things are even. I wonder why they think he invited them to take a sail; for conversation? Because he's a nice guy who wants to share what he has with others? Sam wants sex, a wild time. The women want their adventure, their sailboat ride. Dave and I don't want anything, we're just observers.

The party boat of strangers sets sail. We wind through the channel lined with mangroves and enter the ocean of milky-gray water. There is barely a breeze in the sails. We try swimming; the water is cold. None of us is relaxed, none of us is the kind who can sit down and entertain ourselves with conversation. Sam is the type who would forcefully take a woman. I see him coming to that point. We say a few words, eat some cheese and crackers, and go back. I wonder why I can't be friendly, relaxed, enjoy the company of these women. I suppose it is because I don't know who I am, what I believe, what I want to do with life.

Being on the boat gives my mind a fleeting dream. Sam bought the boat for a few thousand dollars on Lake Michigan, sailed down the Mississippi. He has a home and transportation. Crabs, shrimp, fish are his food; the ocean will never allow him to starve. All that he needs from the earth are a few potatoes and onions. He picks up work here and there, makes enough money to keep his boat repaired, to keep gas in the engine that he rarely uses. The ocean is his playground.

For a moment, my mind clings to the idea. Sailing is an art that could never be completely learned, a challenge without end. I say to myself, "So what?" Jacques and Sam are empty people. Jacques knows this, Sam does not. They waste their lives on barren waters. It isn't what they do that makes them empty. It isn't that they are individuals, living outside the machine. It is that what they do is not attached to anything, no idea, no belief, no understanding. Sam sails the ocean to give himself a personality, a uniqueness, to be a rebel. Jacques sails, perhaps, because as a child he loved the sea—a childish attachment never replaced by anything with substance. They are men adrift. I am like them; the roads are my oceans; I wander because I can't find something better.

Adjacent to our campsite is a family from Connecticut. Father, mother, fourteen-year-old son, nine-year-old daughter named Elsa. The father speaks with an accent that sounds French but could be Flemish, which is another language of Belgium, for that is his country of birth. He is a wealthy man; his family flew from Connecticut to the Keys. He spends his money on experiences for his family, vacations, art lessons, not on material objects. He is a kind man, understanding. He is an inventor, a doctor, a scientist. He's been working five years on a heart valve that will prolong lives.

I wonder what it means to make a heart valve. Society says heart valves are good. Men and women are encouraged to make such devices. They are paid well for their efforts. Would my neighbor make heart valves if the pay was not good? That's my cynicism again, but I believe he would. Does he work on heart valves for the intellectual challenge or because he wants to help someone? Or both? My point is, is his motivation selfish and the product of his work only incidentally humanitarian? Why think so deeply? Be happy the heart valves are made.

What if you're making a heart valve that will prolong the life of an evil man? A rapist, child molester, murderer, thief, a budding Adolph Hitler? Why does it matter that we prolong a man's life? We are all dying, none can escape; why do we wish to temporarily escape? I know what I say is wrong; life is precious, an evil man might repent. Why does my mind break everything down, even that which is good?

There is more to this father than heart valves. He has two older sons who ran away from home, who never speak to him. One boy clings to drugs, the other to some Eastern religion that does not allow the son to talk to the father. I think of my parents; as much as I love them, I hate them. Looking at the kind man who is broken inside, I see my own evil. I don't want to hate.

You can have the knowledge to make heart valves, fit the fragments of knowledge together to save or prolong someone's life. While you are giving that stranger life, your children, who came into the world so tiny, vulnerable; the children you fed, clothed, loved, worried countless hours over leave you, leave your soul in fragments.

I meet other people in the park. Theodore is alone, from New York, traveling in a new van. He likes to paint. He has a poetry reading one afternoon for Jack and Larry. I listen from my campsite. I liked poetry at one time. I listen, and for the first time see clearly that some poetry is just men loving their own confusion and wanting you to love it also. To many, this passes as the intellectual mind.

There is a fifty-five-year-old man in a camper, with TV, traveling alone. I meet him through Jack and Larry. He told his wife he wanted to be alone. He doesn't love his wife as he did. He has had open-heart surgery; he's been retired from his company. He's fifty-five, has nothing to show for his life, is lost, confused, empty inside. Depression hangs upon him. He held to his wife, his work in the leap, and they failed him. I know I won't be lost and confused at fifty-five because I couldn't take the pain that long.

Tommy is five or six; he's the park ranger's son. I watch him ride his tricycle behind my tent, the big mud puddle is the attraction. Tommy judges the depth of the puddle to be shallow, he goes tearing through, full speed. Suddenly his bike hits a hole. He is up to his knees in water, the tricycle wheel is stuck. He is thrown off into the water.

He is completely wet. He cries. He is fighting a war within. He has made a mistake, an error in judgment. He hates himself for being stupid. What will Mother say? Will she scold him? Will she still love him? Tommy says, "God loves me," over and over. With those words he will fight his war.

I was like him as a child. God was so real to me. The words Tommy says aren't enough—you have to think about the meaning of the words. The words have to war with all the pain: mistakes, errors, bad breaks, circumstances, evil people you find in life. In me, those words never won. I tired of thinking, just gave up when life didn't go my way, blamed God. A part of me still loves God, and I know, sometimes at least, that He loves me. Perhaps someday I'll think it through again. Maybe the second time around, I'll understand.

One night we have a fire burning in the raised charcoal grill that is standard to the campsites. We burn scrap wood from the construction of the new concession stand. Jack and Larry are cooking fish that they caught on a charter boat cruise that day. Dave is squawking on a harmonica. Sam comes along and tells stories of the black people of the North Carolina backwaters. No TV, no electricity; wood is burned for heat and cooking in the shacks called home. They speak a pidgin English, slave dialect mixed with an African language. Sam's stories end and he leaves, looking for a wilder time. Dave leaves.

Jack, Larry, and I go across the campground to invite a young, eighteen-year-old kid to our gathering. We saw him earlier in the day with a guitar. He's hesitant about coming. He doesn't pay the guitar well; I had seen the kid the day before with his uncle, who is in his sixties. The uncle was carrying a heavy ice chest and was straining. I watched the kid take the ice chest from his uncle and carry it. I saw a spark of goodness and thought the kid a good person.

The kid comes along. I am drinking beer. He gets high. He takes a dislike to me; everything I'm for, he's against. He's trying to make some conflict between the straight guy, me; and the counterculture drifter, him. To him stealing is no crime, just a way to distribute the wealth. Lying is better than honesty if it gets you what you want. Distrust is better than trust—you don't get burned that way. On and on it goes. Why do I take offense to his attitude? I should walk away.

I am a fool. The beer has mingled with the empty mind, and what comes out is foolishness. A fool with no control over his emotions, no understanding, no mercy, no restraint. This kid is immature, confused, hateful. His personality has been twisted since his birth. I see all of this yet cannot let his words pass. I wonder how much of what I hear is real. It doesn't matter; I fail. We argue loudly.

Then I think of the heart-valve man and his family in their tent, on their cots, listening. I think of little Elsa, innocent to the ugliness in man, listening to the raging of two animals, listening to the filth that comes out of our mouths, the curses. How much have I frightened her? I am ashamed. I have a younger sister, while growing up tried to protect her, and did.

The Silver Cord

The next day the kid is gone. He stole his uncle's expensive camera and left without a word. The kid has been a runaway for years. His uncle was his only friend, the only person who had touched something good within the kid. Did I ruin the chance of recovery? I'm the person who has said that I don't want to give pain to anyone. The kid is adrift again, on the road, a thief, liar, beggar.

The next day I buy a used canoe from the canoe rental stand. I buy two weeks of groceries; in the evening, under moonlight, I leave, bound for the Everglades. I have been thinking of the canoe trip since Sam told me of people paddling the Intracoastal Waterway, some on surfboards. I had attempted to interest Dave but couldn't.

I see schools of fish under my canoe. I see roiling water, water gurgling like a stream out in the harbor; then quiet; then farther, the roiling water and the sound, like the crumpling of cellophane. I see silver shadows. I see big fish, eight feet or more, their dorsal fins breaking the water, chasing the schools of smaller fish. The wake of the big fish rocks my canoe.

Day comes with huge cumulus clouds. I ask myself if I know what I am doing and why. There is no answer. I see beauty around me, but my heart is on empty. Speedboats pass as I enter a large lake or bay. Three Seminole Indians pass, dark skinned, black hair held by red headbands. The older Indian looks at me with admiration. He is telling his passengers, "That is the way to do it. The old way." But I can't enjoy the admiration. I pass yachts, pleasure boats with high, canopied roofs above the cabins. At a marina, I buy a nautical map.

In the late afternoon I am on the fringe of the Everglades. I see thick mangrove jungle, dark green, close to the flat water, narrow beaches. Indentations in the mangrove hint of passages. Highway 1 is to my right. I see two white-trash "swampbillies" in a beat canoe with an electric motor. A boat comes out of the mangrove, sleek, modern, with a uniformed man aboard.

The two swamp rats laugh at the sight of the boat, The sound carries over the water to the ranger. They are playing a game with the ranger. They are poachers. They land on the shore near where I am sitting in my canoe. They hide a twenty-two in some old clothes, and a gaff. I imagine the gaff is to snag the dead gators. They give me the once-over intimidatingly. They bleed a park that belongs to a nation so that the nation will own nothing but a corpse. They curse the ranger, pull their boat up and are gone.

I hear the cars whizzing by, above me and behind me. I don't want to go into the Everglades. There is nothing in the mangrove tangle for me; I know nothing about surviving in the glades. I don't need solitude, I need peace, peace within my mind. The peace has to come from within me; an environment of solitude can't give me peace. Even in solitude, my mind will rage, cough up the ugliness of the past. If my mind did not think, remember, I would have emptiness, not peace.

My mind can never think good thoughts, remember good experiences, without the ugly fastened like a parasite. When my mind is empty, I can only think of a wasted life. Why do I live? What am I supposed to be doing? What is life? Why is there no peace? Why does everything I think turn to dust? How do other people survive? They don't ask questions.

I've got this canoe that I don't want. I want to walk away, go home, even though there is nothing at home. Day becomes night, rain comes. I sit in the rain. At three in the morning, I stand by the road with my thumb out. A van stops, three guys; I sense they are thieves, stopping to roll me. I act unafraid, tough. I get in.

They ask questions. What is in my pack, in the grocery bags? They ask me what I 'm doing on the road. I tell them my story, including the canoe. They drop me off at the first motel. I say thanks. They look at each other, marveling, "Does this guy know how close he came to being robbed and beaten?"

I lie on the bed of the motel room as the air conditioner spews out ice-cold air. I was made to pay in advance. I wonder where in the hell I am in my life. The next day, I go back to the canoe; it is gone. I don't care, I'm happy it is gone. And it hadn't cost much—no more than a night of beers and clams. I stand beside the road, my thumb out. I want to leave Florida, leave it to those who want something from it.

CHAPTER 15

I am in Harrisburg, back in the dollhouse. My parents show no emotion at my return. You would think they would be happy, would embrace me with smiles upon their faces. Even my youngest sister doesn't seem to care that I am home. Can't they see the emptiness in my face? Why don't they have the words that can make me whole? What do I expect them to know? Why should they have an answer?

I get my old job back. I apply to a local college within commuting distance. I think of joining the National Guard, serving my country, making some extra money, playing soldier. I'm set to take the tests and back out. I think of registering to vote but I don't. I try to show more love to my parents, try to be conscientious at work. I want to be responsible, loving, and I fail. Life seems like foolishness, without worth or purpose.

Work is the same—I've been gone less than two weeks. I find moments of enjoyment. My body grows in strength, working outdoors is good. I like the smell of lumber, overturned earth that smells of the cows who once called the fields home, the mason's cement, even the smell of diesel exhaust. I like watching the change from winter to spring. I work around the craziness of our foreman and the pettiness of conflicting personalities.

The Silver Cord

I go to my classes, but knowledge does not thrill me as it once did. I know my college days are gone when I pay my older sister to write a paper for me. She has the brains, likes the fragments. Knowing the fragments gives her self-worth. Having the paper written for me degrades my self-worth. I just want the piece of paper called a diploma.

I go to the bars on weekends with friends. I don't like going to the bars, searching every woman's face for that spark of interest in me. She would have to be a loser to hold onto me, two losers clinging together. One night I'm out with some friends. Kit is one of those friends—he drove me to Wisconsin during the winter I had planned to leave college.

We are drunk. I want to take a pitcher of beer outside. The woman at the back entrance won't let me. She says she'll call the bouncer. The tone of her voice is, "He'll put you in your place." That tone is like a red flag to a bull. I walk out with the pitcher. Meanwhile, Kit has broken the glasses on our table. He comes out to the parking lot with me. There are plastic flowers in a long flower box by the door. I rip them out.

The owner and the bouncer come out. They want to fight. Kit and I want to fight. The police come. Kit is raging, pacing. He is handcuffed, he continues to rage. I don't rage anymore. I sit in the police car without handcuffs; I know why I have acted as I have. I hate my job, college, society, my life, my very self; the hate and frustration have exploded. I am a fool. I don't want to hurt anyone. I don't want to cause trouble.

Three days later, we stand before a district justice. The fine is three hundred dollars for the damage done to some plastic flowers. I know the flowers aren't worth that much. The owner wants me to pay for his humiliation, and that is his right. I study the district justice; he seems like a good man. For a moment I believe, hope, he is going to say something to us that will make sense, will be true, will put my life together. He doesn't tell me what I need to hear. He doesn't have an answer either.

My name is in the arrest column of the paper. My mother is berserk with fury. I have shamed her and the family name. She is worried about her image. She doesn't understand that I hurt inside, that I need an answer. If there is any good in this incident, it is that my father is a better man than I had thought. He asks me why I didn't come to him, tell him of the fine. He would have gotten estimates of the damage, shown them to the district justice. We never could talk to each other; a nameless hate or revulsion on my part keeps us apart. I suppose it comes from my childhood. Never a positive word, an encouraging word; always belittling words. I never remember my father holding me in his arms.

Looking back, seeing it again, I am thankful the police were patient, restrained. We would have fought them if they had challenged our rage with their power, and we would have lost. They didn't challenge; they talked. Maybe we made them appear as wimpy fools to the people watching, but they talked. They are better men than Kit and I.

I realize I can't make my life at home work. I can't fit in. The road is still there, that place where the good memories are attached. I might find the answer on the road. Kit is like me, he doesn't fit in, he wants to live. The time is right for him. His mother is moving from their home into an apartment. It would be awkward for him to live with her.

He has broken his engagement to his fiancée. He had bought the rings, china, furniture; the wedding day was planned, and he backed out. He felt the machine closing in on him, and this particular woman's love could not hold him. He has never admitted it, but he is lost, confused like me; he needs the final answer, the reason why. We sell most of what he owns at a flea market. He doesn't want to leave anything behind; nothing to come back to.

In the summer of seventy-seven we leave, in a used Datsun pickup with a homemade plywood cap. We travel the magic road, I-80 West, my road, the yellow brick road. The mountains of Pennsylvania are still there, the flatness of the Midwest hasn't changed. Rain follows us across the Midwest, the wipers pound their rhythm like a metronome, the tires hydroplane, motorcyclists gather under bridges. We see a convoy of nineteen trucks unbroken by a single car. We eat meatloaf sandwiches, courtesy of Kit's mom; watch the storms come and go.

We loop around Chicago, enter Milwaukee, sleep in the back of the truck in an underground parking lot. We see a huge lake trout pulled out of Lake Michigan. We tour the Milwaukee Zoo, meet some girls who are attending a polka festival.

The Silver Cord

We are in Madison. I remember my college days, it seems a lifetime ago, not slightly over a year. I enjoy showing the city to Kit. I want to say, "This was a piece of my life." I know the streets, buildings, restaurants, parks. I suppose there is pride in in these feelings, in knowing intimately a city so far from your home.

We stop in and see Ed, the friend who stashed my belongings on the first trip. Ed's from Lebanon—the country. He's traveled the Middle East, managed a cocoa plantation in Africa, knows four African languages. He's worked in California on the large farms. He wants to come along but has other commitments. We stay in Madison for a day and a half. We eat lamb from the Greek restaurant, listen to street musicians, walk the lakefront, the university grounds.

We wander through the Wisconsin farmland, tour a Frank Lloyd Wright home and a home built on a sandstone outcrop. We cross the Mississippi, camp on the bluffs, gaze at the river till the sun sets. We hike trails at the Effigy Mounds National Monument. We leave the East behind. We drive and we sip beer, listen to our eight tapes donated by friends, on a tape player sold to us for five dollars by a friend. We pass through Iowa, into Nebraska as we listen to the tapes.

The tapes are of mellow, black, southern soul, of longing love; rejuvenated cowboy songs sung by a generation coming back to the earth, the country life; southern rock, smooth, with a message. Blues, white and black; folk rock; first rock sung again, subtle, yearning, hurting, haunting. The wheels roll, we melt into the hum of the engine, which has melted into the music, which has melted into the alcohol.

The land passes, our windshield is a movie screen. The land is vast and beautiful. We are looking for something that we can't name. Something that is our need, our need that hasn't been filled. I am in the leap called life, and I haven't pushed off hard enough, and I will not make the far cliffside. I drink to put the spirit back into my body. I want to feel life, I want to live life because it is so short. Time is running out. My spirit has died, and I revive it, or perhaps replace it with the spirits of the dead earth—hops, barley. Products of the earth that grow and die according to the cycles of the earth's seasons. I have a sadness in my heart because I need alcohol to bring life back. I know I am hiding from my own ugliness, my failings, my emptiness.

I become obsessed with the drive. The sound of the tires on the road, the buzzing of the engine, the hot wind speeding by the windows, the music, the changing movie screen are all I want. We stop at the historical or scenic places, Scott's Bluff National Monument, by segments of the Oregon Trail, by reservoirs, badlands, the Badlands, fossil beds, the Black Hills, but it is the drive that owns me.

All I want is a full tank of gas, a bag of groceries. People are a waste of one's time; they know nothing I need to know. All their knowledge is dust. I follow the line on the concrete. I am Dorothy in the empty house, swirling in the tornado. I grasp the sensations of the road in the leap called life.

North, through the Great Plains, towns are no more than gas stations, farm machinery repair shops, modest bars, a store. One moment the land is flat, covered in sage; the next moment, undulating troughs, covered in grasses. Beside the brown grasses, gray soil scarred by the plow for uncountable acres, nothing in sight except an empty pickup truck. Sometimes you see a tractor out in the distance—enclosed cab of tinted glass, big fat wheels, ridged tires seeming ready to burst. The short stubby body of the tractor is engulfed in wheels.

Within the machine is a man, on the endless sea of grass. What does he think when he is out there staring at the earth? Is the mind empty, dull, resounding only with the pulse of his blood? Is music playing within the cab? You are gone; he is left to corrugate the earth, think his thoughts. I think of this man feeding little black and brown children of bellies and bones. I want to think of him as good, even though I can't see his heart.

The road becomes a ribbon—when you see it eight or twenty miles ahead, a loose thread trailing, it seems aimlessly, until it touches another weave of thread or a town. Sometimes the road catches the sun, then it shines like a silver band, a cord, a necklace. The glistening road is the backbone of our nation. Sometimes you see nothing but barbed wire, a windmill with cattle clustered at the watering trough like crumbs on a kitchen table. Or you see an antelope, appearing small, delicate, tan, black eyes, white throat and rump, looking curiously. The cattle by the road stare complacently. Sometimes, just sometimes, their minds are in an excitable state; you can push the horn, and they'll turn their heads or blink dryly.

The Silver Cord

Bump. A crushed snake on the road. Rolling land, buttes in the distance, trees in washes, thick herds of cattle, pine-treed ridges, yellow flowers leaning over the road, bees smashing into the movie screen. A hawk above it all, brown or reddish, traces of white, square tailed, no movement, just slipping through the air as you slip over the land, frictionless. To him you are crawling like an ant.

Dirt and gravel roads lead back into the plains. Small rectangular wooden signs, sometimes five or six to a post, say, "Johnson's Ranch, 7 miles" or "Stewart's, 3½." Then maybe you see a Johnson or a Stewart in a big Chevy or Ford pickup with a jacked body going home, into the plains, driving fast, kicking up clouds of dust. The dust hangs long after the truck is gone.

You think of the natives of the plains, who lived from the backs of horses, were fed, clothed, housed by herds of buffalo. You try to imagine the land thick with buffalo—rivers of beasts, flowing where the rain has greened the grass. The buffalo attract the coyotes, wolves, even bears. Teeming life on the barren plains. Thick grass following the rain clouds. The clouds follow the wind; the wind, the cycles of the earth; God sits above it all.

West into Montana. In Yellowstone there is a blizzard; in the Tetons, the air is crisp, clear, the mountains sparkle. Never leave space between a German and an exhibit—they'll wedge between you and pride themselves on the maneuver. In Billings, there is a fair; we see the swirling, whipping rides, the crowds.

North of Billings, outside the town of Lavina, we enter a bar. The patrons buy us beer, Red X. We talk to two brothers in their fifties, one married, one not, who tell us of the moose shot one hundred miles up from Yellowstone Park. The moose must have walked the entire distance. We are talking to a mother, who tells us about her sons, one in the rodeo circuit breaking bones, one in a touring bluegrass band.

Kit becomes buddies with Manly, a sheepherder, the first white man born in the territory, in 1906, he says. Manly wears a straw cowboy-style hat that finds its way onto Kit's head. We leave, too drunk to drive, we pull off the road and sleep. The sounds of horns awaken us; we enter the truck and are gone to Glacier National Park.

The weather in Glacier is poor—rain, sleet. We decide to wait until the weather breaks before we pack the high country. We go to a bar crowded with Indians from Canada. They are playing pool with a style I have never seen. They crack the ball with strength, speed, power, almost uncontrolled. Even finesse shots are done with speed and power. They invite me to play, I mimic their style, they seem to like that.

Three Indian women, late teens, early twenties, are sitting in a booth. The fine shining black hair reaches down their backs, almost to their waists. Their skin is smooth, brown, with a hint of copper. The eyes are large, dark, flashing, yet innocent. They are lithesome, with no hint of frailty. The hips have a nice curve; the shoulders are wide, without bulk. They are beautiful women, demure, quiet, smiling among themselves, flashing white teeth.

Kit and I talk to a big Indian and his common-law wife, who makes it clear she is not attached. Then the father of the man joins us and tells us a story of a mountain goat's love life that has some ironic joke buried within that I cannot find. These people fade away, and a young Indian, intelligent, sits with us, and we talk about poverty, illiteracy, tribal ways. I think all Indians are like me—wanting to live as first man in the Garden of Eden. The Garden is gone, the earth is dead, revolving in its cycles. Alcohol is the spirit of the earth, the earth has no answer for the soul. That is why the original plainsmen ritually skewered their chests with eagle bone and hung from a pole. Outside of this earth is the Spirit with the answer.

Day turns to night; the rain has not abated. We sleep in the back of the truck. The next day we go into the high country, into snow, hail, sleet. The magic is gone for me—the earth is dead. I am happy to come down from the mountains.

We shower at the bathhouse of the Saint Mary hotel employees. We go to the restaurant on the hill, drink beer, dine on "all you can eat" chicken. As we walk outside, Kit says, "Did you pay the check?"

I say, "No, I thought you did."

We're in the truck when we realize neither paid, we had both left tip money thinking the other was paying for the bill. We don't go back. We laugh as if it is a big joke. Laugh because we're too rotten to go back and pay—as if we deserve something for nothing. We are thieves. It is that simple. I am saddened by my conduct.

We drive into the night, just because we want to listen to the sound of the engine, just because our minds are empty. Somewhere in the early morning hours, we stop for coffee. I watch the other patrons eat, and I think taste and fullness are inducements to eat and to live. If taste and fullness were not present, would people eat? There seems to be a contradiction—as if we need some inducement to live.

In the morning we are west of the Bitterroot Mountains. The land is dry, the soil light in color like diluted chocolate milk. Sandstone rock rises in ridges, small plateaus. The sandstone layers are unchanged since the sediments settled. Floating within the stillness of the rock are sea creatures, fish, even dinosaurs. If the sea returns, the rock become saturated, I think the sediments will dissolve, the creatures will hydrate, swim, crawl, walk away.

We see the places the map tells us to see—fossils, caves, rock formations of Utah and Colorado. We go up craggy mountains through aspen groves, through bare-rock canyons; streams hurtle downward over truck-sized boulders; pines grow big but are sparse; lush meadows hold fat sheep. We see sluggish rivers of green water. We tour Rocky Mountain National Park in the rain, trailing along with the other tourists, and then we are gone, gone west to Las Vegas.

We are on the straight road through the desert. Flatness, sand, ground-hugging cacti, sage, mesquite; on the horizon are jagged, barren mountains. The wind is furnace hot. We drink beer. My palm is sweaty on the steering wheel; my left arm, resting on the window ledge, melts into the truck.

We both feel the drunken rush at the same time, like a sensual demon my body feels the wonderment. My head is out the window, the furnace air blasts me. I give rebel yells to the desert. Kit is laughing in amazement as he says, "The air feels like it's coming from a furnace." He has his torso out the window as he attempts to climb onto the roof.

You could ride the cap of plywood, sit up there like a genie on a magic carpet, feel the hot air blast you, watch the land stream by. Kit's shirt comes off. He can't be destroyed; the truck isn't moving; only the earth is moving. I say, "You can't go up there." His eyes tell me he can't perceive a reason why he cannot. I hear him yelling how wonderful it is. Some sober thought of truth cuts my brain; I slow, Kit crawls in, the truck rolls.

I would like to run across the desert, naked—run until my body can take no more, till it collapses the final time. Let the body shrivel to dust. I am thinking this when Kit says, "I'd like to run across the desert till I can't run anymore. I want to feel the heat blasting me."

Then the alcohol falls through itself, the mind descends from the euphoria. The desert becomes monotonous, looks like the background to some cheap western you watched as a kid. Our bodies are just machines tanked with alcohol. We would run them to death, into the dust from which the body machine was made. Dust to dust. The alcohol is a deceiver, gets you euphoric, laughing, leads you to foolishness—to death, if it has its way.

I just want to feel life, feel the extremes. If I feel, then I know I am alive. I'm losing my line, the line like the white line, the yellow line down the middle of the road, the speed limit sign. I am the broker between the earth and the machine body. The earth wants me back, will trick, fool, deceive me to get me back. I don't want to run till I explode. I want to live! What is life? I've got to follow the rules until I know. If I cross the line, I'll never live long enough to know.

Las Vegas sits on the flat desert; in the distance, sharp hills cut the horizon. The city is bleached in the afternoon sun. The streets are wide and seem barren. A temperature sign at a bank flashes 106 degrees. The air is dry, the heat is not unpleasant. An East Coast summer's day in the eighties is more uncomfortable—because of the humidity. Las Vegas is a wide town, spread out. We pass gas stations, fast-food restaurants, motels, gambling casinos, big name hotels. On the fringes of town we see suburban streets and homes.

Near the end of the main strip, we find an inexpensive motel with a pool. In the evening we walk the strip. The hotels, gambling casinos are lit up; neon signs flash. Cars, taxis are on the wide streets, people are

The Silver Cord

moving about. We see black prostitutes on a corner. They don't solicit but discuss us between themselves.

At another corner is a white prostitute sitting on a bench at a bus stop. She wears a red dress, smooth against her skin, low in the front, high on the thigh. I smell the faintest touch of perfume. Her legs are crossed. Her body seems to exude warmth. She has dark-blond hair, a light tan. She says nothing, her eyes look inward. She has an innocent, attractive face.

We walk by, I stop and look back. A sadness overcomes me when I think of her and the black prostitutes. I see these women as children growing up, little girls wanting a daddy and a mommy to love them, tell them right and wrong, to care about their problems, share their good times, their small victories. I see them with their dolls, or playing house, or skipping rope, having dreams of a happy future.

But it is never to be—for Daddy or surrogate Daddy has probably raped them if he is at home at all, and Mommy is on drugs or has a different man in the house every night. Curses and slaps, cutting words are the only communication. The little girl's soul begins to die. The high school boys whisper behind their backs, calling them sluts, whores, laughing at intimate knowledge from broken confidences. The soul winces. Shame, tears. The spirit dulls, the conscience scars, there is no real love for these girls anywhere. The drugs take away the pain.

I want to say something to this woman but don't know what to say. I keep walking. Now I am perceiving Las Vegas in a totally new way. It is all a sham, a lie perpetrated by immoral men who want power, wealth. I wonder how many of the big men of Las Vegas are criminals laundering money, telling America that Las Vegas is harmless fun. These men attract big names, celebrities, entertainers, to legitimize their schemes. People come, and it is all so innocent, so glamorous. Forget the heroin addicts in New York City, forget the coked-out athletes, forget the prostitutes, forget the child porn, forget the gamblers with ruined lives, forget all this and much more. Take in a show—see your favorite Hollywood star.

It is odd, I think of Jesus. I haven't thought of Him in a long time, but I believe I am seeing all this through His eyes, His perceptions. Kit and

I go into the hotels and gambling casinos. We see limousines driving up to the doors, rich men and women stepping out in tuxedos, evening gowns, looking so elegant. We walk through huge gambling rooms, dark, with plush red carpets, thick velvet curtains, beautiful change girls, counter girls. The door men look sharp in their uniforms, as do the dealers in black suits, crisp white shirts, bow ties, dealing a hand. I wonder how a man could hold onto a deck of cards and a crisp white shirt in the leap called life. It seems a worthless, foolish job, taking money from people who have nothing better to do with money than lose it, or who are consumed by the disease called chance, luck, and who have sold all to this insane obsession.

The next day we wander around. The swimming pools are crowded with sunbathers. At the tennis courts behind a hotel, I see a famous tennis star, long since retired from competition, giving lessons to a tanned young woman. I walk into a metal prefab building and find a boxing ring, speed and heavy bags. I step into the ring, bounce off the ropes, feel the canvas beneath me.

A few people are standing around. I talk to a man named Cleo Sanz, once a contender, who now runs a grocery store in New York City and interests ghetto kids in boxing. Cleo says ghetto kids need to hit—they have so much hurt inside. A swarm of people enters the building, the future champion in their midst, Larry Holmes. An aura hangs upon him.

The aura comes from other people watching his every move, talking about him, making their living from him. The aura comes from doing great deeds, overcoming obstacles, being a part of history, the nation's consciousness. This champ has humility and pride, greatness and earthiness, strength and vulnerability, cockiness and maturity blended into a righteous, precarious balance.

The champ hits the speed bag, which breaks free and sails through the air. Everyone laughs. He spars lighter opponents, working on his speed, not giving them his full power. He is just playing, giving half of what he has; it is not time to peak. I watch him dance on the canvas, exhaling loudly as he throws his punches. The workout is short, the champ exits, followed by the mob.

The Silver Cord

Kit and I walk through the front lobby of the hotel. Three other heavyweight contenders sit in the midst of the busy front entrance. One sits with his hands folded, contentment and dreaminess in his eyes. One is leaning over in his seat, his eyes darting; the other contender drums his fingers on the edge of the sofa, bored. Holding them together is their promoter, frizzy hair standing on end, Don King. This is my brush with celebrities, a story to tell the people back home.

CHAPTER 16

We are on the black macadam that is the desert highway to California. Flatness, white light, creosote bushes. Creosote is uglier than sage or mesquite—stubby branches with a dark stem and a sickly green color. The opposite lane of the highway is crowded with California people destined for the desert and Las Vegas. Many of the vehicles are towing huge boats for use on Lake Mead. It is strange to see boats in the middle of the desert. A steady stream of vehicles is returning to California; the stream thins as people race for home.

We are in California, Los Angeles is bumper-to-bumper traffic, tight exits, short entrance ramps; cars speed into the flow, catching an empty piece of concrete or forcing openings. You cannot enter the flow without speed. To stop is to never start. Sometimes we move above the speed limit, sometimes we crawl. My hands are tense on the wheel. We see the big white letters on a dry hill, "Hollywood." Palm trees make their appearance. We are in Santa Barbara, then Goleta.

Kit has an uncle who lives in Goleta at a retirement center—a modern complex with a swimming pool, cafeteria, well-designed rooms. Kit's uncle is retired from the US Air Force. He treats us to a steak

The Silver Cord

dinner. Kit stays in his uncle's apartment, and I sleep in a guest room. We spend time walking around Santa Barbara and the University of Southern California campus.

Kit likes California, Goleta, the university. He wants to remain, establish residency, attend the university, if possible. I understand, he has a dream, life should be about taking chances. I stranded him once in Madison, Wisconsin. I am not bitter at losing a companion—I was born alone. Early one morning, I say good-bye, good luck. I get into my truck and ride.

I go east through small towns. On the hills, in the narrow valleys are fruit trees, most young, swaddled in tape. I am on Interstate 5. I remember little but dryness and hills, then the flat valley and green fields. I pass Bakersfield, a name on the map. Grapevines in endless rows. I remember Fresno because I went down a one-way street the wrong way. East out of Fresno, the grapevines begin again. The names on the mailboxes are Armenian. I see a sign in front of a home that says, "Help Wanted." I stop.

A young guy, twenty or twenty-one, dark skin, black hair, brown eyes, Armenian name, gives me a knife, some sheets of brown wrapping paper. He takes me out a dusty road onto the flat valley floor covered in rows of grapes. He points out some rows and says they are mine. Cut the clusters of grapes from the vines, lay the clusters on the sheets of brown wrapping paper. A sheet of brown wrapping paper is called a tray. The grapes turn to raisins in the sun. Each tray is worth sixteen cents.

It is early morning, the sun is hot, the air humid, the soil sandy. I cut the jade clusters, spread them on the brown paper. A Mexican comes by. He says forget the knife, it is too slow; use the fingers, snap the clusters from the vine. I say thanks. I continue my search, peering into the grape vines, pushing leaves away. My back begins to ache, my hamstrings hurt from the stooping. The sun beats down upon my head. I eat a few grapes; they are sickeningly sweet. My hands and forearms become wet, sticky with sweat, dirt, grape juice.

Two families of Mexicans work across the dirt road from me. A grandmother, kids from four to eight years old, men and women. Grandmother watches the young kids. The older kids and an older woman spread trays in advance of the pickers. The men and women pick three to four times faster than me. When they are on a row, the entire arbor shakes. Their hands shoot out; completely ambidextrous, the brain is equally divided between both hands. The two hands work singly, sometimes far apart, never supporting or aiding the other. Never a wasted movement, never a groping, never a failure to wrest the cluster from the vine. No daydreaming, no interruptions, no pause, no rest; they move like machines.

The women stare at my hairy legs. I'm wearing shorts. Their men wear long pants and would never show their legs. The men are friendly, helpful. The children are cute, obedient, well mannered. If I were to judge all Mexicans by these families, I would say they are good people.

I last one day, pick up my check for twelve dollars, and head north and east toward the Sierra Nevada, Sequoia, and Kings Canyon National Parks. I spend one night in the dry hills covered in brush. The hills, boulders, brush remind me of the sets of B-movie westerns from the forties and fifties. I am awakened by a truck, hear the low, mournful whimper of hounds; I am challenged by a gruff, belligerent voice. I call back, identifying myself in the same tone of voice used upon me. They say they are hunting coon. I think mountain lions or coyotes are their game.

The next day I am in Sequoia. I walk among the giant trees. God makes me feel small just as He does with the stars. I drive into Kings Canyon. White and gray granite, bald domes, the gray-green vegetation can't cling to smooth rock. The rock shines in the sun as if it were newly laid snow. Swift, pure water cuts the rock, scoops out pools, runs around huge boulders; deep water is green-blue; water foams, roars, falls. Vehicles are parked all along the road near the water. People are on rocks sunbathing, or swimming or tubing. In the evening I drive back to the Sequoias and camp nearby.

A guy next to me, slightly older, from California, shares his supper with me. He bought too much hamburger and is afraid it might go bad if he saves it for another day. I am wary of him; he is so straightforward, ingenuous, that I think it must be some kind of ruse. Is the world in a sad state or is it my state of mind? I sense I have a deep problem, not only with suspicion but loneliness.

The Silver Cord

Nearby is a group camp-out, a group of people from eighteen into their early twenties. They sell magazines, are flown all over the country to sell magazines; on their days off, trips are organized for them. Hard to believe but true. In the group is a woman who catches my eye; long, fine, black hair, thin frame, dark eyes. I want to approach her, try to converse, see what kind of person she is. What kind of person am I? What is the use? I'm so lost in my head I have nothing to say, don't know who I am or what I am doing. Who would like me except from pity? I don't even like myself.

I am Yosemite bound the next morning. Yosemite is a circus of people, crowds in the visitors' center, crowds in the campgrounds, crowds at the scenic areas. Europeans, Japanese, Americans from every state. Rock climbers proudly carry their epaulets of coiled ropes. The backpackers carry their bright, nylon, aluminum-tubed packs. Some people dress in the latest fashions of outdoor wear, wearing the stiff-soled hiking boots that give them the clunky gait. A drought is causing leaves to fall, the spectacular waterfalls are barely falling.

I drive east through the mountains, through cold and wind; I pick up a female rock climber, who had been at base camp with her friends, until she became bored. She didn't say why she wasn't climbing with them. Somewhere down the road, I leave her out. At Tuolumne Meadows I pick up a backcountry permit from a stern, harried, and attractive park ranger. I ask her to check on my truck while I'm gone.

I head into the granite mountains, through dark pine forests, across open meadows of brown grasses, by clear, meandering streams. The hills spew out rushing, frigid streams—boulder strewn, pools deepening to six feet or more. Little falls rush over the lips of the backed-up water. Some of the pools are cupped in solid, unbroken rock, like a natural bathtub or swimming pool. Trout speed in and out of the shadows. At places, the water slides down long chutes of flat rock for twenty or thirty feet or more.

The trails are powdered dust; footsteps are muffled, feet slip when trying to gain traction. I camp by a narrow lake more like a pond. One of those lakes that sits out in the open. At the far end are some storm-blasted pines. I camp in the pines, listen to the wind rush through the trees.

John Johnson

I wish to begin the "think." What I do to hide from my problem of "the leap." There is nothing else to do. I want to think, and my mind is blank, empty. The realization comes that I have exhausted all that my mind possesses. The land could not fill my mind, distract me from the emptiness. The earth has beauty, interest, but these last only seconds; and how many seconds in a day? To fill the void, I begin to classify people into personality types. I project how these types will behave in certain situations. I determine what motivates them. Fragments of truth are in my thoughts, but ultimately the thoughts turn to dust.

I lie on my sleeping bag, see a jet trail high in the cold blue sky. The jet catches the sun, sparkles. The stewardesses are serving the passengers food or drinks. The pilots watch the dials and gauges. The businessman, the student, the people who are mothers, fathers, sons, and daughters are talking to each other, or reading a magazine, or listening to music, or staring out the window. Why do they live? Why did God make me? I know He is alive—watching. What does He want from me? To help others? I'm too confused to help others. Night comes.

In the morning, I leave the mountains, turn around and go back the way I came. Snow falls; by the time I am in my truck, four inches of snow is on the ground. I drive through the snow, past the high peaks that loom over me. The snow ends when the mountains are behind me. I am on the eastern side of the Sierra Nevada.

The land is vast, barren, beautiful as my eyes go east. Huge fluffy clouds stretch, it seems, into infinity. Coming through the clouds are yellow beams of sunlight. The clouds have gun-barrel blue bottoms and cast dark shadows. The sunlight is honey- to daisy-yellow. The sunbeams seem like searchlights scanning the brown, open land. Out on the vastness are herds of cattle, huge flocks of sheep, and tiny shepherd wagons.

I go north, past Mono Lake. Mark Twain once visited the lake and the Sierra Nevada; it's all in a book called *Roughing It*. I remember snatches of the book and laugh to myself. I skirt Lake Tahoe, the gambling casinos, ski resorts, silent pine forests, expensive resort homes belonging to the people with money. The lake itself is beautiful. On the way I see powerboats, skiers, even sailboats. The mountains around Tahoe are lumbered. I see lumber mills and fresh-stacked pine boards.

The Silver Cord

Outside of Tahoe I give a ride to a woman in her thirties, wearing a red bandanna, and her little girl. At first she isn't sure she wants a ride with me; she thinks I am drugged. I tell her I'm tired from driving. I wonder if it is my depression, the emptiness of my soul, she sees upon my face. At her feet she notices a book of Thoreau's writings and asks me if I have read it. I say yes. She seems to think this is a worthy feat. The final answer is not in Thoreau; he was just a lonely recluse, absorbed in the workings of his imagination and perceptions—like me.

I follow I-80 to Reno then get back to US 395 South. I pick up another female hitchhiker, the woman and her kid were left out in some lumber town before I-80. This hitchhiker is in her twenties, long legged, dark black hair, brown eyes, attractive. She says she is a student at Berkeley, studying physics. She says she met a woman by I-80. The woman, in her forties, was crying, begging for a cigarette. She had just been raped by a truck driver. The woman had just broken up with her husband. I assume that is why she was beside the interstate.

I can't figure this attractive hitchhiker. She seems to have no destination, no baggage but her handbag. She tells me of a ride with a cowboy. He took her to his ranch, then she mentions something about whips. What is she trying to say to me? Why doesn't she tell me more? Why would a young woman go to a stranger's home? Is she hitchhiking to find sexual adventure?

At the setting of the sun, she tells me her destination is near Yosemite National Park. We stop for coffee at a Spanish restaurant, one for the tourists—Spanish-speaking waiters, stucco interior, logs burning in the fireplace. I notice her check me out as we enter the restaurant. We drink some coffee, eat some tortilla chips. We are the only patrons. I make no proposition. I take her to the long driveway of an expensive-looking home, one of those homes with a well-manicured lawn the length of the driveway. One of those homes that probably has a stable in the back. I see lights in the home; darkness has fallen. She doesn't even seem sure that it is the right home. I sleep in my truck farther down the road.

There are other hitchhikers as I move south: a cook going to work; a perspiration-smelling, mental casualty of the drug culture; a dispirited, sullen, bitter longhair in bib overhauls, in his twenties, leaving the marijuana of California for the wife and kid on welfare in Oklahoma. The creosote and sand return. My head is empty. I think it strange that we can't help but live, no matter how ugly, how barren life gets. What is this urge within us to live? What man hasn't thought of killing himself? And yet most don't. Why don't we?

I go east, through the Mojave Desert. Creosote; bleached soil almost white; black, pitted volcanic rock. Buzzards circle the highway; the cement is the buffet table, the cafeteria line. Foolish life served up, fresh rodent, skunk, coyote. I see a coyote trotting along the shoulder of the road, glancing over his shoulder a few times before moving back into the creosote. Dust devils swirl up in the flatness then dissolve into the burning air. East of the Needles, I drive off the road and sleep in the desert near the Colorado River.

The next day is the hum of the engine, desert, sage, juniper, short grasses, plateaus, pines. I stand on the lip of the Grand Canyon. The Canyon is impressive but washed of depth and color by the bright afternoon light. I make camp in the park. In the evening I walk along the canyon trail. I'm not alone; everyone wants to see the setting sun bring out the colors in the canyon. Most of the tourists are Germans, men and women in their fifties and sixties.

I am walking behind a young couple; a guy my age, tall, gangling; the woman is short, petite, with long, black hair. I hear them speaking French. As I am passing them, the guy speaks to me. He asks where the campgrounds are. I tell him, adding that they are probably full. I extend an invitation to share my campsite if they cannot find one. I give them my campsite number. That evening they drive up to my campsite. A French woman has given them a ride; they are hitchhikers. They introduce themselves as Soupy and Ninette.

We talk briefly that night over tea and apples. Soupy and Ninette live in a small mountain village in France. They have lived and worked a year in Quebec, saved their money. They traveled across Canada, down the Pacific Coast of the United States, into Mexico, Central America, Venezuela, Columbia. They are on their way back to Quebec. Soupy has an interest in entomology, the study of insects. He likes photography and has slides of their travels he wishes to show me.

The Silver Cord

Soupy moves loosely, without the appearance of strength. He tends toward vegetarianism but seems to eat little of anything. His state of constant semi fasting explains his looseness, lack of energy. He speaks English well but usually speaks French to Ninette until Ninette thinks this is unfair to me. Soupy has manners, is thoughtful, introspective.

Ninette has a petite frame with a softness in all the desirable places. Her eyes are dark, almond shaped, and always sparkling. Her nose is dainty, small yet straight, sharp. Her skin is a flawless white. She is always ready for a joke, or laughter, to be astounded and amazed at the simplest of things.

The next day we walk the rim of the canyon. I invite Soupy and Ninette to travel with me as I visit the archeological sites of Arizona, Colorado, New Mexico. I will leave them off in New Mexico, and they can continue east. They agree.

I drive, Ninette is beside me, Snoopy is by the window. Ninette's bare arm rubs my arm. Her skin is cool, soft; my arm is hard muscled and hot. She likes the contact as much as I do. I turn off such thoughts and drive. We listen to the tapes. We pass through Monument Valley, the towering plateaus, sculptured points, turrets, rise from the red flatness of the valley floor. It is like being in a rowboat as ocean liners pass. Along the highway are booths made of scrap wood, nailed together, covered by blankets or tarps. Indians are selling turquoise, silver jewelry, blankets, cedar beads.

I think about Ninette. Could I take her away from Soupy? If she leaves Soupy, would she leave me when the excitement is over? Would I be constantly struggling to hold onto her? Is she a woman who blows with the wind? I don't know who I am. I can't take care of my own life, let alone another. I've got to have the final answer, know what life is, before I can give a woman love.

I am a man. A man is to be strong, rooted. He must know himself, his purpose, so that he can give his strength to others, be responsible for more than himself. I am not yet a man. I couldn't handle another life, a shadow following me. I have too many shadows in my mind. It hurts to know such things about myself. I know what I say is truth. If God made truth, then the realization comes from God.

I've been thinking about where I got my line that divides truth from untruth. The line didn't come from schooling; it did not come from my parents, though they reinforced, added, confused. The line was born within me, deep within my head. When I was a child, deep in my head I prayed to God, talked to Him, and He was working. He was always there when I was a kid, always inside.

You can call it *conscience* if you realize even conscience has a framework, rules to know what is right from wrong. The younger your conscience, the more pristine and truer it is. I'm sure there is a thief whose conscience bothers him because he has been slacking off in his thievery and there are bills to pay. The pristine conscience, the one the thief was born with, said stealing is wrong. Period. I'm sure there was an SS commandant of a death camp whose conscience bothered him because the graph showing people exterminated wasn't climbing. The pristine conscience said, "Don't kill people, you fool." You can have a conscience and no sense of right and wrong. What I need is truth and the power to live it.

We leave the paved roads, go back into the desert to the ancient towns, now deserted. We pass over flat plains, ravines, ridges and enter the valleys, ravines, gorges where the towns were built when the land was forested, the fields irrigated. We see apartments, ceremonial houses, homes within natural caves. Soupy and Ninette are enjoying the scenery. Ninette is always so appreciative. After a meal, or at a scenic spot, or at a campsite by the fire, Ninette will look at Snoopy and say, "*Bon?*" And he will answer, "*Bon.*" Ninette always washes the dishes; I never ask her to. Always fun, laughter in her eyes. I began to understand her French simply by her expression. Where is the source of appreciation? How do you acquire it?

Somewhere near Farmington, we climb a gravel road into the mountains. The pines are thick, the air cool. When the trees thin we see meadows, rangeland stretching for miles, dotted with cattle. Streams gush out of the mountain; the stream rocks are moss covered. We find a grassy clearing within the forest with a picnic table and a fire pit. Soupy searches the woods for edible mushrooms. I gather firewood, Ninette unloads our gear.

The night is cold; I build a huge fire, not my usual small cooking fire. We have a supper of rice, beans, and round loaves of Spanish bread dipped in coffee. We sit by the fire, contented, except for Soupy, who has found no mushrooms. He didn't necessarily want the mushrooms for food. He uses mushrooms as a drug and has tried every form of drug in every country he has visited, marijuana, cocaine, cocoa leaves, peyote, and mushrooms. I wonder what he is searching for. Perhaps just an unusual experience. Drugs only rearrange the chemical stains within your mind; nothing new is added, even if effects are heightened, but always something is taken away. I'm a lost man but I know that much, yet I drink my beer.

We tour more ruins, have more good campsites by ancient Native American towns. We pass through Durango, head south. We are on a plateau, pinyon-nut trees stretch over the flatness, the protruding rocks and ridges, and into the canyons. Many people are under the trees, gathering nuts. We are in Santa Fe on Interstate 25, stop at an old mission, then move on. East of Las Vegas, New Mexico, I leave Soupy and Ninette by the road. At Ninette's prompting, Soupy begrudgingly gives me money. I don't need or want the money, but they will not take it back. I make the good-bye quick. I don't look at Ninette—it would hurt too much. I am gone.

CHAPTER 17

I drive south, Albuquerque, Socorro, Truth or Consequences, Las Cruces. The sun is setting, colors come out of the dry land. The sky is purple-red, desert flowers or cacti are blooming and scenting the air. Dusk, the highway is strung with beads of white headlights glaring into my eyes. The highway widens, a sign says, "El Paso City Limits"; I pass an aluminum or steel mill and see hot liquid metal glowing orange-red. Chemical plants border the highway; white paint, piping everywhere. I see hotels, department stores, restaurants; the warm air carries the smells of exhaust, factory, food, gasoline. My eyes catch on neon signs of reds, blues, yellows.

In the early morning I drive across desert, salt pans. The Guadalupe Mountains rise before me. Guadalupe Mountains National Park is before me. Huge upthrusts of rock, like walls, looking desolate and grand. El Capitan looks down on the highway, Guadalupe Peak—8,751 feet of it—stands back from the road. The vegetation is sparse, prickly, knife-bladed plants; yucca, sage, creosote. Elk live within the mountains. Pine trees grow in the highest sheltered canyons. A spring sits in the desert, a round pool of water. I read of the Apaches who were surprised and slain by Texas Rangers as they camped beside the water.

The Silver Cord

I meet a fellow camper at the campsites, John, from Colorado, who is traveling by motorcycle. He just graduated from college and is out for an adventure. He's the kind of guy who goes up to anyone and begins talking, about anything, just to see where it will lead. We drink a beer together, hike to the summit of Guadalupe. He attempts to score with every woman he meets. He pursues a young park ranger. She invites me to her place to eat, John is already there. She is happy I have arrived—I am her protection from John. John and I travel to Carlsbad to see the caverns, then we split company.

I go south through Van Horn, Marfa, Alpine, into Big Bend National Park. I camp in the emptiness of the desert by Glenn Springs, a place where water comes up from the earth. The water is surrounded by trees; the water trickles down a wash, cutting deeper as it goes. The water disappears. A few frogs call the trickle home. I suppose other desert creatures visit, but I see no tracks. At one time a town stood by the springs. I camp in the remains of the town, read of the raid by Mexican bandits in 1916 that killed four soldiers and a boy. I spend the night in the incredible stillness and silence of the desert.

I drive into the greenness of willows, oaks, shrubs, bulrushes that follows the Rio Grande. Roadrunners are speeding through the thickets. I walk out on a sandbar of the low, muddy Rio Grande and gaze on Mexico. I see a shack or two, some people on the shore. Two riders on mules see me and begin wading the river.

I wait as the mules come up to me. The Mexicans are teenagers, dark skinned, wearing straw hats. The older and bigger rider wears chaps, boots, sits in a well-used saddle. They speak to me in Spanish. I flunked Spanish in college. They know some English. "Marijuana, kilo, tequila." They are offering to sell me bricks of marijuana, cases of tequila. I say, "No." They are puzzled; who would come to such a desolate place for any reason but booze or dope?

They are suspicious; the younger one begins to move into the thicket where my truck is parked. The alien sensation between us is palpable. I follow the younger, the older follows me. At the truck I make them peanut butter and jelly sandwiches, which they like. They like my tape player. They marvel at the smallness and toughness of my truck. I mangle a few Spanish phrases in an attempt to communicate before we say goodbye. I tell them I worked in Yucatan when I meant to tell them I wanted to go there.

I think of wading the Rio Grande, walking around Mexico, just to say I did it. I walk along the river. I see men jumping into a fifties Ford sedan, right before my eyes. Seven big men, burly, with thick forearms of tattoos, long hair. They look like ex-cons belonging to some outlaw motorcycle gang. I guess they had just made a buy or were going to, and I spooked them. The car scrapes as the sand kicks up from the tires.

I leave Big Bend and go east. The land is open, the temperature somewhere over one hundred. The railroad tracks of the Southern Pacific shimmer. A gang of dark-skinned Mexicans in bright-white T-shirts works the rails and bed with shovels, sledges, crowbars. They are of a uniform size, short and stocky. They work in the heat but not at a pace that would melt the fat off their torsos from the good-paying job.

Somewhere I buy gas, and the beautiful Mexican girl working has never seen a traveler's check. I drive, and Texas seems to have no end. I see water, the Rio Grande dammed. I pull off the road, though it is only late afternoon. Good campsites, picnic tables, pavilions are located on a peninsula that reaches into the lake. The campsites are empty except for a group of four—two women, a tall guy and another, shorter guy with long hair. The long-haired guy waves a greeting. His name is Paul; he's thin, regular features, has a Dutch accent, Holland is his home. He says to stop in and visit.

Besides Paul, the free spirit, there are Pam, William, and Joyce. Pam is tall, large framed but not heavy, with an ample chest, large brown eyes, blond hair. Her English is good. William is over six feet tall, thin, with a slight hook to his nose, a nose of character. Dark hair and eyes like Abe Lincoln. He is moody, with a touch of sullenness, but is not unfriendly. Joyce is petite, of average height, with a beautiful figure, bold, loud, exuberant. I notice a tension between them, understand traveling together has become a strain.

This is their story. They came to the United States from a sense of curiosity. Paul thought the US was filled with gangsters; this is what songs

The Silver Cord

and magazines had led him to believe. He expected to find Americans businesslike, and they are—but not in the way he expected, not strict like Germans. They enjoy commenting on the lack of culture—Jellystone Park Campgrounds, Frontier Towns, Reptile Lands. They have a feeling of superiority. I think they needed that feeling for confidence in such an expansive land. They had spent a few days in New York, where they had bought an old station wagon with a cracked windshield. They got the car at a good price because of the windshield.

Someone's parents had given them an early 1950s road map of the US. Consequently, they had no idea of the interstate system. They thought they could drive across America in a few days and see everything, while taking their time. The US is bigger than they had expected. I wanted to chuckle at their naivete but saw that it would hurt. I would have been laughing at the slowness of change in Europe as compared to the United States, not at them.

They have problems. Pam and Joyce don't get along. They are a contrast in values. Joyce is free sex, steal if you can get away with it. She tries to shoplift the next day in a supermarket and gets caught. Joyce has been on her own since seventeen, has known a few drugs and men. Joyce can sew and cook; she sews an Indian-motif patch on a pair of my jeans. Pam is motherhood, modesty, honesty. She has a line within her but it doesn't seem to give her peace.

William is easy to understand; he's in love with Pam and homesick. His English is poor, and this makes him feel stupid, inferior. He is down on himself for whatever reasons. Paul keeps his nose out of these problems, just tries to enjoy the trip.

In the evening we all sit in the station wagon, as it rains. Paul and I have a discussion, first on philosophy. He says life is absurd. I don't argue. Then he asks what I know of Holland. I say not much. I give some geography, mention dikes, tulips, diamond buyers, hash parlors, legal prostitution. I touch on history, mention that I respected the Dutch who tried to protect their Jewish citizens during World War Two. Within the hate, fear, they chose to cling to what was right. The entire nation even went on strike; in turn, the Nazis cut the food supplies off. I say it took courage.

Paul says it was a fear of God more than anything else. They feared going to Hell, so they did the right thing. God's wrath was feared more than the Nazis' wrath, Paul says cynically. To know and believe there is a Hell and a righteous God does not mean that you can't do what is right from a love of God's righteousness and His love for mankind. I say to him that if fear was the only motivation and not love of what is right, then that was poor motivation—certainly better than *no* motivation—to do right. The old Bible truths come into my head. I was taught fear of God is not a physical fear but a respect. Respect comes from admiration and love. You've got to be willing to obey truth, and God is truth, even if a part of you doesn't want to do what is right. Paul understands. Pam is smiling.

That night, lying in my tent alone, when Joyce could have been beside me, I think about Hell, fear, respect, and truth. If there is a Hell, then God judges. What does He base His judgment on? By how much I want to do what is right? By how much my soul hates what I do wrong? Christ atoned for that part of me that does evil and even likes the doing of evil. Isn't that what they tell you? If you believe this, what more is there?

Should I try harder, be more diligent—if it is possible? Then would God be real in my life; showing me the truth; talking to my soul, my conscience; showing me the reason for life? Are my travels a flight from God in the leap called life, when it should be God I grasp? When I was a child, I grasped God. Did He let go of me or I, Him? I hate God as much as I love Him. I am indifferent to Him more than I think of Him. Why don't I want Him to be a part of my life? Would it be a burden to take Him along? I don't know anymore. I've just got to keep going, do the best I can, try to do what is right?

As I drive south, the land changes to scrublands of oaks, ranches, oil derricks. Then there is the scent of fertile land, mown hay, fat-humped Brahma cattle, creek beds filled with tall rushes. Among the greenness are dirty villages, single gas pumps before one-windowed grocery stores. Chickens running about on the hard-packed trails behind the road. Fading signs peeling from white walls. The children are barefooted, dark-skinned Mexicans in hand-me-down clothes. The children have dirty faces and hands; they are at play.

The Silver Cord

The Rio Grande is only miles from the road; fields stretch over the abnormally flat land. I see leaves blowing across the fields; the leaves blow into my windshield and splatter yellow paint. Butterflies, the leaves are thousands of butterflies! Lines of palms tower over the land, rain comes, the ocean is near. I feel the vast water's presence. The towering cumulous clouds tell me so. Brownsville, Texas. I check the newspaper, try to land a job harvesting cotton. The man says the jobs are filled.

I go north to Corpus Christi. I become disoriented on the beltway around the city. I want to be at the south end but find myself at the north end. I see a steel bridge arching before me. An ocean ship is passing under the bridge, up a slip of green water. I look up the slip and see oil storage tanks, refineries, grain elevators, chemical plants, a sprawl of pipes, storage tanks and containers, buildings. Ships are pressed against the edge of the slip.

On the other side of the bridge I exit and turn around, go over the bridge again, then exit. I am in a neighborhood called North Beach. North Beach is upon a flat of sand facing the bay. Rundown motels, motor courts are rented as apartments; weathered cottages are scattered about. I see two bars and two modern motels. I stop, walk out onto the jetty that protects the entrance to the slip. I look up at the bridge I have just passed over. I watch a ship coming through the bay, making for the slip. I see Corpus Christi across the water, a low spread-out town of few high buildings.

The vibrancy of the harbor, the slip, the big ships, intrigues me. The slip collects the bounty of the land, of southern Texas, and exports this bounty to the world. This is life, basic, honest, raw; wrestling wealth from the earth, placing it upon ships that sail the open seas.

I get back on the beltway, go south of the city to Padre Island. Padre Island is a long, thin stretch of sand, a national seashore. I spend a week on the beach. It is October, the sun is bright, the water warm. I don't do anything in particular, scan the horizon for ships, trawlers, schools of dolphins. I walk the beach; study shells, shriveled jellyfish, dead fish, human debris from the sea—weathered wood smelling of creosote or tar, fishing buoys, pieces of rope thicker than a man's wrist, nets, shoes, bottles, hats, shirts, a coconut or two. I study the sky, the clouds, the weather patterns.

This should all be fun, satisfying; but it is not. I have nothing to do, no purpose, and a lifetime to do it in. I am a hollow piece of flesh. Life has its wonders, pleasures, joys; but I can't live for them; they aren't life. I tire of the beach. I have an impatience of depression and confusion. My mind is so empty that I think it will cave in. I must drive. When I drive, I am forced to think of the road. I drive north. There is nothing north that I want, but I go.

Small towns, scrub oaks, pasturelands. Sugar Land and chain gangs working by the road, Houston rising from the flatness. Traffic. Everyone has someplace to be, but no one is going anywhere. They are machine parts in their grooves. Beaumont—a horizon of cranes, barges moored in backwaters, wet swampy land. The Mexican faces are gone, replaced by black faces. Diked fields of rice, cotton, soybeans. Pines become plentiful. Louisiana—rain, night comes, I sleep on the front seat in a field. Baton Rouge—follow the Mississippi, high levees, big ships, barges in the high water; chemical plants sprawl, and between the plants, old plantation houses that are museums now. Cane fields, green, dense. Down every dirt road, in every shack, in every car, black faces. People just hanging out—like me—with nothing to do. New Orleans, a domed stadium. Mobile, Alabama; an old navy ship, battleship gray, a tourist attraction. Pine woodlands. A young black mother on her rundown porch plaiting the hair of her daughter. Daughter feels the pull that is her mother's love. Frost, sleep at a roadside rest. Good-bye, Montgomery. Atlanta is, in my eyes, looking modern, prosperous. Pick up a hitchhiker, well dressed, no bum.

Greenville, South Carolina, visit an old friend from community college, fraternity days. I think he is more lost than I am. He has a good-paying job. The machine justifies his existence, he's a success. I sit in his apartment, listen to him talk of work, life, and know he has nothing I want. The Smokies are six-thousand-foot peaks and ridges, row on row. The Smokies are smoky; the fog gathers in wispy gray-white shrouds or as a hazy blanket. Deep ravines, rushing streams, broadleaf valleys, coniferous ridges, black bears, wild boars, deer, elk are the Smokies. There are coves within the mountains, recesses, small valleys, or a level place hemmed by the mountains, where people once lived. The coves have worn out soil, derelict barns and homes, the ghosts of people from the past.

The Silver Cord

I enter the national park, leave the main roads, camp at a site where I am the only person present. The weather is cold, raining, as I walk into a cove where the mountain people once lived. The clouds hug the tops of the trees, filter into the forest; I follow a trail up a small hill so that I may look down on the collection of buildings, a one-room schoolhouse, a church, a home, and old dilapidated barn. I find tombstones of gray and white marble, brown sandstone upon the hill.

Who are these people buried beneath my feet? Inbred hillbillies, common folk, the handsome and beautiful, the homely, the intelligent, the slow? What did they wear, store-bought suits, hand-me-downs, homespun? What did they want from life? What passed through their minds? What did they grasp in the leap?

The eroding tombstones give ages, dates of birth and death, relationships, and epitaphs. The little scraps of information expand. If a birth date says May, then you can smell, see spring in the cove. You know this person's family collected on a spring day. There was a birthday cake, a birthday meal, perhaps; presents? And if you know a little history you can picture the clothes worn, the world events that might be the talk at the table.

If the person was born in May, then he or she was conceived in September or thereabouts. You know the parents of this child lay in bed and loved on one of those cool nights that tells you summer is dying, the garden is near the end, the corn harvest is in the near future.

You induce and deduce from all the scraps of information. You can make yourself a mother, father, sister, brother, friend and feel the relationships a family feels. When it is a child beneath your feet, or a mother dying in childbirth, or a son who died in the war, a sister who died in the 1918 pandemic, you hurt a little more. In a small way, you can feel what they felt, experience another time not your own and yet the same.

I think of the shortness of the leap called life, the utter foolishness of humanity grasping all that is worthless as the sleet pounds upon my poncho, knocks leaves to the ground. I wonder where these people are now, in Heaven or Hell as the Bible says? I want to believe there is a nothingness, a cessation of being. Is that a fear that I will not see Heaven? They're dead—so am I; I think this as I rock to the caffeine pounding in my heart.

My breath condenses in the raw air as I walk around the buildings. The barn still smells of cows, pigs fifty or more years dead. The porch of the home would be pleasant on a summer's evening. A wooden bridge spans the clear water of a rivulet. The wet grass soaks my pant legs. The church is a simple wood structure painted white. A tall steeple; tall, thin windows, one room, wooden pews broken by a central aisle. A plain altar, a pulpit, a piano. The Bible lies open on the pulpit at Ecclesiastes.

I read Ecclesiastes. It is the story of Solomon, a man in the leap, a man who has the opportunity to grasp all that life has to offer, a man who has pounded the fragments of knowledge to dust and has not found the final truth, the final satisfaction. He finds good in life, pieces here and there, in work, a full stomach, in all the little things I have found pleasure in. Like me, none of these small pleasures adds up; none gives him the answer; none destroys the futility, the vanity; none moves his spirit.

We cling to life, and most of what we do is vanity; something we grasp in the leap because it appeals to us, to some selfish desire. We are the present cast of the great play called Life. The props, costumes change; the actors' lines change, but the content of the words is the same. Life goes on and on.

"Remember also your Creator in the days of your youth, before the evil days come, and the years draw nigh, when you will say, 'I have no pleasure in them.'" That is me, a young man with the mind and body of an old man. In the end, I am told to fear God and keep His commandments. I can't keep His commandments, probably don't want to. I fear God and hate Him. I want the final truth. I want a new spirit put into my empty soul.

I leave the Smokies as the snow comes. The snow is heavy, wet; it lies on the colored leaves of the trees. Interstate 40 carries me west. I think of going home, but I can't; there is nothing for me at home. Perhaps I have something to prove. When Kit and I had first planned this trip, it was our intention to work in Texas for a while, then head into Mexico to the Yucatan Peninsula, live on a beach for the winter months. Why change the plan?

Forty seems to be sliding down the length of Tennessee, as if Tennessee tilts from east to west and will dump me in the Mississippi. I

The Silver Cord

see Nashville near dusk. The autumn clouds are solid, low, ominous, cold. The tall buildings of downtown must sway in the cold wind that comes from the west. The skyscrapers catch the yellow light of the setting sun. The light is friendless, without warmth on the western faces of the buildings. On the east the buildings are in the shadows of night, a purple blackness. The city is frightening to me, a lonelier place than my truck. Buses pass, with the names of country-western singers upon the sides.

I pick up a hitchhiker, twenty-two, says he like to work construction when he works. I don't think he's ever worked, just slinks around acting as if he's working; you know the type. His story is: He was drugged up on an animal tranquilizer, went into a convenience store, demanded money, threatened the girl working. He got fifty-two dollars and caught. He skipped his court appearance—didn't think the money was worth a year of his life in jail.

Then he gives the hard luck tale—put in an orphanage at the age of thirteen. He has a daughter in Denver. He shows her picture. She is cute, has a hearing impairment. Says he loves his daughter. If he loved his daughter (if she really exists) he wouldn't be taking drugs, would have found a job. How we deceive ourselves. Somewhere down the road, he gets out. I hope he finds the power to change.

In the morning I pass by Memphis. The alluvial plain of the Arkansas shore is covered in brown, dried-up stalks with cotton tufts clinging. Soybean fields are extensive; huge, red harvesters vacuum up the beans, spit them out into the long beds of trucks. Somewhere past Little Rock, I camp back a power-line-access road.

The next day I enter the pine woods and Texas. Unending pine forests, small towns hugging the road; the trucks carry fresh-cut pine boards. I stop at a roadside rest in the woods. A couple from California invites me over to their picnic table for lunch. They work in Houston. He is thin, small build, intelligent. Still speaks of the sixties, radicals, war protests. He was an orphan, raised in the South. He entered college in California and found his southern education was inferior. He couldn't pass the college English test. He rose above all obstacles. He denounced the southern lifestyle as he experienced it, booze, cars, football.

The couple leaves hurriedly and angrily as a carload of black high-school boys, drinking and smoking marijuana, aim laughter our way. He had gone to a predominantly black high school, and being small, frail of build, and white, had been picked upon without mercy. I leave, pass through the Big Thicket. A historical marker tells me Civil War draft resisters hid in the swampy land. On the southern border of the Thicket I stop again at a roadside rest to study my map before passing by Houston. Two little girls come skipping up to me, twins, six or seven years old. They are of uniform size, have long, reddish-brown hair with straight-cut bangs. They wear straight dresses to the knees, bright-blue socks. They are poor white and speak like poor black. They talk to me, want me to watch them play, run down a small mound of dirt. I am reminded of my younger sister and her childhood. I see the beauty again in life.

Grandmother, always within sight, comes over to me; puffy-faced, huge stomach, chest drooping seemingly below her waist. We talk, she tells me of her family, her sons working on barges, oil rigs, driving trucks. She tells me where I can find a job driving a truck. Her friendliness revives my spirit.

Then Granddaddy comes out of the swampy forest in rubber hip boots, camouflage hat, twenty-two in hand, hunting vest bulging with squirrels. The squirrels will be supper. The little girls wave good-bye.

CHAPTER 18

I am on Padre Island, buying a Corpus Christi newspaper at a convenience store. I have walked to the store for exercise. I intend to live in Corpus Christi. I will daily search the help-wanted section of the paper, fill out applications, go to interviews until I have a job. The beach will be my home for the time being. I am walking back to my campsite when I hear a car approaching. I put out my thumb.

A ragged, foreign sports car, paintless save for a primer coat, pulls over. I climb into the back seat, sit beside a frail young woman. Two men, my age, sit in the front seat. The driver is short and stocky; the passenger is bare chested, wide shouldered, long haired, holding an infant. The woman glances at me a number of times. I look at her. She says, "Were you in Glacier in seventy-six?"

I say, "Yes," even as I recognize the woman beside me: Mary, the maid, the woman with the racing mind, who loved Kerouac, who wanted to live intensely.

We talk. She is not the girl-woman of 1976. She has lost weight; she is thin and weak. Her baby is only months old. Mary's body is covered in red bumps, mosquito bites from some roadside night. She met her husband, the short stocky guy, at the Rainbow Gathering. They've been traveling since then. The car is all they have; it breaks down often. Her eyes hold no sparkle. Her mind doesn't race anymore, not because she has found peace. Hopelessness has tamed the mind.

She has a child, no home, no money, no possessions but the clothes on her back. The last job was working for a cooperative bulk-food store. Mary, her husband, and his friend were accused of stealing. For a moment she is bitter as she thinks of her accusers. She says they were set up, made to take the fall because they were drifters. They spent time in jail.

She asks about me. I tell her of the past. I tell of the future, how I plan to work in Corpus Christi and then travel to Mexico. She says, "Viva Mexico!" Her eyes hold excitement, her mind races for a brief moment. Mexico can only be a dream for her. There is the baby, no money, no place to call home, not even reliable transportation.

She wanted to live wild and free, to smell the sad sweetness of the lilacs. She held to her emotion in the leap called life, and I see in her eyes that she knows the sad sweetness is hollow. What does she cling to now in the leap—her child? Has she been awakened from the dream world by the cries of her baby? The car stops at the turn to my campsite. I say good-bye, wish her luck. I briefly wonder if she took the money; no, she would not. I wonder if her husband and his friend stole the money and never told her.

I watch the car disappear around the bend and have a sadness. I wish I had the answer to life so that I could have given it to her. I am thankful that on that night in the tent nothing happened, or I may have been the one with a family and no hope. I thank God that I am not like her. A voice within my mind laughs. I *am* like her, a wanderer, in love with my dream world, running from life—not to some truth. I am without purpose; my spirit is dead. I tell myself I will find a job, take pleasure in my toil as Solomon did.

What kind of job doesn't matter to me. It should matter. But work is work; you receive pay; the money is used to feed, clothe, house you. Some will be left over for your whims. That is the nature of the machine. I can't see any difference between business executive and janitor. The business executive will make more money, so he may fulfill more of his whims, desires, lusts. His work may be more subjective than the janitor's, certainly more complex. But a job is a job. Learn the procedure; do it as quickly as possible, without hindering the product or the outcome; and the soul will be as empty with one as the other.

Secretly I hope that within life there is a job I can devote my being to, a job that would be a passion, work that would have some lasting effect, work outside the machine. I can't envision that job. I don't know where mankind is headed or what mankind needs. I don't know those things about myself.

I drive up to North Beach, searching for the address in a help-wanted ad. By a cotton warehouse I see a guy on a forklift, call out to him. He's not familiar with the address either. Just for conversation, I ask him if he knows where to find an inexpensive place to live. He says he has an extra room, kitchen privileges included, for forty dollars a week. The place is in North Beach; he gives directions.

His name is Randy, he's from Chicago. He talks with exuberance, and I sense a hustler at work, a guy always looking for an angle, wanting to make opportunities happen. I find he doesn't have a vehicle and sense he would like to have that convenience. I say I might be back in the evening to take a look.

I drive around the sand flat called North Beach, looking for the address, which I never find. I like being close to the power and vibrancy of the harbor. I watch a ship pass under the bridge and into the slip. I drive the one main road of North Beach. The stucco is crumbling on the old motels, the auto courts of the fifties. I find two convenience stores, one grocery store with empty shelves, one liquor store, a used-book store named Slim's, a used-work-clothes store that I hadn't seen on my first drive through.

I find Randy's cottage, one of four crammed between the back walls of two well-kept older motels. The cottages are livable if you're not squeamish. The woman who runs the units next door has weekly rates slightly higher than forty a week, which is what Randy is asking for. Her rooms are clean, well kept, air conditioned, but I'd rather have the money. I return to Randy's apartment in the evening to ascertain if he is trustworthy. I'm tired of the beach, sand in my sleeping bag, and rain.

Randy was born in Chicago, adopted. His adopted parents look Jewish, have dark hair, eyes. Randy has short, reddish hair, a close beard on a ruddy face. He says he grew up in a tough neighborhood of factory workers. He dropped out of college, wasn't drafted. He tells of union activity at a warehouse, protests, violence. He talks about New Mexico, working at a racetrack, living in a communal house. He has a dog that resembles a coyote, given to him by a friend. Everything he says seems vague.

I listen and I judge. He exaggerates, has unbounded enthusiasm, which he uses in an attempt to pull you into an emotional closeness. He makes you believe his life is a colorful adventure. He has no worries, but the underlying vehemence of his conversation speaks of a desperation. There are few possessions in his room, even fewer cooking utensils. I don't see any tendencies toward violence or homosexuality. He will attempt to use my resources. I can control that tendency. I would be gaining a dirt-cheap place to live, near to where I want to find work. I have access to great entertainment—the ships coming up the slip, a beach to walk, a bookstore. I tell him he has a deal. If it doesn't work, I can always move next door.

I am hired by a meat-processing plant on the outskirts of town. A tall, thin man with a German accent interviews me. He seems as weary of life as I am, and only some deep instinctive will keeps him in life. I have the feeling that life isn't life to him, only an illusion created by other people. He remains in their illusion. Later, I find he is the owner of the plant, along with his brother; both survived Nazi concentration camps as children. Both brothers still have their tattooed numbers on their forearms.

This is my work day. Up at six-thirty, eat breakfast, pack my lunch— two sandwiches and a piece of fruit. A twenty-minute ride in moderate to heavy fog and light traffic. Few mornings are clear. I park, smell the slaughterhouse smell, see the cattle in the slaughter pens. The cattle know something is wrong; they've lived wild and free on the Texas plains all their lives, and now they are rubbing bodies and smelling death. The air has a thick, greasy, bloody, calcium smell.

In the plant I am given my equipment—hard hat, plastic stomach guard (you don't want a knife in the stomach while wrestling with a piece of meat), cotton gloves, chain-mail glove (for the left hand), knives in a plastic sheave strapped to the waist, sharpening steel, wrist guard for the left arm, white frocks. Underneath the white frocks you wear enough clothes to keep you warm in a near-freezing environment.

The equipment is on by seven, when I punch in. I think it is strange that we must buy new gloves everyday—they become bloody, greasy, ripped. We must pay for the washing of our frocks. All this money is automatically deducted from our pay, as is money for any equipment we damage. Our sharpening steels are inspected to see that we keep them rust free. I don't know if money is deducted for the fine sandpaper used. I suspect it is.

The majority of the workers are Spanish speaking. There are a handful of gringos on the processing end; most are in management. The few blacks seem to be at the slaughtering end of things, though I saw some in the offices. I am trained with a group of whites who work together, then I am demoted or graduated to the line.

I stand before a belt. Meat comes down the belt; you pull the pieces that are your responsibility, trim them as they are to be trimmed, cut them as they are to be cut. After a while, nine hours of standing becomes easy. The cold braces you up. Every now and then I space out; the meat on the belt seems luminescent. I see beautiful reds, browns, whites, purples. Sometimes the knife hand cramps, the feet ache, and it seems the thermostat is below freezing.

The Mexicans talk to each other, joke. We have a joker, Pepino, a wide-eyed, thin guy who likes to joke with one woman in particular. She's Cuban; left Cuba in '59 on a small boat to escape Castro. She's attractive, been married, divorced. Once, Pepino sends a bull penis down the belt and makes some smart comment. The tone of her voice could peel paint; in rapid Spanish, the words come, like lead from a machine gun. She cuts Pepino to silence, wipes the smile from his face, totally emasculates him. He is never the same.

Sometimes my pieces come in a huge rush at the end of the day. I believe someone is doing this purposely; someone dislikes me. Or perhaps

The Silver Cord

I am slow, and they withhold the pieces so I'm not overwhelmed, and then I have to make up for it. I don't know, I'm never told anything by anyone. I have no idea if I'm doing my job well or not. I think not. I think I don't have the blue-collar dexterity or mind.

The buzzer sounds at the end of the day. You've got to clean up your area, clean your equipment, turn it in. I feel so good getting into my truck; I reflect on whatever small incident broke the monotony of the day; a female federal inspector who was appreciatively whistled into embarrassment; a tumor that was cut open, stank, and caused an evacuation; a truckload of dirty meat, spilled in a highway accident, that had to be cleaned; a group of men playing the harmonica at lunch.

That is my schedule, six days a week, nine and sometimes ten hours a day. I go home, cook a feast, then sit in the ripped easy chair with a cold beer. Randy is rarely seen. Sometimes I read books from Slim's. Read one on Chesty Puller. Read another on the French and Iroquois interactions of the 1600s. Sometimes I turn on the radio and the music carries me away. I think of where I've been, the country I've seen, the people I've met. I laugh sometimes because I'm in Corpus Christi, and a year ago I didn't know the city existed. I wonder where I will be a year in the future.

I am content again. I have friends from work, I feel useful. I enjoy managing my own life, paying rent, buying groceries. When I begin to drink too many beers, I find the will to join the YMCA, shoot hoops, or run at night around North Beach. I don't count mileage. I work up to an hour and a half of jogging on the jetty, along the beach, back in the scrub on dirt roads.

In the paper is a help-wanted ad for laborers at the grain elevator, only a mile or two up the slip from my cottage. The elevators rise up into the sky like a mythological castle. I enter a room surrounded by a console of lights, buttons, diagrams. Men sit by the console. A tall, quiet Texan, a gentleman, listens as another man of rude manners and bearing tells me how hard the work is, tells me I won't last. The rude man looks at the tall man, and the tall man nods his head. I have a job that pays twice what I was making at the meat-processing plant.

The next day, they put me with the grain trucks. The grain trucks are lined up in the morning when I arrive and lined up when I leave in the evening. The trucks wait to be put on a ramp. I open the gates of the trucks. The wheat spills out. The entire truck is tilted, and the wheat gushes out, falling down the grates, where belts carry it away.

Then I am on the opposite side of the elevator, by the railroad tracks that run parallel to the slip. An engine pushes grain cars under an overhanging roof by the elevator. The grain cars sit under a grate, the three hoppers hanging like square teats. An electrically operated rod is inserted in the spindles, the hopper doors open, the grain spills out. Sometimes the electric rod doesn't have the jism, then we use steel bars and muscle.

In time, I am in a room where the grain is dumped into one-hundred-pound bags. A crew of Mexicans is lined up; one pours the grain into the bags, the top of the bag is pulled together by another, another man sews the top of the bag, and a man loads the bag onto a pallet. The job has a rhythm. The bags say, "Made in America." The bags go to starving people all over the world.

A group of men is sent into a room beneath the earth. The dry, volatile grain dust hangs in the air like a fog. We wear cotton masks and wade into the powder. One light bulb hangs from the ceiling. Someone says one loose current of electricity, and the room will explode. We shovel; men are coughing, no one can see. We are told to go deeper, we lower ourselves through a narrow opening, to another room. The dust is to our knees. We shovel, stopping to gasp for breath. A voice yells down to us, we hurry up to the clean air.

Grain dust makes the job miserable. The dust enters yours clothing, causing an itching. The dust turns my eyes red, raw, sore, itching. My eyes hurt, water constantly. In the night I listen to the sounds of my bronchial tubes. I breathe deeply, exhale; only a portion of the air is expelled. Then my chest wheezes, and the remaining air pushes past the dust.

I work overtime in the grain elevator. Thick, black belts run everywhere, carrying a stream of grain. I sit underground by a belt within a long corridor; I watch that a spill doesn't occur. The grain falling off the side of the belt can divert all the grain off the belt. A button must be

The Silver Cord

pushed when this occurs. I listen to the rushing sound of the grain on the belt in the early morning hours.

After two weeks, my eyes and bronchial tubes have had enough. I go to a doctor; he writes a note saying keep away from high concentrations of grain dust. I go to the office; the quiet Texan isn't there, only the rude man with the bloated stomach and florid complexion, southern drawl. I show him the note. He tells me to get the hell out. I am fired. I ask if I can work in some other department, like bagging. He says there's dust there too. He's a liar. I think of hitting him—every man deserves respect, and I wasn't getting any. I don't hit him—his own rage makes him a fool. Insecure men rage. I walk away in a hurry, before I reconsider hitting him.

I have some good memories of the place, like watching the ships come in from Japan, Poland, Russia to load American wheat. Tugs push the ships up the slip. The ships moor against the side of the slip and slightly below the elevator. The wheat is pushed through long tubes into the deep holds. The Japanese ships are modern, clean, the crew in uniform, their actions crisp. The Polish ships have rust and crewmen that stare longingly into America. The Russian ships always seem deserted.

My best memory is riding the vertical belt up to the top of the grain elevator. The weather is clear, cool, a sparkling day, no clouds in the sky. The wind is from the Gulf. I see for tens of miles, up the slip till it can't carry ships, becoming just a trickle; the chemical plants, oil tanks gone. I see all of North Beach. The water in the bay sparkles. I watch the shrimp boats and pleasure craft. A big ship moves up the slip.

I go to the top to help clean the grain bins. A man is attached to a harness, given a long pole with a scraper on the end. He is lowered, dangles as he scrapes loose dust. Everyone is serious; I ask to go into the bin but am not sent.

It is over, and I am satisfied. I made my little pile of money; no job is worth your health. I live day to day, search for interesting jobs. I go out to Aransas Pass, a Gulf Coast town, to see about getting on a shrimper. I am told you wait around with your clothes packed, and if a captain is leaving for the Gulf and a crewman is missing, you have a job. Back in Corpus Christi, I visit the harbor master's office. The big room faces the slip, sees every ship that passes under the bridge. The harbor master sits by his big window with his radio and talks to every captain bringing a ship in. The ships wait out at sea, anchored by a sandbank, waiting for their turn to dock. Sometimes as many as nineteen ships wait. The guy working is friendly and tells me to get on a ship, you must belong to the Seafarer's International Union.

I want to get close to one of the ships, maybe even board. I drive dirt roads back through the chemical plants, refineries to a gate with a security booth. A huge ship, the *Amoco* something, looms. The guard lets me through.

I stand before the black hull; huge ropes are wrapped around moorings. I hear the hum of pumps moving oil into the hold. The superstructure rises like a stubby cross. I walk up the steps; there is another security guard, a retired machinist. He tells me about the ships of the twenties and thirties, the coal burners. He tells of his son, who works with ships' engines. As we are talking, the ship's doctor, in blue uniform, leaves for shore, then the navigator. I've gone as far as I can, seen enough, wish I had become a merchant seaman.

When I am not searching for jobs, I explore. I walk across the Harbor Bridge, go to the museum, a new building by the bridge. The waterfront is lined with cement steps. I come to a dock where private boats are moored. I meet four young guys who bought an old boat and couldn't get the engine to run. They eventually got out into the bay, the engine quit, the Coast Guard towed them in.

From the North Beach jetty, I watch the ships come in. I like to stand out there at night, see the lights of Corpus Christi. To the east, the lights of the oil rig construction company burn, revealing steel frames, piping, cranes. The plant seems a futuristic city from planet Xenon. Up the slip, natural gas is vented; the sky glows from flames. The big ships come, and I listen to the powerful engines thumping, the water turning from the big screws.

Sometimes I read all day and night, books from Slim's Used Books. I break the day with a walk. Once, a Mexican naval frigate slide into the slip, gray, sleek, missiles and guns bristling, the uniformed crew lined up

The Silver Cord

on deck. Once at the grocery store of empty shelves, two gringos wearing serapes try to sell me peyote buttons. The buttons, at least thirty of them, are in a burlap sack. Once, I help the Mexican woman who lives next door dig her garden. At Christmas she sends over some Mexican food.

I strike up a conversation with the old man who runs the laundromat across the street. He's ninety-seven, tall, not fragile, big bones, lean frame. He's posted signs all over the place, US MONEY ONLY! DON'T SLAM DRYER DOORS! DON'T SIT ON FOLDING TABLES! DON'T LEAVE WASH UNATTENDED! He enjoys making people do it his way, likes to tangle with the customers. One day he tells me his story. It goes like this:

Born on a Texas ranch, good life, wild, free. A pack of Irish wolfhounds always following his horse. Two or three steers a week are killed for dog food; his family eats beef every day. He becomes an expert pistol shot, wins medals at local contests. He fights in the Spanish-American War. He studies engineering in Heidelberg, Germany. Comes back to the US to enlist in World War One. He is a veteran of World War Two.

He has been taught to never back down from anyone. He shoots and kills two men up in Amarillo in 1903, when the country is still wild. Lefty Smith and Whitey Jones are robbing a bank. He walks in to deposit some money, they shoot at him, a bullet knocks his hat off his head. He crawls out "like any good ol' boy," draws his pistol, goes in the back door. He shoots one in the neck, the other in the heart.

He remembers the trial vividly. The jury is only out about a minute. The jury leader, close to seven feet in height without his Stetson, big boots, protruding Adam's apple, is the funniest-looking man he has ever seen. This big Texan tells the judge, while moving a wad of tobacco from cheek to cheek, "This country needs more men like the defendant." My laundromat man is acquitted, has a reputation that stands for decades. The pride is still evident in the feisty old man.

I find another job, as a janitor, at a Padre Island beachfront motel. I work from three in the morning to eleven. I pass the sleeping night clerk, punch in, go to the closed and empty bar, drink a beer, plan my work. Then I jump off the stool, work fast—vacuuming, mopping, dusting, emptying trash cans, the works. At six, the cook comes in, and I have a free breakfast. After eating I go outside on the pretext of picking up trash or washing the windows—which I do—but I really go out to see the sun come up over the Gulf.

The sun rises out of the water as an immense orange or lemon-yellow ball. The water and clouds are stained with subtle colors, oranges, yellows, pink, red. The surf roars in. I keep tabs on the water's color and consistency, the surf's height, the clouds, wind direction. I watch the shrimp boats far on the horizon.

Some good people work in the motel, some oddballs, some with noses in the air. A janitor finds out who the high and mighty are quick enough. Most of the cleaning ladies are Mexicans. One is a gringo, in her fifties, divorced. She has lived in Nicaragua; her ex-husband owned a lobster business. They sent out divers in scuba gear to gather lobsters.

The day's work seems over before it begins. I go home, eat, sleep, read, run, listen to the radio. Randy livens things up. He hustles himself into a head chef's job at a motel restaurant by conning the woman in charge of hiring. The employees see right away he's a phony. At the end of the first day, he has burned all the rolls the motel makes fresh for their tables. He's fired. He begins to pick up strays, befriending anyone, so that he can squeeze them for a few bucks or a favor. There is a list: an overweight, semi-blind girl from Iowa, who receives a disability check; a guy from Minnesota looking for a job on an oil barge; an alcoholic camped in a recreational vehicle down the road.

Then there are the Smiths. Dave is forty; Sue is twenty-two, with close-cropped blond hair—an Indiana girl who went to California and stayed. He is an electrician, helped to build a mass-transit system in a California city. Workers died in the tunnels. He became disillusioned. They left the machine, began traveling, went to Baja in a dory; a storm shipwrecked them, they walked across Mexico. Sue feels fortunate that she did not die from thirst and hunger.

They wanted to belong to a well-known Tennessee commune, but it was like a prison camp, a business more than a spiritual existence. The attitude was, "What can you do for us?" She is pregnant, they are receiving food stamps. They travel in an old Valiant, collect things from junkyards and Dumpsters.

They are camped up the road at a public picnic area. They come to the cottage to take showers, use the stove; we share a few meals. Sue pays for the kindnesses by cleaning the house, cooking. Indiana small-town virtue remains in her; I like her. She stands by her husband as he searches. She doesn't know how to complain, she is practical within her impractical lifestyle.

A part of me thinks they are foolish, especially with a baby coming. Yet, I know what Dave is searching for—truth—for I have the same search. It isn't that men died in the tunnel, but that they died for a few bucks, so they could buy a few more earthly toys they don't need. Or that they died because the safety standards weren't strict, so a few more bucks could be saved. It's not that the commune was strict and run as a business, but that the earthly was put before the spiritual. That the commune was more concerned with increasing its wealth than reaching out to people in need.

Dave sees my Bible lying around the cottage. I have had it in my truck the entire trip, have never read a word. He asks if I read it. I tell the truth and I say that I should. Why don't I? It means enough to bring along, but not enough to read?

We talk of going to the Yucatan together. I want to wait until February when the weather is good in the Yucatan. Sue says, "Listen to him." But Dave wants to go now. He wants to go to a country of poverty, without money, with a pregnant wife. What if Sue needs modern medical care? Even a case of Montezuma's revenge might be fatal. Without money, they will be nothing to Mexican authorities, even the Mexican people. He is bound to go, go somewhere. They cook a meal for Randy and me at the picnic grounds on a cold, overcast evening. I say good-bye and good luck. I hope life has been good to them.

CHAPTER 19

Sometime in February I quit the janitor job. I spend a couple of weeks lying around the cottage, reading. I decide not to go to Mexico. I am going home, and I don't know why. Do I plan to settle down? Man isn't made to wander the earth, concerned with his own pleasures. He is supposed to give something of himself to the world, to make the world better. To be true to himself, he must give, even if the world remains as it is. These thoughts were put into me a long time ago; I can't escape the truth. I should not want to escape.

I think of becoming a teacher. Where will I find the strength to enter the machine, wade through the forms, papers, hassles, work, school, the living at home? Where do I find the discipline to work and be satisfied, leaving the childish things behind? Can I have the will when I don't have the final answer, that truth that puts all of life together?

How can I make the world better when I am so confused? The little good I do will be washed away by the good I don't do and the evil I consciously or unconsciously commit. Truthfully, I can't imagine me having any impact on anyone. What can I tell anyone about life? My spirit is gone, my soul is dead. I go north on faith, or is it fate? I drive, thinking that I might be in control, I might be able to make it at home. I made it in Corpus Christi, lived, worked, had enough happiness to survive.

In Virginia, darkness comes. The temperature is in the low twenties, the earth is covered in snow, moonlight shines on the fields, ridged mountains. Small towns are tucked into valleys, lights shine like the stars. My heater goes, I think nothing of it. I'm in the machine, and the machine says, "Don't stop." I don't stop—till my engine blows. What little confidence I possess disappears.

My engine blows because there is not enough antifreeze in the radiator. My engine blows because I have stared dumbly at the temperature gauge. The engine blows because I'm not in life. The engine blows because I am a stupid man. The dead engine seems to condemn me; a thousand thoughts call me worthless, eat at my self-esteem.

I have my truck towed to a service station. I ask how much to fix the machine, they say six hundred dollars. I say, "I'll be back to pick it up." I walk to the highway, put my thumb out. A trucker stops, he has his belt unbuckled, his zipper down. A forty-five-year-old man playing with himself as he drives. I scowl at him. He says he has indigestion. Sure, buddy. He zips up, buckles the belt. I get in. We bump through Virginia doing seventy-five.

I am home, the dollhouse hasn't changed. Kit, left in California, has already come home. No one is truly happy at seeing me, family or friends. I can honestly say I am depressed. Knowing I'm depressed doesn't help. I can't lift myself up. Two weeks later, my father drives me down to pick up my truck. We don't talk. I wish he had the answer. I love him but I wouldn't tell him that. I know I am losing some inner battle. Coming home in my truck, I am stopped by a state trooper who sees my registration has expired.

My birthday is March 30. Another year will have ticked off the clock, another year with no answer, another year closer to death. I try to get my life moving. I make contact with a college within driving distance of home. I contact the National Guard, thinking some extra money would help. I contact a shipping company for part-time work. There is no joy in what I do, no feeling of purpose, energy, will. No feeling that I am doing what I am supposed to be doing.

I do most of these things to appease my parents, especially my mother. She wants to lay into me, give me hell for my life. She does once, tells me to be responsible and to do all the other things I know I should be doing. She doesn't realize how much I hurt inside. She can't tell me why I am alive, what I am supposed to do with my life. Neither of my parents know why they live. They just do what the machine tells them to do. They aren't happy people.

I stay in my room to avoid my mother. I lie in my bed. I don't want to think anymore. I sleep so much my head hurts. I try to hide in sleep. Food has no taste, all of life seems an inconvenience. I awaken from my sleep with cold slobber on my pillow and my face, like an infant. I awake with a vast emptiness inside, a chasm. All that I am is draining down into that hole. I know my soul is crying. I have rages where I punch into my bed till I can't punch anymore; I can't look people squarely in the eyes.

On a night of emptiness- I reach for my Bible. The Bible I have had since the age of five. The Bible I carried in my truck all over the United States and never read. I think of the church in the Smokies and turn to Ecclesiastes, Solomon, who is in the leap called life. Solomon, whose wisdom becomes dust. God wouldn't leave a man in such emptiness, hanging in midair, in such pain.

I want to read about Christ, Jesus. He's got to be my hope. I can't read. I know what the New Testament says, read it in Sunday school, church. I cried to Christ in my pillow as a child, talked to God in my prayers, and my life never changed. I make myself read; anger and bitterness flood my soul. I goad Him with the seeming inconsistencies of the text. I am angered by His demands. He insults his enemies, promises them Hell, speaks in parables that few understand. I ask Him where He's been in my life. He can't help me, I say to myself. I deserve what I've gotten. I must keep on living.

Toward the end of March, I decide to leave home. I have a friend, from fraternity days, Moe, whom I have talked into traveling with me. He says he wants to see some of life before he settles into the routine. I encourage him, I do not want to go back to the road alone. I judge him. He has a lust for life, likes to be amazed, likes to learn, explore. He's athletic and an outdoorsman.

I know his faults. He's a two-hour outdoorsman, then he needs his creature comforts. Rain, cold, an empty stomach will bring complaints. He has never deprived himself. He has strength but is low on stamina. In his search for knowledge, answers, truths, he can slip into an argumentative, quarrelsome, bickering personality. We will leave with a group of friends, see a fiddlers' convention in North Carolina with them. Then we will leave with backpacks on our backs, thumbs out.

I want to leave home, yet I want to get my life on some track, some course toward truth, toward work. The tugging in my mind is pulling me apart. One day, at the supper table, my parents gang up on me, tell me how ridiculous my plans are, how I must be responsible. Responsible to what? I shout back at them in a rage. I tell them to shut their mouths, to be quiet. I jump up from the kitchen table, turn to the shiny new refrigerator, and slam my fist into it, denting the metal. The pain feels good in my hand; it is the only feeling I have had in a month. They are silent. They know, if only for a moment, how much I hurt inside.

***

The Chevy Scout, loaded with camping equipment, moves south along the interstate, through the night. We leave the interstate in North Carolina, roll up and down narrow roads. Traffic, flares on the road, an entrance point into the convention grounds. Men are taking money from the vehicles. Our driver, Doogie, drives by; when the flares can no longer be seen, he leaves us out. We give him money to pay for his ticket. Then Moe and another friend and I take off across the stubble of a cornfield.

We see lights, fires, hear rebel yells. The yells are eerie in the night air that smells of woodsmoke, dampness. We run across the open fields in a crouch, walk the woods quietly. We come to a smattering of campsites, see the Scout. We have our campsite; we are in free. I suppose I didn't pay because none of the others wished to pay. Or did I want excitement? Or was the price of admission outrageous? My actions are wrong.

The next day the clouds are gone, the sun shines, the air is warm. The field that was half empty the night before is completely full. Radios, tape players blare; car doors bang. Woodsmoke is in the air. People wear shorts, Frisbees are sailing. Moe and I tour the grounds; every field is packed with vehicles, tents. Collections of people attempt to maintain a togetherness, a separateness by placement of belongings, clotheslines, vehicles. People flow around between campsites.

The convention attracts gangs of motorcyclists, diehard longhairs, back-to-the-earth people, teenage kids, people in their thirties. I see groups of men with banjoes, guitars, fiddles, dulcimers playing for each other, listening and learning. One field has rows of booths selling food, souvenirs. Someone has taken wire cutters to the fence that surrounds the big pavilion that is the center of the convention. A security man stands by the hole, cursing at the people who come through when his back is turned. Moe and I follow the fence to a gate. Six men stand by the gate. They look at us, we look at them and walk in. We don't do this defiantly. I would have turned around if challenged.

Inside the fence, people are jammed together along a road that leads up a hill. The people face the same direction and stare at something. We hear whistles and splatters of applause. We edge in, see a small trailer, only eight to ten feet long, shaped like a half circle. In front of the trailer is a bearded, long-haired man exhorting the crowd in a straining, hoarse voice. His neck veins are popping through the swollen muscles. A wild look is in his eyes, and a fistful of money in one outstretched hand, a cane in the other. He sometimes points, pokes it at the crowd.

I see the reason for the crowd. On a chair, near the man, sits a naked woman. Her dark eyes are wide in amazement, drugged eyes, I think. From her seat the wall of people, faces wild with lust and delight, must seem comical, bewildering, gratifying. A trace of a smile is at the corner of her mouth, a mouth that wants to grin. A hint of self-appreciation is in her eyes, as if the audience isn't looking at her simply because she is naked, but because she has beauty.

Her rib cage is narrow, the ribs are delineated; her waist is tight; her breasts sag, then regain size and firmness at her nipples. She sits upright; her posture would have made her first-grade teacher proud. Her legs are crossed under the chair. Her face is attractive. Her white, flawless skin, in a state of excitement—as if the slightest touch would begin a process she could not control—holds the crowd. It is this incipient voluptuousness,

The Silver Cord

the body wanting to be touched, that mesmerizes. I realize the faces of the crowd are half crazed, less than human, and my face probably looks the same. I leave.

I suppose the naked woman is the highlight of the Fiddlers' Convention. I never did hear any fiddlin', probably because I didn't have the drive to seek it out. In the pavilion where the music took place, we do see a guy in gym shorts lying on a bench long after the warmth of the day has gone. His skin is burned red. He doesn't move, though his eyes stare out into space. The eyes don't blink. I suppose he is a casualty of too many drugs. We alert some medical people. I don't know if he lived or died.

The rain comes. My friends are interested in drinking, smoking, shooting off firecrackers. I don't want to do any of those things; the emptiness inside makes me brood. The weather is so bad we decide to leave a day early. The fields are slippery; the roads are churned-up mud, slick grades, deep holes filled with water. Watching cars, vans, motorcycles struggle up the hills becomes a favorite form of entertainment. People cheer, applaud; cars fishtail, sink into mud; tires spin, mud and water fly. The mud acquires the consistency of newly poured concrete or chocolate pudding. I am always amazed at how fragile the machine is; put a car in a wet field, put a city in a snowstorm, and you will understand.

We watch a motorcyclist in faded jeans, black leathers, with long brown hair, a thick beard, earring, looking like a Viking, attempt to ride a black Harley up the slick hill. His eyes are wild as his bike bucks the hill. He is afraid of failing before the hundreds of people who watch him. He makes the climb.

Doogie wants to find warmth and escape the rain. We drive across North Carolina and into South Carolina. By dusk we are by the ocean. The rain stops, but the clouds press the earth. Palm trees, palmettos, sandy soil touch the senses. We camp on a flat island consisting of picnic tables, pavilions, electrical outlets. Of the hundreds of campsites, only a handful are occupied. We cook a meal, walk up the beach to a modern, high-rise motel.

I notice Moe is anxious. He knows that tomorrow, he will leave his friends, his familiar world. There will be only him, me, the road. He has never left home for any extended period of time, has never traveled more than a few miles from home. His father laughed at him when he said he wanted to see the country, then dared him to go. His mother is against the trip.

If Moe returns with everyone else, his father will laugh at his foolishness, give him the I-told-you-so, even as he secretly prides himself on the control he has over his son's life. A son who obeys his wishes, his perceptions of life. It is funny, his father thinks he knows everything about life and forces his knowledge upon his son; my father seems to know what life is and tells me nothing.

I am anxious about tomorrow. Will Moe back out? If he does, will I continue? Where am I going and for what purpose? Moe is good in a crowd; he feeds off people, they are stimulation, they keep him happy, his mind thinking. Can he be happy in his own thoughts? Can he adapt to new circumstances, new and changing faces? We will see, I tell myself. We will see what he is made of. He will, by his presence, delineate me, tell me what I am made of.

The next day the clouds are higher, lighter in color; a hazy sun shines through to the earth. Doogie drives to Interstate 95. I look at Moe; he hasn't said a word all morning. I wonder if he will back out. I see the struggle inside. He wants to back out badly. Why do our parents bind us? Let us live, make our mistakes, if we must. He can't back out, or he won't. Doogie pulls off the highway. We unload our new modern backpacks. We shake hands; they wish us good luck. Neither of them knows if he would have the courage to do what we are doing. We watch them drive off. We are alone beside the highway.

CHAPTER 20

A few minutes pass, a van pulls over and stops. The guy driving wears wire-rimmed glasses, has hair of moderate length. He is soft spoken, friendly, offers us sandwiches made by a friend's mother. He is going to Florida to visit his fiancée. He attends MIT and is originally from Indiana. He talks of his father, who was a great inventor, tinkerer. Moe asks him if he wants to get high. He says no and asks us not to take offense. He realizes that to ask someone to smoke is a token of friendship. He has given his life to Christ.

I ask if there is any special reason he did this. He says it was just time to do it. I say that many give their lives after a traumatic experience. I believe he had such an experience but would not admit it, as if crisis somehow is an invalid reason for seeking God. As long as we are happy, we want God's hands off our lives. When we screw up, we don't want to admit we're fools, not even to the God who knows everything. It stands to reason we've got to be brought to the end of ourselves before we call on God.

It is strange that in the leap a man can give his heart and soul, his passion to a hobby, a job, a profession, a philosophy, creed, a person or people, even a religion, but not to God. Perhaps he doesn't want to seem foolish to the world, dedicated to the invisible. I suppose as much as my life hurts, I want it to be *my* life. No, that isn't true. God can have my life; I don't want it. Our driver talks, he's interested in the metaphysics of thinking and God working through our minds. He talks, but my mind is dead. I know God, and He has never helped.

We stop for gas. The cement by the pumps is spotted thickly with grease and car fluids. I think that odd. Something is wrong, but I can't put my finger on it. The attendant is shifty eyed. I think someone should remain with the van, but I fight that thought, attributing it to my distrust of mankind. We fill our gas tank and leave.

Down the road a few miles, our van begins to cough and sputter. MIT notices that the pump hoses at the service station were cracked, flaking. He borrows a screwdriver from a worker at a prefab metal building off the highway. In the gas filter, we find a big hunk of hose. I know it isn't an accident; that is what the gobs of oil and grease were telling me. The tourist from the north leaves his car to go to the restroom; the attendant spreads some fluid; tourist returns, and the attendant says, "Your car has a leak." Before you know it, your car is on the lift, and you have a big bill. Years after this event, on TV, I see this scam revealed and investigated by a news show.

Toward dusk we leave MIT; he is continuing to Miami that night. We want to hit I-10 West at Jacksonville. We are a good way from Jacksonville, but I know better than to end up near a city at night. We say goodbye; he says, "Good luck."

We hop a fence, plow through sand and pines—a just-harvested pine forest, now covered in seedlings—make camp by a pond with a sandy shoreline.

We gather firewood, set up the tent; the air is warm, the sand cool. We smoke some marijuana. The smoke means nothing to me, does nothing good to my mind. I don't really want marijuana in my life. Moe continuously asks if we are safe; he thinks a crazy man might be prowling the night. He asks about tomorrow. I tell him tomorrow we will be in Mississippi. Our plan is to stay south, visit Corpus Christi, the Southwest, Southern California. In California we will visit a friend of Moe's. After that, plans don't really exist, except maybe to build a log cabin or adobe home and rough it.

The next day I'm first out of the tent. The day is cold, but the sun is up in a cloudless sky. In the sand I see footprints, shoeless, standing before our tent. I backtrack; the footprints have come from the interstate. I follow the tracks forward till I lose them in the pines. I figure it is some poor, local man. Poor because the ground is frosty, and shoes are needed. A man, by the size of the feet—wide and long but still blocklike. Curious about a tent in his environs. The tracks are only three feet from the tent; that is too close. I show the tracks to Moe. He thinks I made the tracks to frighten him. Maybe it is better he believes I made them. Maybe we're lucky to be alive.

The first ride is in a heavy, blunt, tail-finned car of the fifties, with a New York plate. The interior is red vinyl, studded with red buttons. A young man drives, a boy sits beside him. Both are pale, scrawny, with shaved heads that have sprouted a black stubble. The driver says it is his mother's car. Could we spare a dollar or two for gas? They are passing through Jacksonville on their way to Miami. The driver is punchy from lack of sleep; he's been driving all night.

They are of the New York City race, Hispanic, black, white mixed together; whitish skin with a darker pigment within, straight black hair, elliptical eyes, a nose close to the face, wide nostrils, lips of medium thickness. They speak Brooklynese—dey, youse guys, dawg, boid. I know these guys are both just out, legally or illegally, of jail or some halfway house or reform school. The car is stolen, the missing radio has been sold; you don't sell your mother's radio. They have no money. They've been driving all night to make a clean getaway. We get in and at the next gas station give them some money for the gas.

The ride ends, our driver speeds away. In the Florida warmth he will steal from the tourists, make a new life of crime for himself and his buddy. An old deaf black man, shining black skin, in a fifties Ford pickup, give us a ride. He says the Lord wanted him to give us a ride. He has a kind heart. Then there is a ride on top of a stake-bed truck piled high with scrap, junk, driven by two black men. We sit high on the junk and roll west on Interstate 10.

A navy man gives us a lift all the way into Mobile, Alabama. He picks up two more hitchhikers, a scrawny guy in his early twenties, who is

The Silver Cord

traveling with a good-looking eighteen-year-old woman with plump thighs. They travel in the pickup's capped bed. I look back through the window and see her back against the window, laying on her side, the scrawny guy is out of sight but not far away. Her body moves in spasms, back and forth.

Outside of Mobile the ride ends for everyone. We talk to the couple. She is from a boarding school for the handicapped. She is deaf and does not speak clearly due to her hearing problem. He is a southerner, just drifting. He spent a week in jail a few days ago. A sheriff searched his pack and found a bong. The sheriff put him in jail, never did let him call a lawyer. We camp with the couple at a rest stop of picnic tables, grassy lawns. Chickens run loose. We think of eating one of the more tender-looking hens, but it doesn't seem worth the trouble.

The next day is sunny, warm; a guy driving produce destined for an oil rig gives us a ride. Somewhere in Louisiana, we shoot down a dirt road, past thick-branched oaks draped in Spanish moss. My mind goes back to my sixth-grade reading book about a family that traveled, had adventures across the US on their way to Dad's new job in California. They had stopped in Louisiana. Our teacher, on summer vacation, had been to Louisiana and brought back Spanish moss for us to examine. I think in sadness of the sixth-grade boy who was me.

We come to a dock where there is a small resupply ship. Water stretches to the south of us. The truck doors are opened, apples and oranges spill out. Our driver gives us one apiece. We watch as a side of beef, boxes of hamburgers, pork chops, bananas; big containers of ice cream, countless boxes, tins of foods are unloaded. Our driver takes us back to the highway, and we wait.

Four Mexicans, crowded into the front of an economy-size pickup, stop for us. In the capped bed is another hitchhiker, who says nothing. We stop for still another hitchhiker, a kid with a speech impediment. He lives with his aunt. I wonder if he is a runaway. The back of the truck is hot. The Mexicans seem irritable, as if there has been an argument between them. Later, one tells me they were short on cash and didn't know if they could make it to Brownsville, their destination. Some wanted to kick us out to lighten the load, another wanted to collect money from us. My informant thinks one of his buddies is holding back some cash.

A good many miles from Houston, we are ditched. The truck is out of gas, we are told. One of the Mexicans walks over to a service station to make a phone call to solicit money from a friend or relative. We stand by the highway, a hot wind blows, the land is flat. The land is diked, the fields plowed and brown. A trucker in a beat-up, gas-engine rig stops.

The trucker is in his thirties, fat face, fair skin, red neck. His eyes are red, tired. We get in, discover he is higher than a kite. The cab is hot, the windshield glazed with gray dirt. We hear every tooth of the gear wheel, hear every piston working. The truck bounces over the cracks in the cement; we jounce along, our guts shaking, doing 40 miles an hour. Near dusk, fifteen miles outside of Houston, at a crowded, dirty rest stop, the ride ends. We leave the rest area, jump a fence, go through trees, up a hill. We sleep upon an unused road that is upon a dike. A long pond runs the length of the road on the other side, a rice terrace not yet planted.

Problems are beginning to surface with Moe. He doesn't like waiting for other people to give him a ride; too many uncertainties, wasted time. A man should have wheels, a machine, be independent. What he is telling me is his self-esteem is wrapped up in a vehicle. He wants to get where he is going as fast as possible. He doesn't understand the journey is the destination, not a place.

In the morning Moe is covered in mosquito bites, and I have none. On the road, a guy who is going to work at a bakery picks us up. I think he is a homosexual; I don't like thinking the thought. He leaves us off in a concrete maze in Houston, among morning rush-hour traffic. Moe looks stressed out. A guy in a new jeep with a roll bar, top down, gives us a lift. He works on the oil rigs, is just back, out for a good time. He takes us out of Houston, drops us off on a flat plain. A Mexican in a pickup, dragging a compressor, picks us up. We travel through oak-scrub lands, then on a coastal road where the land is dead flat, greener than any land I've seen in Texas. Cattle graze, and in the small inlets, shrimp boats are docked.

The Silver Cord

In Corpus Christi, at North Beach, we buy a bottle of cold wine, walk the beach, watch a ship come in. We stop in at the cottage; Randy still lives there, jobless, scrounging a few bucks here and there. He owns an old sports car without a hood. We buy a bunch of things at a supermarket for dinner. Randy keeps adding to the list, knowing there will be unused ingredients, portions from the meal that he can live on for a few days. I had suspicions before that Randy was involved in illegal and or immoral practices. I once saw him do the "I handed you a twenty" routine on a cashier. The cashier was savvy and didn't get gypped. Randy knew a guy at the meat-processing plant who I knew was a homosexual. How else could they have met? That Randy is still jobless and yet surviving without food stamps says it all. Moe and I leave the next day.

A Texas girl gives us a ride. She is going to classes at a college somewhere on the outskirts of the city. She deposits us in the country. That is all I can remember about her, and this brings sadness—I want to remember everything. The land is beautiful, a swelling, vast, treeless plain. The road, a black band by our feet, rolls over hills miles away. In the distance the black band turns to a silver cord in the sunlight. In the near distance I see a farmhouse, silos that shimmer and blur in the rising heat. The day would be warm if not for the wind.

Sage and cacti grow by the road. Plowed land stretches out from the farm, then there is nothing but yellow-brown grass. Moe cuts up a prickly pear cactus and begins to eat. I write about the road, the land around me, the moment within. Moe reads what I have written and says, "Is that what you see?" in a pained, disgusted, questioning voice.

I say, "No, that is what I see and feel."

He says, "All I see is a road, emptiness, a farmhouse, heat waves."

It is then I realize he will never understand traveling, never enjoy the trip.

He is correct, we see objects that can be identified, that have substance. But a man's mind can color what he sees by emotion, perception, state of mind, intelligence, need. If a man could be perpetually objective, then he would no longer be a man but a machine. And yet a man's mind can be so tainted that he may color life with the lies of his own heart. Moe's way is not right, and yet perhaps my eyes, fleeing the emptiness of my soul, the bitterness of my heart, have skewed reality. Perhaps I am floating through a purposeless dream world. I guess I need to see life through the eyes of God, for if He has a bias, it must be called truth. That's all I want—the truth.

A guy our age gives us a ride. In San Antonio, two Wisconsin women in bathing suits, returning home from their spring break at the Gulf, give us a lift. Then we are with two teenage kids who are on their own, working, with an apartment, who act road wise, and seem in awe of us. The next ride is with a man on his CB, talking to his wife and kids, who live outside of town in a trailer. At dusk we sleep in a stand of oaks, beside a fenced-in cattle pasture.

The next day brings an India Indian, who works for the state of Texas at some institution; then a goat herder; then a gold-chained, well-dressed Mexican in an El Dorado, going to Los Angeles. The car breaks down, the radiator is bone dry. He's slightly panicked. A Texas-plated RV stops. A man, his wife, and two little girls step out. The man discusses the problem with the Mexican while the two little girls, by their mother, show me plaster-of-paris forms of skunk tracks they made. They give me a form as a gift. I make a big deal over it. The girls light up in happiness. The Texan takes the Mexican into a town for help. He comes back and asks if we want a ride. I decline; I don't want to burden him and his family. Perhaps I'm afraid of his kindness. The man and his wife have a peace. I don't ask where the peace comes from even though I need peace desperately.

A van stops, the driver is in his mid twenties, a guitar is beside him. The man beside him is in his fifties, he stutters, he is thin, wears a baseball cap with an electrical union logo above the visor. The driver, Gary, was picked up by the older man, Pete. To start a conversation, Pete says, good naturedly, "Gary hears things in music most people don't." You know Pete is quoting Gary from words spoken before we arrived. Pete is jokingly making Gary appear as a weirdo. Gary smiles. Pete stutters, "Do you have any M&Ms." I look blankly at Moe. Pete sees my puzzlement, clarifies that he wants speed, uppers, amphetamines, bennies. I wonder what went wrong in Pete's life.

Pete says to help ourselves to the beer in the cooler. We drink a beer. Moe gives me a look that says, "Let's get out of here—this guy isn't right." Pete is all right; he's just a fifty-year-old electrician who has never grown up, wants some company for the long drive. I get Pete talking. His family is back in Houston; doesn't see his wife often—they're on the outs. She is religious, born again; she and her daughters sing in a gospel group. One daughter is trying to make a living in gospel music. The family doesn't like his traveling all over the country and his drinking. Pete will have nothing to do with religion. Pete's headed for a mining town near Gallup to wire a new building.

On the outskirts of Stockton, Pete has Gary stop at a restaurant. Pete says, "Order anything you want; the bill is on me." The other two look unsure of Pete's motives, but I know kindness is the motive and the reward. I order a moderately priced dinner, Gary and Moe follow my lead. In Fort Stockton, Pete leaves Moe and me out at a supermarket and is gone. The plan is to stock up on food, make an excursion into Big Bend National Park.

We walk outside of town, past a radio station, into the sage. The next morning, two mules are standing over us—we are in their fenced-in pasture. They have not trampled on us, peed on us, or bitten us, though I'm guessing the traffic is hoping for a show. The mules are better neighbors than some humans. The day is clear, cool, with a strong wind. I begin walking the road. Moe says, "Why walk? " He's had a reluctance to walk the entire trip. I explain walking is a part of the attitude you must have, that you'll get to where you're going with or without people. The exercise can't hurt, will tone our bodies for any backpacking in the park.

He continues to drag his feet, lag behind. Depression hangs about him. Few vehicles pass. If we do get to the park, I can't depend on Moe to hike the backcountry, so what is the point in going? We walk back to Fort Stockton, stand beside Interstate 10. Two Mexican girls drive by; they come back in a few minutes, hand us giant Cokes with plenty of ice. We talk awhile, the talk goes nowhere, they leave.

I coax Moe into walking farther, to a hamburger joint for another coke. The sun is hot, the temperature in the high eighties. Beside the hamburger joint is a restaurant. In the parking lot is a car with New York plates. The dealer sticker says Canandaigua. I have an uncle who lives in Canandaigua, a town in the Finger Lakes region. A man and woman come out to the car. I give my uncle's name; they know him. The man owns the bowling alley in town; I know exactly where the lanes are located. The man has a puzzled look on his face, unable to believe the coincidence. They get in their car and drive off, without offering a ride.

Two nurses from Wisconsin, on vacation, pick us up. One is short, plump, with curly hair; her name is Alice. The other is tall, broad shouldered, well built; her name is Janice. Within ten miles, I have them talked into going to Guadalupe Mountains National Park. We have a cookout, climb Guadalupe Peak, sit around the fire in the evening. Alice and Janice are good people; I haven't met many nurses who aren't. Moe perks up, as Janice likes him. He enjoyed the hiking. Alice and Janice drop us off in El Paso. They give us their addresses in Wisconsin.

At a fast-food restaurant, we hitch a ride with a Mexican in a pickup. He wants to show us the Rio Grande, the levee, have a few beers with us. I have a gut feeling, say no thanks. Outside of El Paso, when the sun is gone, a jeep stops. Our driver is Lyle, an oil corporation geologist. We ride with him to Las Cruces. The night is sky is covered in stars. Moe and I camp in the desert, four hundred yards from the highway. Moe is worried about the bogey man again, as he has been every night.

In the morning a step van stops, a floral shop advertised on the sides. The guy who steps out is short, thin, with a shaved head. He is either just out of the military, a prison, or a Hare Krishna commune. He says he's never been in the military, no Eastern mysticism is heard or seen in his actions. We deposit our packs in the back, the van is empty of flowers. A few miles down the road, he tells us we are in a stolen vehicle. He has just escaped from jail, his crime—car theft. He is bound for California, to some canyon outside of Los Angeles. He says there is money to be made stealing cars in California. He intends to dump the van when it runs out of gas.

We exit when only fumes are left. We watch the van go down the road half a mile, then it is ditched under an overpass. We see the driver put out his thumb, he's picked up almost instantly. Across from us is a restaurant and a pay phone. I go over to call the state police. It bothers me this guy

The Silver Cord

is getting away. Moe says the van is covered by insurance. Insurance can't make up for the inconvenience, personal belongings lost, the red tape you have to endure.

    The pay phone is out of order. I don't go into the restaurant to call because I begin to have second thoughts. Our fingerprints are in the van. We will be under suspicion. We will have to give a description, perhaps search through endless photographs. I decide that if I see a state police car pass, I'll flag it down. None passes.

    A car stops, ten guys are crowded into it, one lying across those sitting in the back. I wave them on. A Scout, hauling a flatbed trailer with a crushed Volkswagen, stops. Two guys, a woman greet us; the woman is the one guy's wife. The two guys are soldiers, picking up the crushed bug from their last duty station in Texas. The bug was crushed in a night of fun; now it must be hauled to Oregon, the new duty station. I would have junked the bug.

    Somewhere out in the barrenness of rock ridges, sand, creosote, cacti, we leave the soldiers, hook up with a young kid, in the navy, bound for California to board his ship. He's never been on a ship or to sea. I tell him of a friend who went into the navy, was stationed on a ship, and liked it. This knowledge relaxes him. The desert is thick with huge cacti, standing like men with hands raised in the air. Evening comes, and California waits.

CHAPTER 21

Navy leaves us outside of San Diego, before the concrete is thick on the land. It is night. I am in a state I do not trust. California, to me, is like a giant playpen, full of children oblivious to each other, intent on playing with their expensive toys and fads. Play is more important than work; work is for money, status, power; appearance is everything. California is a place where everyone appears happy, everyone is convinced his or her act is together. Californians can be friendly, but it is a friendliness to sell themselves to you, or it is a boast. "Look how normal and well-adjusted I am. I don't do anything wrong, have no problems. I'm on top of the world."

The next day a landscaper going to work gives us a lift. The highway is clogged with traffic; everyone is behind schedule, brake lights stutter, horns blow. We are deposited in the suburbs; NO HITCHHIKING signs are everywhere. Moe is leaking anxiety; he feels like a bum without a car. A black man in his fifties stops; his four-year-old grandson is with him. The man is calm, placid amid the rush around him.

He stops at his church, leaves us with the four-year-old boy. He judged right with us, but I wouldn't leave a child with a stranger. As we wait, we see a man come out of a duplex, eyes darting nervously. By his garage, he lights up a joint and smokes. When the joint is gone, he turns back toward his home. Grandfather returns, takes us farther up the road.

We are deposited again by NO HITCHHIKING signs. Moe is wearing a knife on his belt as if he is still on the Texas plains. I suggest he take the knife off; he thinks it is okay where it is. The knife is his security. A motorcycle cop pulls over, dismounts, walks over to us. Expectation in his eyes. He's trying to figure us. His eyes go to the knife, then leave quickly. He is a small man, short in stature, and light in weight. He stands before Moe, looking Moe in the eyes; his hand reaches out quickly, unsnaps the safety strap, pulls out the knife. A plan and decisive action negated his stature and weight. Once the knife is in his hands, he apologizes, says he can't take chances. He writes out a ticket, knows we won't pay, but does it anyway. We begin walking.

A woman in a Mercedes slows; she has long black hair, dark eyes. Her eyes run over our bodies, she decides we're not quite what she's lusting for and drives away. We walk, the city thins. To the left is a city park and a bay; we rest on a bench. We watch a man on a Jet Ski. The engine buzzes, changes sound as the craft is airborne. We hear the slap of the fiberglass onto the water. The guy is zigzagging, wiping out, whooping, hollering. His exuberance seems an attempt to convince the world and himself that he is having fun.

At a supermarket, we call Moe's friend from high school. Sandra comes within minutes and picks us up. She runs over a median strip, as she talks a mile a minute about friends in Pennsylvania, smiling the entire time—happy at seeing a face from the past. She takes us back to her mother's house, a townhouse in a development beside a prestigious golf course. The townhouses are well built, sturdy; no corners cut. A major, nationally televised tournament is held on the immaculate course. I'd say the homes were expensive.

Sandra's mother is moving out. Her mother is thin, nervous, flighty. Her speech is fast; she smokes one cigarette after another. She owns a small poodle—thin, nervous, flighty, with a fast bark. The poodle has urinated all through the house. The stench of urine has soaked into the carpet fabric. The stench stings the nostrils. The dog urinates from nervousness.

John Johnson

We meet Sandra's boyfriend. He seems a calm, friendly person. We meet Sandra's mother's boyfriend. He wears a business suit on a short, stocky, fifty-year-old man build. The hair is graying, the right hand is in a cast, a black bruise surrounds an eye. He was recently in a barroom fight, or rather, a cocktail lounge altercation. Here is a man who spends his time in bars, cocktail lounges picking up women, drinking. In the morning he puts on a suit, goes to work, looks like a man, talks in a man's voice, and has found no purpose in the leap called life but to be perpetually eighteen. I am just guessing—the worst. I don't know who he really is.

The next day we move furniture; a piano must be moved, steps are everywhere. At the end of the day, we cook steaks on the grill. The next day Moe and I bum around with Sandra in her MG. We go to the supermarket, drive along the beach, stop in at a college library. The following day we go to Los Angeles to see the exhibit of Egyptian artifacts that is touring the country. A special pass is needed to see the artifacts, so we wander around some side rooms.

Our next adventure is Mexico. Sandra and her boyfriend are our guides; they go into Mexico often. We cross the border into Tijuana. The streets are filthy; trash lies in the gutters; the roads are potholed, unpaved; the buildings rundown. People crowd the street; the blackness of their hair hits my senses—nothing but thousands of black-haired heads bobbing. I see so many cripples, deformed bodies, so many unsmiling faces, or harried faces carrying an arrogance, the conceit that is armor. I believe I have just witnessed a difference in cultures. I think what nations think and do may decide everything that will be their present and their future. Shacks are perched on hilltops and hillsides; one-room, cardboard shacks ready to slide or topple in the next heavy rain.

We are on the highway south. There is no speed limit, no guardrails; small painted rocks border the road. We see long stretches of beach below us; sometimes shacks are upon the beach. We're in Ensenada. Young boys rush to our car, wanting to shine our shoes or wipe the windshield. The evening we spend at a bar, drinking Dos Equis, a Mexican beer. The bar is a mix of Mexicans and foreigners, who are mostly Americans and Canadians. Sandra's boyfriend speaks fluent Spanish and talks to some Mexican friends. Three undercover police officers sit at our table. I don't know if they're local or federal. They want to know why American tourists come to their country. Sandra's boyfriend does most of the talking. One wants to know the color of my sweat shirt. I say, "Salmon." Not my favorite color but a gift from an aunt. I assume he wants me to say *pink*. I'll leave it at that; you can read between the lines. Every now and then, Moe and I go out to the street and eat burritos from a small stand. While we are standing outside, a Canadian woman comes out of the bar dopey, sloppy drunk. She bumps into a Mexican guy who just happens to be walking by. His eyes go wild with fear, anxiety, hatred, disgust. She is babbling as she staggers to the ground. Her friends come and pick her up.

We sleep in an old Mexican hotel, clean, sparsely furnished. The next day we buy breakfast from a small bakery, walk the streets, eat lunch at the harbor. Sandra buys a bottle of tequila to take back to the United States. She hides the bottle under the seat. The customs agent sees her nervousness and checks our car. He finds the bottle, tells her she didn't need to hide it. Then we are in the States, and I am thankful that I am an American.

In San Diego we say good-bye to Sandra and her boyfriend, thank them for their hospitality. We stand beside the road, Los Angeles bound. The road stays close to the beach. The beaches are empty; a few surfers, in wetsuits, paddle about in the cold, gray water. One ride is with a tall, thin, longhair who had just broken up with his live-in girlfriend. His heart and soul have been broken.

Two girls, sixteen or seventeen, pick us up. They ask what I think of free sex. The question is unmistakably a proposition. I say it is a good way to catch a disease. I study them; they aren't attractive but not ugly. Their clothes are unkempt; their hygiene seems to be lacking something, no clean soap smells or perfume, no combed hair. I sense an emptiness in them that saddens me.

We stand at a street corner of a four-lane highway slowed by traffic lights. Across the road is a mall. Rush-hour traffic streams by. I see people looking at our huge packs. We are studied by the backed-up traffic. We stand for an hour and a half. A bicycler stops. He says we can ride a bus all the way through Los Angeles for thirty-five cents. He says we can forget being picked up.

John Johnson

The bus comes; we drive through the worn heart of the city—warehouses, old factories, dust, smoke, drabness. Poor people enter and exit the bus. At an unused brownstone school we hop another bus. By nightfall we are in the center of Los Angeles. Another bus will be by in an hour.

We are in a small park that faces a cliff. Below the cliff is the coast road and a public beach, complete with bathhouses. We can see white lines of surf rolling in, hear the sound of the crashing breakers. Before us is downtown Los Angeles, deserted. We walk the deserted streets to an all-night supermarket. The women shopping wear furs, high heels. We go back to the park and sit on a bench.

I realize that a crisis is building within Moe. It was difficult for him to leave the security of his life in Pennsylvania. He is always asking, "What now?" or "What's next?" I know that in his mind, he did what he came to do—make it to California and visit a friend. I don't know what is next; this trip has no purpose for me. I saw the parts of California I wanted to see on the previous trip. I've seen the beaches of the Pacific. There is nothing I want from this trip except not to go home.

Moe has been a burden the entire trip, even though I needed his company. In his hometown, he is full of life, always wanting to do something, always talking to people. Taken from his protective environment, he has the opposite personality; he can't make things happen, can't see the adventure, can't grasp the moment, can't relate to the people he meets. My first time on the road was one long high. The strong, confident Moe of home has been replaced by a confused, enervated complainer.

I see the conflict coming. A tension has built between us. I am tired of defending the trip, every move we make. We have different philosophies of life, different perceptions, different qualities. I know in my need I subtly influenced Moe to make this trip, knowing he probably didn't have what it took. Yet, he is right from a certain perspective. To hitchhike is truly stupid if you have a vehicle and the money. My first trip I had no vehicle. To be standing still in your life when you should be forging ahead says something isn't right.

The bus comes, we ride the night; passengers are picked up, left out, it seems every hundred yards. The city is left behind; the final bus stop comes. We step out onto the coast road in the darkness, I move off up a hill covered in high wet grasses. I lay my poncho down, unroll my sleeping bag. The anxiety and panic on Moe's face is so evident. The field is what the road has given, and I am satisfied.

The early morning is cool, the road is silent, gray mists come in from the ocean. Expensive homes line the road on the ocean side. We can only see high iron fences, lush gardens, shrubby flowering trees, driveways leading back to barely glimpsed homes. Expensive foreign cars pull out of the driveways. I say, "Let's walk."

Moe's face wears the pained expression I am so familiar with. "Why?"

Calmly I explain the reasons I have been giving since the journey began—to keep in shape, to keep the scenery from getting stale, to see what adventure or discovery lies around the next curve, to find a fresh artery of traffic. He doesn't want to walk. I begin walking, knowing he is so afraid of being alone he will follow.

Along the road I discover a high, lush grass that tastes like licorice along the bank of an expensive home. All the vegetation is lush, green. A car stops, the driver asks us if we are naturalists. We are still clinging to the licorice grass. The driver says he picked up a guy who hitchhiked around, picking up plants, cataloging them, discovering their uses.

As we sit beside the road, Moe begins to talk. He wants to end the trip but can't come out and say it. He can't admit he doesn't consistently have what it takes to travel the road. I know he needs me to go back with him; then he wouldn't be a failure. Then his idea of life would have been proven superior to mine. He wants, needs the security of being right. I have shown him another philosophy of life, and it frightens him. I can't condemn him; I'm on empty. I hoped his enthusiasm would rub off on me; unfortunately, his enthusiasm dried up the moment he stood beside the road.

He brings up the vehicle argument, an argument I have heard all the way across the country. A vehicle would have made us independent; we could have traveled in comfort, without effort. I say what I have been saying: that we wouldn't have met as many people, or saved as much money, or tested ourselves encased in a steel box.

His next tactic is to use guilt. "Don't you feel like a leech, taking something for nothing?" His voice is sharp, quick. I must have said something in my previous answer that struck a nerve. I answer, "If they are going my way and want to share a ride, how is that leeching? I've given plenty of hitchhikers rides. I don't force anyone to give me a ride."

He is silent for a moment before beginning another argument. "Don't you think we should be doing something useful? Everyone else is working."

I ask why they work. Work is what they grasp in the leap. Some work to survive, some for money, status, power, security. Some enjoy knowing something well; some enjoy the game. How do I owe these people my life, my behavior? I need to know what I am to do and why. I need to know the truth. I want work to mean something to me. No, to the ultimate truth—to God?

Moe would do anything, work in any field, if the money is right. The value of work is based on dollars; the money brings status, self-esteem. I don't believe morality or ethics—let alone purpose, responsibility—have a part in his thinking. If he is moral and ethical, it is because it is easier to be moral and ethical than not to be. I try to tell him that you should do what is within you, what has been put in you from birth. I call that the intrinsic value and believed it then.

Intrinsic value fails because it simply means that this quality comes from so far back in a man's past, he has internalized it so much, that he forgets why he likes what he likes, why he chose what he chose. A man who builds a house might like to hammer because as a kid he saw his father hammer, or his dad praised him for hammering. Or did the hammering release frustrations? Or perhaps he likes to build because he does it easily, has a knack, and so he likes what is easiest to do, because he is content. Intrinsic value can be as corrupt as any other human motivation.

The intrinsic philosophy breaks down, at least for me, when pitted against the problems, sufferings you will face as you pursue that innate gift. I don't have the strength to bull my way through the hard times if what I do is solely based on intrinsic pleasure. You want to be a musician, but the record companies don't want your kind of music. You

The Silver Cord

open a restaurant because you like to cook, produce good food, but the economy is such people can't afford to eat at a restaurant. Whatever you choose to do, it will have its hard times and suffering, either placed upon you by an outside source or your own inexperience or bad luck.

Some men go through the bad times on pure ego. "I want it, and I'll get it." I have no ego. What I do must serve something greater than myself so that when the hard times come, I can say, "What I am doing is necessary; it is the truth; it will make the world a better place. God wants this done." I'm full of crap—just hiding from my fears.

Moe has repeatedly interrupted my talk, stressing my faults, raising objections to halt my flow of thought or to sidetrack it. His words are bitter. He says no one has to suffer, just plug yourself into a high-paying job category and go through the steps. He says I like to suffer. He has always believed this. It is not true, but I know if you are going to remain separate from the machine, live the truth, then suffering is bound to come.

People like Moe don't suffer; they are machine parts, made to fit into the whole, interchangeable. Moe says I got this suffering philosophy from Christ. He says I want to be a martyr; that is why I walk when I could be driving, that is why I live near poverty when I could have a high-paying job, that is why I wander aimlessly when there is work to do. He says I want to be miserable. He says this with as much disgust as possible. There is a physical intimidation in Moe's stance and tone of voice that angers me.

I think on what Moe has said. I wonder how Christ has entered the argument. I have never talked to Moe of Christ in all the years I've known him. We've had philosophical talks before, God has been a part of these talks. He is real, and a part of the way I think. Did I mention Christ somewhere in those discussions? I think of Christ dying on the cross for a humanity that could care less about the sacrifice. I think not of physical pain but of the pain of responsibility, duty, subjecting yourself to the truth, wondering what it will mean. Moe asks me if the suffering Christ is the kind of God I worship. I didn't realize I came off as a Christian type.

I answer that I don't think God wants us to suffer, but life doesn't give us much choice if we see it truthfully. Christ is there to comfort us when life is full of hurt. I don't tell Moe that Christ has never taken care of my hurt. My mind is bitter toward Christ, even as I defend Him. One part of me says, "I didn't ask Him to die for me. I don't want to owe Him anything. I don't want Him ruling my life." He had his chance when I was a kid, and nothing but pain came from it. I justify myself by believing that I have given God as much as there is to give.

I tell Moe suffering is a part of life, suffering to find the truth, or live the truth, or simply to live outside the machine. If this is being a martyr, then I am a martyr. I know Moe has never suffered, because he has never believed in anything that is contrary to what other people believe, never acted in a way antagonistic to the machine. I speak calmly; the argument's intensity has become dangerous. I apologize for any personal attacks made. We both try to remain objective, but contempt and viciousness are evident—I believe more on his part. I believe that Moe has no principles, beliefs; he does what is easiest, what causes the least commotion and the most praise. He looks to the machine for guidance, not truth or God.

A stopping car ends the uncomfortable silence. We are given a ride into Santa Barbara. The afternoon sky is gray, promising rain; the air filled with exhaust, sticky moisture. We stand where Highway 101 is slowed by a succession of traffic lights. Across the highway is a park and then the ocean. The park is full of bums. I watch a man, long hair, thirties, beard, in a dirty jean jacket and jeans, walk over to two Mexican bums. One of the Mexicans has a bottle in a brown paper bag. After a long talk, the three men go behind some trees, smoke the long-haired man's roach, drink the wine.

I notice brown paper bags lying everywhere, at the base of stop signs, streetlight poles, on steps into homes, in alleys. Bums, transients wander around in differing states of intoxication. We walk beside the highway, through the noise of honking horns, revving and idling engines. At one street corner stands a sixty-year-old woman in a heavy overcoat, a plastic bandanna on her head. She carries a plastic handbag, wide, deep, with a bold flower pattern on the sides. Her dress comes below her knees, then there is flesh, ankle socks, worn-out sneakers. She is a street person, mentally ill. She is attempting to make eye contact with the people who pass. She yells out, "Jesus saves!" as she pulls a pamphlet from her bag.

The Silver Cord

Moe, who is in the lead, slows so that I will take the brunt of this woman's behavior. I lead. A stern look is upon her face, as if she is not happy. I come up to her, look her directly in the eyes. She is silent. She looks into my eyes. Hurt is in her eyes. I say hello. She says nothing, hands me nothing. When we are passed, she begins again.

I wonder why God has worked no miracle upon her? Why isn't she sane, or calm, or at peace? I suppose He can only do so much with us here on earth. If He broke the laws of nature, did so consistently, life would no longer be for man. Is it God *in men* who must care for this woman? If Christ healed all the insane, all the mentally ill, then everyone might believe God is real, but would they give Him their hearts from love? Is this, then, the purpose of life? To give your heart to God from love? Or is life for the testing of the soul?

If life is a test, am I passing or failing? Do I love God with all of my being? Maybe I haven't gone the whole way. Maybe I like to suffer, don't want good things to happen. Maybe I would rather have my own suffering than God's peace, my own confusion rather than God's purpose for my life. Perhaps I left God; perhaps He never deserted me. Maybe I'm responsible for the emptiness in my heart. I think these thoughts now, in the town called Mechanicsburg, not then in Santa Barbara. Then I just kept on moving, kept on living.

Moe and I wait at the last traffic light. Countless hitchhikers have waited at this spot. Their feet have killed the grass, worn a hole in the ground. Their soda and beer cans are scattered about with their brown lunch bags. On the traffic light pole, on the highway signs, the hitchhikers have written their names, the dates, the hours they waited, their destinations. Now we wait.

CHAPTER 22

A guy in an economy-sized pickup changes lanes to come over beside us. He has greasy, streaked hair that dirty hands push back from the forehead. He wears a black T-shirt, a jeans vest that carries a motorcycle club patch. He is tall, thin, thin faced, greasy skinned. He is rancid in odor; more than a few days have passed since he has bathed. He studies us, our expensive packs, and knows we have a little cash. He says for three dollars he'll take us to San Francisco. We throw our packs in the bed, slide into the cab.

We stop for a woman hitchhiking. Moe and I had talked to her minutes before getting in the truck. She carries only a shoulder bag. She is attractive—firm chest, thin waist, rounded hips, blond hair, a lioness nose that is sexy. Her lips are pink, fleshy—not to an excess—and cracked slightly so that you would like to wet them. Her one eye is slightly crossed. Moe and I saw her step out of a Jaguar convertible, hurriedly, cursing the driver, who dressed like someone from the fifties and had an arrogant look upon his face. She walked up to us, pulled two beers from her bag, and gave them to us before walking ahead.

Our driver says, "Hey baby, do you need a ride?" His eyes leer. I offer her a front seat, as much from chivalry as to get away from the rancid

The Silver Cord

smell. She doesn't want any favors. She has met one gentleman today, she says sarcastically. She hops into the bed. We are on our way.

I ask about the truck. Our driver, Mike, says it belongs to a friend. I think the truck is stolen. The truck is new, yet Mike is beating it; when he shifts, you hear the gears thud; the gas pedal goes to the floor. The engine is at the apex of revolutions before a shift. He's traveling fast—wants to get away from where it was stolen? No one treats a friend's truck like he treats this truck. A stolen truck might explain his bathless state, the motorcycle club patch.

Rain comes, the rain stops. We pass through saturated land. The sky is low, the clouds come from the west, the ocean. The hills are lush, green, with high grasses; Lone trees are wide spreading, with smooth bark. Thickets crowd the crevices between hills. Somewhere back from the highway are ranches.

We stop at a service station in a small town across from a military base. The land is sandy and flat. The woman leaves as Mike puts in three dollars of gas. Even with the beer in her, the ride must have been cold. She wanders off. Where will she sleep? What will she eat? I suppose as long as she has her good looks, she will survive. I have a sadness for her. If only I had some truth to give her, something to put her wandering soul to rest.

Back on the highway we see two hitchhikers; Mike tells me to hustle up some money. The two men are short, fat, with angelic faces highlighted by colorful serapes. The hitchhikers are Germans or Austrians by their accents. They don't want to pay for a ride. I tell them they will be waiting a long time, and rain is coming. No, they will wait. I say, "Good luck."

Farther up the road are two more hitchhikers, a woman and a younger man. She is an Indian, dark skinned, long black hair, probably from the Washington coast. He has a scraggly beard, a baby face. I can tell he is a fat guy who lost a lot of weight quickly, so much so that he is weak with hunger. She says they have been fasting, haven't eaten in days. Their eyes are wide open in the fatigued stare that a combat soldier might have. The faces seem tired; the aura of hunger, exhaustion, drugs hang on them. He has trouble thinking fast; she does not. She talks slowly, heavily. They know the score, come up with some money, hop into the bed.

We move away from the ocean, through lush fields and small, poor-looking towns of pool halls, churches, store, Mexican faces. We pass through a forest on level land. The forest seems enchanted, with dark, strange trees, no undergrowth. Moe continues the conversation with Mike. Mike calls his common-law wife his "old lady." He drives trucks, the big rigs, occasionally; that is his legitimate work. He belongs to a motorcycle gang but doesn't want to talk about it. He makes LSD at home. This untamed man, whom you know can barely read and write, knows his chemistry. Moe becomes interested; they discuss making LSD, its history, chemical makeup. Moe, in his younger days, experimented with drugs.

Mike sells vials of LSD. He drops the chemical into his eyes with an eye dropper. He boasts about how wild he gets when he is tripping. He will do anything, fight anyone. His friends always keep a close watch on him. They enjoy his antics. He holds onto this reputation of wildness as if it were something good, his uniqueness, his identity. He makes good money from selling drugs—enough to buy, in cash, a tractor and trailer.

Night comes; I hear the ocean pounding the beaches, the rocky cliffs. The road winds, we pass through an area burned by a forest fire. Charcoal stumps stick up out of the weeds. A rabbit is upon the road. "Watch out, little bunny," says Mike with tenderness in his voice. I think of Mike on a drug trip, pounding human flesh bloody with his fists. Where did the gentle man come from and where did he die?

Up a steep grade, the engine sputters. We pull over at the top of the grade, where a single naked bulb burns under a high-roofed porch. The roof is attached to a white, shed-like structure. On the periphery of the light's glow are 1940s-vintage gas pumps, rounded, solid. The gas station is closed. Mike wants to steal gas from a parked car but has no siphon. We will wait for morning.

Three slender teenage boys, who were by the bulb, drift into the fog and darkness across the road. I sense expensive homes across the road, beyond the thickets. The two hitchhikers talk to us. Fasting cleanses; everything becomes better—a cigarette can make you high. The Indian woman tells of drugs, hallucinations. She has seen, met the devil. She tells of a monster with a huge head, the future course of life on earth. Her

The Silver Cord

story reminds me of a science-fiction movie plot with special effects. Because this experience happened within her mind, involved her emotions, it is the truth.

I listen. The future she has seen hasn't changed her, made her better or worse; it hasn't motivated her. The event within her was colorful, emotional, a chemical stain within her mind. She and her baby-faced partner are going to the Renaissance Fair in Seattle. The fair is a month away; they will work until it begins.

In the foggy morning, an unkempt man comes from the shed, unlocks the pumps, writes down some numbers, gives us gas. We pass through dank forests, open hillsides; drive past rustic shops, coffeehouses, inns. Expensive homes are hidden away. The hitchhikers bail out by a restaurant—the smell of food too alluring.

A tramp is upon the road with his thumb out. He's forty, has a fluffy, thick beard, a tanned face roughened by the weather. He wears baggy pants, overly large shoes; his shirt hangs out under an imitation-sheepskin coat with imitation-fleece collar.

Mike needs to get high; he pulls over. The tramp says he might have some marijuana if he's given a lift. Mike's voice stops short of intimidation. "No marijuana, no ride." The tramp rummages his pockets slowly. He holds out thick, weathered hands with a yellowness coming through the tan. In the deep creases of his hands are three roaches, three marijuana butts, more paper than weed. He pretends to be flustered, checks all his pockets again.

Mike's anger rises; he feels as if he's been lied to. Or is he trying to flush more marijuana out of the tramp? The tramp feels the presence of violence, reaches into his pockets and pulls out three little stones of jade he found in the hills. The tramp looks at Mike expectantly. Mike takes the three flat stones and the three roaches. The tramp gets in the back of the pickup. We deposit him before a hillside shack only a mile away.

The hills are gone; we are on the outskirts of a city. We pick up a woman who hitchhikes to college classes every day from her hillside home. She wears a peasant skirt and blouse, has long, brown hair; she has beauty.

Her eyes sparkle; she likes the excitement of meeting new people. Her ride is short. Then there is a little guy—dark hair, eyes; pudgy; with tiny hands—who carries a portable typewriter. He has been living in Central America, writing a book. Then we pick up a Jewish guy in a tweed coat, wearing a porkpie hat, who speaks with a New York accent. He says he is a carpenter. He doesn't have the hands of a carpenter. Somewhere down the road, we drop off our riders. At a store, Mike steals a handful of candy bars.

We are in San Francisco, driving up steep hills. The streets are crowded with people. We are on a wide street of small shops, tightly packed together. The shops turn to homes of pastel colors. Trolley cars run up the middle of the street; people stand in the aisles, on the stoops. Mike asks Moe if he wants to come home with him, try some LSD in the eyes; his old lady won't mind. Moe says no thanks.

Mike leaves us out at the top of a hill, on a crowded street. We don't know exactly where we are. Moe is uneasy. I am uneasy. It is a week into April; my youngest sister's birthday is on the sixteenth. I buy a card for her at a Ukrainian book and card shop. I go to a candy store and send her a box of candy. I don't know why I do this; no one would have expected this of me. I once loved her as only a brother can love his little sister. I would have fought anyone to protect her, done anything to make her life easier. Of the family, she was the only one who loved me. Somewhere I lost my ability to love, to care. I don't know why love died. Buying the candy and the card take every bit of my resolve. I want to love my sister as I did before I became lost in myself.

We walk the crowded street; few women are in the crowds. Men are blinking quickly on my right and left. Does everyone have eye problems? Is it air pollution? Then I realize these blinking men are showing their sexual interest in us; this is San Francisco. These one-tracked mind zombies are like human fireflies, blinking, blinking, blinking. I pick up the pace; the street ends; we come to a gas station, buy a map, get directions, buy a soda, try to relax.

We move down a street until it becomes a deep ramp, almost a tunnel. We stand on a narrow shoulder as cars whiz by us. A woman stops—young, blond, attractive. She is a secretary. Her eyes are lustfully running

The Silver Cord

over Moe. She likes cocaine. Of all the subjects she could have chosen to talk of, cocaine is what gives her life taste. I figured she just snorted a few lines. She takes us across the Golden Gate Bridge. The wind is strong from the ocean; a few fleecy, white clouds whip through the clear, blue sky. I look back at the bridge; it doesn't seem as long as I imagined it from TV, pictures. But its color, height, iconic placement on the land and water is powerful to my mind.

Within two rides (a gray-haired granny in a van, a Samoan guy slightly older than we are) and a supermarket stop, where a drugged-out longhair almost makes a play on our packs, we stand before Point Reyes National Seashore. We camp that night at the park entrance. I see Moe's mood swing back to anxiety and fear. We have another one of our talks that leads nowhere. We cover the same ground; his bitterness toward me seems to increase. He asks me what I am running from.

The next day bad weather hits the coast. We walk the trails, over fields, hills. We see the ocean—wild, untamed—and sandy beaches below the cliffs. The rain comes, the tent leaks, the sleeping bags are soaked. The night is cold, damp. In the morning we eat breakfast bars. In the porta john are two young guys claiming to be staying out of the rain, but I think they want to see other male apparatus. By midmorning the rain stops. We explore some thickets, some ponds. At dusk we go down to a campfire on the beach. High school kids, with their teachers, have made the fire.

The rain is coming down hard as we walk out of Point Reyes. We are completely wet, numb to the pounding. We climb into the bed of a pickup, the rain stops. Stores, homes, cars, signs stream by. The asphalt road is shiny; colors have an intensity. We are on a city street; we enter a doughnut shop squeezed between two buildings. The narrow shop has a dirty, white tile floor; cracked vinyl stools that spin. We drink coffee, eat doughnuts.

The man next to us, in his early thirties, says he traveled like us when he was young, before joining the army. He and his friends went out to Tennessee and had some good times. He offers us a ride. His girlfriend joins us. She doesn't like the idea of our company, but he's boss; she keeps quiet. I say, "Do you want us to sit beside her? I might steal her away from you." He smiles, laughs, knows we are okay. As we drive, he asks if we need a place to stay. He's moving out of his apartment, there is no furniture, but the stove can give us a hot meal.

We sleep in his apartment, wash our clothes the next day, put our sleeping bags through the dryer. The day is overcast, but a light is shining through the clouds, promising clear weather. We buy two six-packs. Moe is in an elevated mood. I know that for a few brief moments, the trip will be good.

Somehow we end up in Oakland, in a downtown section, nothing but offices. We both need to urinate, and there is nowhere to go. We walk into some landscaped bushes beside an eight-story, windowed office building. Like two stray dogs we urinate. We walk back to the highway, catch a ride with an off-duty sheriff. We end up on some side street to the highway in a lower-middle-class neighborhood.

We are in Oakland because we don't want to go farther north along the coast, into more rain and cold. We are turning back, heading south—to where, I don't know. Moe talks more frequently of going home. He says we did everything we set out to do. We can go home. He has his car waiting for him, a warm bed, as many homecooked meals as he wants, his tape player and tunes, his weights, his friends, a girlfriend. He wants to find a job. I have those things waiting for me, except for the girlfriend, but they don't mean anything to me; just props on a stage, things to fill the time in the leap. Am I some kind of freak, that such things don't please me or motivate me?

Moe goes to a nearby grocery store and buys more beer. We will booze it up, travel on the spirit of the dead earth—fermented hops and grain. This concoction will make us soar. Would have made us soar if we could have kept our mouths closed. We begin one of our debates. Moe's mind is seething, seething in confusion and loathing at the idea within me that his logic can't break. He has to break me to go home; he has to be the victor. He says the same old things: I can't make it at home, I like to suffer, I am afraid to go back, I am running away.

"Let's go home. Let's hop on a bus a go home," he says. I don't want to go home. He begins digging into me, belittling everything I believe to be true. He is captious, asks rhetorical questions. His words are fast, bitter;

The Silver Cord

his lips tightly pursed. I try to remain calm, answer with logic, without emotion. I know the truth about myself. I don't have the strength to live in the machine. There isn't anything at home for me. I know I am failing as a man, a person, that my love has died. Life itself has died.

Moe cannot wind down; the bitterness, mockery, sarcasm stream out of his mouth. By sheer vehemence, he will conquer. I don't have an opportunity to speak. Because a part of me wants the truth, I listen, and I begin to believe Moe's evaluation. I strike back, tell him he is without character, with no line within, a follower who does as the crowd does. He ignores the ugly side of life and the ugliness within himself. He is only as good as his surroundings; his purpose in life: the dollar. He is a machine part among machine people.

I've gotten under his skin. We stand, facing each other. I throw my beer can down. I have the wildness in my eyes; my body is tense. He backs down for a moment, then he stiffens. Our breathing comes hard; we stand nose to nose. Even through the drunkenness, the hurt egos and intellects, our friendship conquers. I thank God we didn't strike out at each other. Without the alcohol, we would never have come to that level of anger.

Bitterness doesn't leave easily; it hangs on you. I tell him to go find his bus. I walk away, walk till I can't see him. I know how his mind is reeling, being in a strange city, three thousand miles from home, alone. Once my being alone wouldn't have bothered me, but now I am empty, ashamed, confused, drunk, lost, and three thousand miles from nothing.

I wait by the empty street as the sun sets. The air becomes cool. A car stops, the driver asks me where I am going. I say Sacramento. He smells the alcohol and drives away. Another man stops, drives me into San Francisco, to the outskirts of the business district of towering buildings. The streets and buildings are empty. The air is cold; the sky, a faded blue. An orange-red tinge is upon the sky, the western sides of the buildings. The evening star is out, shining above a building shaped like a pyramid. I wait.

An Asian man, I believe he is of a Chinese background, stops and says, "Where are you going, Grizzly Adams?" Grizzly Adams is the name of a television show about a loner who lives in the Rockies, has a grizzly bear for a pet. My driver is in his forties, stocky, squarely built. We pass under ramps, bridges; pass by exits and entrances as he speaks of life.

He says the Caucasian race is characterized by exploration—geographically, scientifically, technologically. This race—many times, individual men—is always pushing the boundaries of knowledge further. The Oriental race are the workers of the world, the people who keep the world functioning and on its mundane course. They do not explore, are not innovative, but know how to copy; they accept life as it is. Those of the Negroid race are the destroyers. They do not explore, do not maintain; they tear down, enjoy the animal pleasures of their bodies.

He speaks well, has evidently spent much time honing his observations; though I wonder why race is what occupies his mind. I don't argue with him, just listen. I think that if you are Caucasian and come from a culture that believes in a God who made the earth and all within it for you, to do with what you want, to make life better, then you will probably explore the possibilities. If you are Asian and come from a culture of yin and yang, a cycle of life you are not to break out of, then you won't explore. If you live in an overcrowded country, you are satisfied just to achieve a normal life free of hunger. If you are a black child, with no father present, siblings too numerous for working Mom to love, given no values, then a good deal of hate will be in your life. If you're black and living in an Africa of shamans, demons, gods of evil, you might want to destroy.

We should forget history—the primitive tribes of Europe that were destroyers, or Germany in the 1940s. We will forget the innovative electronics of the Japanese, all the Asian scientists and mathematicians. We'll forget the black scientists, men of peace, the black laborers who built this country, the builders of African kingdoms. My driver leaves me off in or near Berkeley before a picket line in front of a restaurant. I stand by the entrance to the interstate.

I am going home; I don't know why. I don't want to go home, but I have nowhere else to go. The street lights blink on, the cold air lies on my flesh. My soul is numb.

CHAPTER 23

A woman in a pickup stops; she will take me to Sacramento. She is studying to be a mechanic. Her name is one that can be male or female. She is a Chicana, brown skin, curly black hair; I remember her hands, so small, like a little child's hands.

She tells me she is a lesbian. She shows me a picture of her lover and her friends. Her lover is a good-looking girl—a stern face, perhaps; pulled-back hair; a prominent trachea in a long, slender neck. My driver grew up with a younger sister, whom she loved—not a sexual love, but when she kissed her sister, a confusing passion arose. She has four brothers. She once saw her mother and father naked and was appalled by the male form—her dad was hirsute. One brother died in drunkenness, killing another person in an auto accident.

She once hated herself. She drives past her exit so we can talk longer. I ask few questions; she seems to want to confess to me. I see a woman, who in the confusion and pain of childhood, chose wrongly. She interpreted emotions, feelings, events incorrectly, was deceived; she tormented herself so badly that in the end it was easier to believe she is a lesbian. Everyone grows up mangled; we are all fallible.

She isn't satisfied with her lesbianism; she does not think it is good. She would not raise a daughter to be a lesbian. I believe there is hope for her. She grew up not knowing God; perhaps knowing wouldn't have mattered. I want to believe God helps us, that we can lean on Him, that He doesn't want us to hurt, to live wrongly. I do believe. I must believe. How else can there be hope?

I step out onto the highway, go into some trees—pines, unroll my poncho and sleeping bag. The night is damp and cold, the wind crisp. I wonder at God. He gave His son to help us live right, didn't He? Why isn't anyone receiving any help? Or is it that I just don't know of these people who are being helped? What do we have to do to have God come into our lives, change us, make us what we are supposed to be?

The next morning a station wagon stops. The man driving is in his forties; thin faced; cigarette in mouth; black, greasy hair; close-set eyes. He is a building contractor headed for Reno and his home office. He and his men just finished a job in southern California. His men are partying away their paychecks in California. He was drunk the night before. At a rest stop he asks me to drive. I don't like driving a stranger's car, but I do this time.

We are on Interstate 80, my silver cord of life, moving into the Sierras. Sharp, jagged, snow-covered peaks shine in the sun. The forests are dark blue-green against the snow and gray stone. So desolate and impassive are the mountains. I don't think a ground squirrel or marmot could be found here. Even winter birds would simply be passing through. The cold comes into the car.

On the other side of the mountains, near Reno, we pull off the highway, go to a home under construction that my driver is supposed to inspect. A custom-built home in pine woods. We get out; he enters the house, walks around the outside of the house, inspects. Only after I'm back in the car do I suspect he had other motives. I suppose my innocence has been my best defense all of my life.

I stand by the interstate; the day is clear, cold; no rides. I walk through Sparks; every other sign says, "No Hitchhiking!" Police cars are cruising nearby. I climb a fence into a railroad yard. I walk along the tracks, a short cut to a spot farther down the interstate. I think of hopping a train, but I know I would freeze to death in the Rockies. A railroad employee, standing beside a panel truck, tells me railroad security guards will throw me in jail, no questions asked. He speaks with no malice. I appreciate the advice. I believe him, remembering stories from the hobos in my apple-thinning days.

A quiet Mexican, whose car has sheepskin-lined seats, who wears a sheepskin jacket, who is a sheepherder, gives me a ride forty miles into the Nevada desert. Minutes, tens of minutes go by between cars. When the traffic does come, it comes in groups. I wonder if these drivers are cognizant that they band together as they cross the desert. A battered station wagon pulls off the road. The windshield is marked with chalk numbers in the corner.

My driver is in his early sixties, his hair a stubble of gray-white. The three-day stubble on his face matches the stubble on his head in color and length. He has a round face; a robust, square build. He talks as he sips from his can of beer. His speech is sometimes redundant. His words trail softly into his own mind. Sometimes when I speak, he doesn't hear. Sometimes he utters an *ugh*—half startled, half a plea for me to speak up. When something he says is good or reflects a past determination or resolution, he says, "By God!" I am sure he doesn't know God; it is only an expression.

His car had been stolen from his home in Montana; weeks later it turned up, was impounded by the sheriff's department in Reno. This explains the numbers on the windshield. His conversation turns to his boyhood. He rode freight trains during the Depression. He was just a kid. He lived in hobo camps and hid from the bulls. He once rode the Chief, the fastest train in the Southwest. He ran a hundred-yard sprint to gain the speed to jump aboard.

He would go into a town, ask for work at restaurants or stores or bars. There were always dishes to wash, floors to sweep and mop. Once, out in the country, a woman, standing on the porch of a farmhouse, hailed him. She wanted her garden dug—"a huge piece of ground, by God!" She was a widow. She said, "Dig up the garden, and I'll give you a meal." She was good to her word, heaped up food before him.

The Silver Cord

He was in the artillery during World War Two. He was shipped to the East Coast, got drunk with his buddies in Washington, DC, on their last night in the States. They almost missed the train to their ship. He didn't want to tell me anything of what happened in Europe. He kept silent. After the war, he drove a taxi in Los Angeles, then he drove a truck for a mover.

He answered an ad in the paper for a chauffeur. He drove a man and his wife and the wife's sister from Los Angeles to Montana on a vacation trip. The man had plenty of money and friends who put them up every night. The wife's sister wasn't beautiful, but she had a kind soul. I think my driver is wondering if he should have walked away from the woman with the kind soul.

He decided to call it quits to Los Angeles. Through the man he had taken to Montana, he got a summer job packing mules into Glacier National Park. All the fire stations and some of the ranger stations needed supplies. He loved this job, where he was the boss, could swear, yell at the top of his lungs any time he wanted. "Mules have personalities, by God!"

We drive past shimmering, white, salt pans; past flats of sparse grasses. Tumbleweed rolls, skips, floats over the road. In the distance are gray, jagged mountains; the high peaks have snow. The sky is pale blue. We stop for a pint of whiskey and a six-pack of beer. Near dusk, a fast-moving sports car comes up to us; the driver looks in at us. He waves, says something, then he slips back behind us. At Wells, Nevada, the mule packer heads north to Montana.

I stand in a parking lot of stone; neon lights advertise slot machines at the building before me; a restaurant and a gas station are nearby. These are the only buildings within the desert. The sports car pulls up. The driver is in his thirties, in the navy. He says he saw me picked up by the station wagon and has been behind me since that time. He signaled in an attempt to pick me up. He was bored with the ride and wanted to make something happen. I get in, even though I think this desperation for company is strange. I see in his eyes he realizes the strangeness and is embarrassed. He is Salt Lake City bound.

I let him talk, prime him with a question every now and then. He is married, talks of being stationed in Japan. He wants me to talk, but I have nothing to say. All I know is dust; my life is dust. God left life in my hands, and it is dust. You can't blame God for putting life in your hands; that would be like blaming the sun for coming over the horizon in the morning. It is the way it is, one of the rules of the game. If God lived our lives for us, then we would hate Him for manipulating us, controlling us. The man from the navy has no answers.

Twelve miles from Salt Lake City, I walk into a truck-stop restaurant, take off my pack. A waitress says, "You can't leave your pack in here. It has to be kept outside." By her tone I understand that I am roadside trash. A guy at the counter, a gas station attendant on break, gives me a look that says, "What's wrong with her?" That unstated question gives me heart; I sit at a table, don't leave my pack outside. That night I sleep in a field; a dog barks from a distant home; the sky is heavy with star milt.

In the frost-covered morning I hitch a ride with an all-American kid—blond hair, blue eyes; wide, easy-going face that smiles readily; robust build, athletic; he's a four-glasses-of-milk-a-day kid. He has baseball gloves, footballs, basketballs in the back of his truck. He hitchhiked in seventy-six to Glacier and the Rainbow Gathering. We could have seen each other in a store, a bar, or passed each other on a trail.

He asks me what kind of people are still on the road. I tell him the outcasts, perverts, the criminals, the romantics. The majority are not bad people, if you don't give them the opportunity to do bad. They'll give you half the truth, and it's up to you to guess which half. He knows the type I mean and laughs. I laugh. He tells me of ghost towns up in the mountains that I should check out some day if I'm ever in the area again. He says good luck as he leaves me out.

At the top of a steep grade, I wait. The grade goes up a bare, brown-rock mountain. Cars, buses, trucks labor up the grade. The air is cold, the sky clear. I watch a bus go by. I am almost certain I see the face of Moe looking out the window. He should already be home, unless he was somehow delayed; perhaps it is my imagination.

A man in a company pickup slows down and stops. Cable and toolboxes line the bed. He works for the telephone company. He is a quiet man, mean looking, blunt featured. He is not his face; he has a kindness. He worked in the steel mills of Pittsburgh during World War Two. He asks where I am going, what I will do once I get there. I tell him I will become a high school teacher of history. He says, "What about the Magna Carta?" This is the piece of history he remembers from his high school days. We talk about the Magna Carta.

My ride ends thirty miles up the interstate. A fire-engine-red Chevy Blazer, jacked up, with heavy, wide tires of thick tread pulls over. The driver is a young guy employed by the US Forest Service as a firefighter. He is coming from California, bound for Michigan. He talks of the machines he uses in his work with an unnatural excitement, as if he admires them like they are celebrities.

He knows all there is to know about the outdoors. He has the latest information on rain gear, insulating materials, boots, tents, survival techniques. When I tell him I sleep in the woods, fields, beside the road, he hides his disbelief. You know he couldn't sleep anywhere but in a camper. His talk of the rugged life seems a sham when compared to his flabby body. Did he ever walk an entire day or sweat for more than fifteen minutes at a job?

As I ride, we come to the crest of a hill. We see a barren, brown valley, stretching for miles. He guesses the valley must be twenty miles wide. He asks my opinion. I say it is probably seven and a half miles as measured by the sloping road. He measures the miles on his odometer. My figure is a quarter of a mile too great. He is terribly annoyed that my guess is better than his.

We see ridges of sedimentary rock; herds of antelope; the Green River; Little America, a fuel and rest stop consisting of hundreds of gas pumps. At dusk we cross into Nebraska. The land is flat; the immense sky threatens rain, sleet, hail, and high winds. The wide Chevy is pushed and pulled by the wind.

In the night we stop at a clean rest stop with picnic tables, windbreaks, restrooms, plush grass. My driver is tense, not knowing what to do with me while he sleeps. He says, "I'm not responsible for you." I tell him I'll sleep outside; if he's still there in the morning, I'd appreciate a ride. The next morning, I'm up and waiting by the Chevy. We drive east across

John Johnson

Nebraska. The sky is clear, the clouds white, the air cold. The Chevy thumps on the silver band.

By nightfall I am standing on the eastern edge of Des Moines, under the pinkish-yellow light of a high metal pole. The cars passing through the ball of light do not stop. I climb a fence, walk through a muddy cornfield to a line of trees in a small ravine. I pile weeds and grasses together for a mattress. The temperature must be in the thirties.

I hear a train whistle, see the light of the locomotive. The whistle is the sound of my life—sad, pensive, lost in the vastness. It is the sound of my soul crying into the darkness. The whistle grows in intensity and then fades into a whimper. I pray my childhood prayer.

The next morning, I put on every piece of clothing in my pack. I feel like a knot-tied balloon man. The wind is strong, raw, ladened with atomized icy moisture. The sky is solid gray; in places, the cold air has given form to the clouds and the darker gray of a winter sky. My hands are stiff; I have difficulty tying my shoes. My jaws feel as if shot with Novocain. The cornfields stretch for miles—rolling fields of dull-gold stalks, crushed and wet. My breath turns to white vapor and is pulled away.

A guy my age, driving a delivery truck, picks me up. He seems happy to be helping me. He never did any hitchhiking, but his girlfriend has been all over the country. He stops at a grocery store in the middle of the country, delivers some items, tells me to get anything I want; he'll pay. I buy a carton of milk and a small apple pie. I pay, thanking him for his generosity.

Back on the road, he expresses his concern for my lack of warm clothing. I may have his coat; I can send it back to him when I get home. He says this so that I will be more willing to accept the coat—he doesn't care if it comes back or not. The coat isn't new but has plenty of wear left in it. I say thanks, but I can manage without the coat. Where did this guy get his kindness, his joy in helping others? When I leave him, he says, "God be with you."

An old man, in his seventies or eighties, stops for me. He wears a raincoat with the lining in and a hat, both from the forties, by their worn appearance and style. He is going to see his son in Dubuque. His son doesn't like him to drive and doesn't know he is coming. He is weak, frail, his mind wanders. He begins talking about unions as if they are new on the scene. He doesn't like them; he tells why. He recounts his past, when he was young, in the work force, and unions were moving in.

We drive along at 40 miles an hour. Within twenty minutes, he pulls off the road. He says he is sleepy and needs to take a nap. His eyes shut almost instantly, his head tilts back. He is asleep. For a moment I think of driving him to his son's home. I wonder if son really wants to see Dad and how will Dad return home. The man shouldn't be on the road. I think how lucky the old man is for picking up an honest hitchhiker. I get out, begin thumbing. Maybe he'll wake up, give up, and drive back home.

A U-Haul truck with Colorado plates stops. The driver, in his thirties, has a ponytail, a tanned face, expensive, rugged outdoor clothes. We put my pack in the truck. I see a dirt bike, boxes, toolboxes. In the cab the heater is blasting. I wait for the warmth to penetrate my body. He shares some raisins, nuts. He is a carpenter. He lives in the Rockies of Colorado at twelve thousand feet, building saunas. He needs more cash; he's going to Chi town to work the summer rough framing. In two months he can make enough money to live a year in the mountains.

Riding his dirt bike is what gives life taste. He likes the speed. He pulls out a bag of golden-colored marijuana. He says it comes from Southeast Asia; expensive, potent. We smoke. My body begins turning inside, relaxing, as if receiving an internal massage. I sigh, I am dizzy. I stare out at the muddy cornfields. I see a farmer out on his fat-wheeled tractor enclosed in a cab. He is turning over the heavy soil.

At Interstate 55, the Colorado carpenter is gone, north, to the big city. The air is colder than in Iowa; Lake Michigan isn't far away. My body is heavy, sodden, lifeless from the marijuana. I feel as dead as a rock. Smoking dope is a waste of time, a trick from the dead earth. Speeding traffic, exhaust billowing, drab sky, drab scenery; suburbs with brown lawns.

A young kid, bound for his first job in construction, picks me up, gives me a sandwich his mother made that morning. Then two women, sisters, attractive, give me a lift. Beautiful faces, feminine voices. They want to travel. They tell me of their lives, their troubles, divorces, men they know. They want to travel but need a push, a man to show them the way. They invite me to Pontiac, Michigan. I ask them if they want to travel to find something or to run away from something. I know the difference; one is happiness, the other sadness. I don't go with them; they are running and don't know it. The road's song is over for me; I am running too.

I stand by the sleet-glazed roadside. The wind comes off the flatness and through me. A big tan-colored car stops. A man in his fifties is driving. He's going to Pittsburgh to visit a sister he hasn't seen in twenty years. They were separated at birth, raised in orphanages. After twenty years, he wants to see her again. He has just been divorced from his wife of twenty years.

He thought their marriage was good, sound. He loves his wife and two teenage kids. He is a self-made man, owns a tire distributorship in Chicago—warehouses, stores, trucks. He has money; a fifty-foot yacht on Lake Michigan, with radar and automatic pilot. Being an orphan, he has always wanted the comfort of material things.

Through his narrative and my questions, I see the reason the marriage came apart. His desire for money took him away from his family. His mind was always on the business, making money, not on the needs, problems of his family. He thought everyone was happy, content. He was a good husband because he was a good provider of material things. He gave them money, a nice home, clothes, cars; they had security—all the things he didn't have as a child. He didn't give them the one thing—the most important thing—that he did not have growing up: love.

There was the problem; all those things were for him, even if he gave them to his family. His wife became lonely, unneeded; his daughter, spoiled; his son, a stranger. He was just a machine part called Father, Husband. Machines can't love. He ignored the warnings his wife gave—talks she wanted to have about their kids, her moodiness. His own words condemn him, and still he doesn't hear.

Emotion enters his voice. The crying is past, but you know he has cried. He lives in an empty apartment without furniture. He is too depressed to buy any, or is he too busy? He will fill the room, perhaps that

The Silver Cord

would take some of the emptiness away. He still can't see that it is his heart that is empty of love.

Even in his moment of blackness, he thinks of me. He could get me a job in Chicago, working for him, driving a van, maybe. I say no thanks. I want to wake this man up, but I don't know how to say it, and it seems too late. I hope his sister can reach him.

We drive into the darkness as a misty rain falls. At a cafeteria-style restaurant, he buys me a meal. I don't refuse, knowing the giving would make him feel better. Outside of Youngstown, he drops me off. He says I can go to Pittsburgh with him. He'll find a room for me for the night if his sister isn't prepared to put me up. I appreciate the kindness, I tell him; no thanks. I wish him luck, hope everything straightens out for him.

He says, "Thanks," and is gone.

I sleep in a stand of trees surrounded by a cornfield. A cold fog hugs the earth. I listen to the wet tires on the wet highway. I wonder how long a man can live not knowing why he exists. The next day is cold, windy; the sky solid with gray clouds. Some kind soul gives me a ride, some easily forgotten face. I stand by the tollbooths where the pay road ends. A coast guardsman stationed in Chicago picks me up.

The mountains of Pennsylvania are just coming into full new greenness; the farmhouses surrounded by greening crops and recently tilled earth. On a country road, walking back to the highway, I see at least fifteen dead deer, drowned, caught in a sharp bow of a swift-moving creek. At Dubois, a seminarian student gives me a lift. He has an interest in history. He is a lonely person; God, Christ seem very far from his mind.

Where I-80 is intersected by US Route 15 South, I pick up another ride, a woman. I am preoccupied with my problems, don't take the time to talk to her. I am going home defeated.

CHAPTER 24

I write from the room within an apartment, the apartment within a building, the building within a block, the block within a town, the town called Mechanicsburg. Summer is fully here. Storms have plagued the land—boiling, seething disruptions in the humid skies. The hot days have come, days and nights of stillness and heat. The heat carries the drying earth, crops, the drying trees, and natural vegetation up into your nostrils. The cement and macadam of roads reflect the steamy heat into your lungs. The fields and trees don't move; there is complete, utter stillness. The shade is sticky, unable to cool. Go into the woods and feel the hot dankness.

The sweat bubbles on the skin. The land, fields, trees, farmhouses are encased within the heat. The heat sits upon the land, a visible thing, like a spirit. The birds don't fly; the groundhogs are sluggish, sleepy; they hide in the deep earth. Farmhouses have their kitchen doors open. No sound, no movement comes from the big white houses. The women do their work early, then lie on their couches.

Mulberries, cherries crushed by traffic, stain the country roads, the semipermanent shadows of the trees. The sweetness of the fruit hangs in the air like a gentle perfume. You can smell the perfume far from the

The Silver Cord

trees. The corn is over a foot high, maybe two. The corn leaves droop. I can smell the corn, a peppery smell that catches on the back of the senses, back where breath has reached its limits even as you are groping for a name for the smell. Farmers have cut hay. Dead groundhogs and rabbits litter the roads. Clover is in full bloom, purple-white flowers giving their sweet odor. I see wildflowers perched on fibrous stems; I once knew their name; the old knowledge fades.

Out in the fields, in the mornings, there might be a farmer on his tractor, looking behind, neck stiff, watching the furrows or the cutting bars as the dust or chaff rises. In town, the women—secretaries, clerks, lawyers, whoever they are and whatever they do—have their hair up, pulled to the tops of their heads, so their necks are bare. Thin wisps of hair fall; soft, delicate ears are seen. People walk down Main Street in the glare of the sun, wishing not to be in the heat and glare of the sun, but in the cool, air-conditioned buildings.

After work I come home, lie on my mattress and wonder when God will pick me up, take me to my typewriter. My body rises—not on my will, my energy, for I have none. It must be God who picks me up. Vanity of vanities is life. I am an old man in a young man's body. The silver cord, the road that gave me purpose, hope, is broken. Twenty-five years old and an old man. With only enough strength to wash dishes for a living.

Isn't it strange that men live even when in despair? There is always something good in the day, even when I won't admit it to myself. I hurt, and yet I live. "Ask and it will be given to you; seek and you will find; knock and it will be opened to you. For everyone who asks receives; and he who seeks finds; and to him who knocks, it will be opened." I've been reading the Bible from the church signboard across the street; that was yesterday's quote. I traveled the United States searching, asking, seeking from my own mind and experiences. The search had its fun, excitement just like the book knowledge, the college days, had their fun and excitement. In the end, after I had my fun, after my mind died, exhausted itself, thoughts of God came into my head.

Maybe my emptiness is the only way in which to travel through to God. Thoughts of God have always been in my mind, sometimes weak, sometimes strong, receding and surging. Now they are the thoughts that have endured. I have never sought, never asked, never knocked. As a kid, I never volunteered to go to church, never read the Bible on my own. "I am the bread of life; he who comes to me shall never thirst." This is today's quote. I think Solomon would have liked to hear these words. What shall I do with this promise?

After coming home from California that last time, I went back to college—just for the piece of paper called a diploma. The knowledge did not excite me as it had. Moe and I patched up our friendship. We painted houses together for a while. We got into more philosophical discussions, work-related talks. He wanted to make the big bucks, I didn't. He wanted a fast pace. I wanted a slower pace. We split again. I student taught at a city school. I intended to be a teacher. I never finished my final semester after student teaching. I had no desire to continue. I wasn't a bad teacher; I would have gotten better. The kids were kids, I handled the situations. There was just no drive. So here I am, getting by.

There is no wind; there is an ominous quiet, a darkness descending. Outside I see the maple leaves that form over the street, agitated by the passing of trucks. A storm is coming, coming out of the haze that lies on the land. The storm will be brief, the rain will wash the earth and the manmade objects. The sun will even shine for an hour or two before dusk. The rain will lift back into the air on waves of heat. You will be able to see the steamy tendrils rising. The air will be incredibly clean and sweet for a time. Billowing clouds will fill the sky. The kind of clouds it is fun to explore, to allow their textures and forms to play in your head.

Swallows will be dancing in the clean air, the sun glinting from them as they dive, swoop. I will listen to their excited chatter. What do they say to each other? They love to take their bodies to the edges of aerodynamic principles. Sometimes I can feel the stress ripping through their wings as they pull up from a dive. I can see the wings shudder for a moment, then they are climbing, soaring upward as fast as they descended. They must be saying things like, "Did you see that one?" or "Hey, watch me!" They seem to take joy in what they do; I hear their laughter; they have more joy than I do.

Dusk will come; I will lie on my mattress and wait for morning to come. I will hear the traffic and voices, conversations from the cars

The Silver Cord

stopped at the traffic light. I will hear the highway's sound in the night, but it will not fill my emptiness.

I've got nothing to lose by seeking God. I'm done with my life. He may have it. Even if I gain nothing, I should seek just because I love Him. I do. Most people probably can't understand this; to them, there is no God. I don't think God allowed my life to fall apart. He was with me so many times on the road, showing me life, giving me courage, keeping me from danger.

Maybe if I seek I will still be empty inside, still have no power to achieve, no motivation. Maybe I will still not have the final answer that puts all of life together. But I must take the initiative. If God took the initiative, then mankind would cry, "Manipulator, bully, tyrant!" So I must seek. "Remember your Creator in the days of your youth…"

I remember a hitchhiker, a kid, I picked up in Pennsylvania, near Interstate 80, a seventeen-year-old kid. Long hair; short, stocky build; a once-broken nose. He's running away from home. He doesn't have a pack or money. I asked him about his mother and father. He says nothing about his mother, just harrumphs under his breath, purses his lips. He loves her and is trying to hide from the pain his actions will cause her. His father doesn't care about him, has no interest. The boy is resigned when he says this. I know it is true because I see no emotion or confusion in his eyes. The kid doesn't like school; he has a few acquaintances with whom he smokes marijuana, but no close friends. The kid is going south—no destination in mind.

I take him to Harrisburg. At a fast-food restaurant, I buy him a hamburger and fries; that is all he wants. Go home, let your father ignore you, criticize you, perhaps beat you. Just love your dad. Love your mother. Try to do better in school, study. Make close friends. Stay off drugs. Stay away from bad company. Where do you get the power to do these things? Discipline, patience, understanding, perseverance, and on and on. Good words, but where do you get the power? How do you live them? Why should you live them? Why should you live?

He asks me how to get downtown. He wants to go to the filth of the city, where the action is: where the drug dealers, junkies, whores, pimps, homosexuals, transvestites, derelicts, thieves congregate by the corners, in the bars, the peep shows. He wants to go where the soulless people rage. In his confused mind, he thinks that is the place to be. That place is life! The musicians he listens to glorify that life; the TV says the action is there; his acquaintances talk of it. I tell him there is nothing down there for him, nothing. He leaves. I watch him walk down the street that will take him to the heart of nothing.

I had nothing to tell him—that is my failure. It is over. The road is gone.

EPILOGUE

I am an old man now. The unfinished manuscript had sat for roughly forty-four years. I was going to throw it away when I was downsizing from a home to an apartment. The stack of papers seemed worthless. I chose to dust off the yellowing paper, clean up the text, unconfuse thoughts and characters with the idea that maybe I could help someone who is in the leap called life. Nothing in the human heart has changed from Solomon's time, and nothing has changed in forty-four years. It is of no importance that likely anyone over forty at the time I met them is gone from this earth, or their bodies are living and their minds, dead. Who of the remainder have died before their time by accident, poor health choices, at the hands of others, or from incurable diseases? I had a heart attack at fifty-four, saw myself leave my body. I was a little higher than the football-field bleachers, looking down at my body, before I was sent back. I had two girls to raise and couldn't skip out early. It was not my time, said the Lord in that inner voice. I watched them graduate from high school, then college, and now I wait for them to earn a master's degree or a doctorate. When we part company or end telephone calls, we say, "I love you." For we know life together is precious, and God holds the weave and pattern of our lives within His hands.

My daughters and I have had fun together: countless hikes, walks, bike rides, train excursions, horseback tours, whitewater rafting trips, long

The Silver Cord

cross-country rides to and from colleges and vacation spots. They've played in countless soccer games. We've seen open-air plays at Boone, North Carolina, and on the Cherokee Indian Reservation. We've hiked Grandfather Mountain, stood on Chimney Rock, slid in the ice-cold waters of Sliding Rock, swum in Looking Glass Falls, strolled the sands of North Carolina beaches. We've motored the Smokies, we've toured Nashville. I tell you this because kids are the best gift God has given us. I tell you this because even my former nemesis—that dreaded machine—allows for time off, a time for adventuring.

I watched my grandparents die. I was present when my mother and then my father parted from their bodies of flesh. Before they departed, I came to understand they did the best they could to raise their family. All parents do the best they can, even as it is never enough. We need to respect that intent, however sporadic or ineffectual it may be. I had the chance to tell them I loved them. I've realized how caring and loving my father truly was, as the Lord brought remembrances to my soul.

I survived the workplace—the grinding machine—and shared some of the same battles my father fought, to win a stable environment for our kids, to give them the ethics and morals that would keep their hearts clean and our country strong. I found a block of time in the workday, early, in complete darkness in the mornings, before my girls needed to arise for school, when I could go adventuring on my bike steed on the green-belt path. I saw coyotes, foxes, deer, river otters, skunks, woodchucks, homeless people, and drug addicts. I saw car accidents, house fires, full and crescent moons, starry skies, the blush of dawn. I felt the power in my legs, the expansion and contraction of my lungs as the scent of the land perfumed the air. That's all I needed to feed that physical part of me—that first man, the native son who wandered and adventured the earth. I went to work, sat before the computer, in peace.

During the ebb and flow of random jobs that made a work history, I wrote five works of fiction, and probably five people have read them. If I were to have a funeral when I die, open to the public, I'd probably have two people attend, my daughters. Maybe my two sisters would show; they live far away. This is certainly no complaint—I'm just a loner;

God's book is filled with them. I know for a certainty that a band of joyous angels will be in attendance—without fail. Simply because that is the kind of God we have.

The silver cord that was the road glinting in the sunlight has broken, permanently. The silver cord that was within me—that backbone of my purpose, life, desire, and self-delusion—snapped. In my nothingness, I reached for my Creator. I know my Redeemer lives, and He lives within me. Soon after that final trip home, I asked Jesus into my life. I invited Him in because I wanted to be a good person. I wanted to be more than my weaknesses. I wanted to know who I was and what life truly is. I didn't wish to hurt others—I wanted answers to give to their hurts.

I had finally admitted I was a fool and on empty; the last sputtering of gasoline was gone, and the machine named John stopped. In the complete emptiness of my spiritless body, in the hollowness of a mind that had no more to think, I gave my Creator my empty shell. Then all the words He recorded and spoke made sense, and I submitted to His lordship. The Holy Spirit hopped in, and away He drove. A trip without end, a trip of discovery. I'm not perfect, and there are hundreds who would attest to that gleefully and joyfully, even hatefully, as that is the way of the flesh, the carnal spirit; but I am forgiven. I have had great trials, disappointments, failures; but even these cannot overcome what I have been given.

Knowing Christ is the best thing that has happened to me. The road without Him has no allure. He picked me up and carried me through these last forty-six years with a peace in my heart that the world (machine) cannot crush. The leap that was my life became the solid ground. King Solomon had wisdom; when you serve *you*, you live for your spirit; all is truly meaningless. How does one leave himself? Ask Jesus. My friend Moe was right on so many points. I was afraid, weak, fighting internal demons of failure; unwilling to start a journey I had no power to win. But the Lord had me endure, and in the enduring, I won, and I am thankful. It's not what you accomplish in the material reality—your salary, the car you drive, the homes you've built or lived in, the trophy partners who hang on your arm, the number of people who take your commands. It is conforming yourself to all that is good within life, allowing evil to die and good to reign. Only then will you truly accomplish. Kind words and

The Silver Cord

acts, giving the respect due to all people because they are His creation, should be our goals. Simply, the focus is not what you do with your life; it is whom you do it with and for. Live for your Creator, your Father.

If you are at that crossroads of life, if you don't know where you fit, what you should be, what you should do; if you only see your weaknesses, your failings, your embarrassments; if someone has hurt you; if the world of politics, religion, social interactions is jumbled and confused, and the past, the present, and the future are so broad a path you are lost...remember your Creator! He has given you a Guide of wisdom and of power.

At some time during the day, late-evening hours or early in the morning, listen to the sound of the road, the hum of tires upon the silver cord. Hear the train whistle course through your soul as a town, crossing, city is approached. Look above, hear the jet engines echo, and see the contrails crossing the sky. Watch the waters as barges glide or ships depart from ocean ports. Ask yourself what is the cord that binds us—individuals, friends, groups, neighborhoods, states—gives us freedom to move, to work, and freely wonder and express without censure. What (or is it who) has brought us such prosperity in the material and spiritual realms?

Though I am not a genius, do not possess wealth or influence, am not a great man as the world designates great men, I ask in all humility that you look again at this Jesus we have used as a curse word or an exclamation of surprise. Put aside the negative comments of others, read for yourself—from His book—who He is. Just take a moment and understand that all the good that was, is, and shall be has come from God. All the evil that has befallen you never came from Him, but from a twisted world and people who will not let Him reign. Know life through the power that flows within Christ and truly live. That is my hope and my prayer—for you.

www.ingramcontent.com/pod-product-compliance
Lightning Source LLC
Chambersburg PA
CBHW071959110526
44592CB00012B/1146